A. M. Hemenway

The HISTORY of the TOWNS of Plainfield, Roxbury and Fayston

A. M. Hemenway

The HISTORY of the TOWNS of Plainfield, Roxbury and Fayston

ISBN/EAN: 9783741123368

Manufactured in Europe, USA, Canada, Australia, Japa

Cover: Foto ©Lupo / pixelio.de

Manufactured and distributed by brebook publishing software
(www.brebook.com)

A. M. Hemenway

The HISTORY of the TOWNS of Plainfield, Roxbury and Fayston

THE HISTORY

OF THE TOWNS OF

PLAINFIELD, ROXBURY AND FAYSTON,

[FROM VOL. IV, OF THE VERMONT HISTORICAL GAZETTEER, NOW IN PRESS.]

WITH MARSHFIELD OR MIDDLESEX PAPERS IN FIFTY COPIES.

COMPLETE IN ONE NUMBER.

Price, Fifty Cents per Copy.

MONTPELIER, VT.:
PUBLISHED BY MISS A. M. HEMENWAY.
1882.

Printed by Joseph Poland, Montpelier, Vt.

THE VERMONT CAPITOL.

THE COAT OF ARMS.

THE STATE FLAG.

PLAINFIELD.

BY DUDLEY H. SMITH, M. D.

Plainfield is a small township, which contained, before the annexation of Goshen Gore, about 9,600 acres. Its surface was uneven, but no more so than the average of Eastern Vermont. It contained but little waste land, and was upon the whole a productive township.

Goshen Gore, by Plainfield, was about 3½ miles long by 1½ wide, lying east of Plainfield, and containing 3,000 acres. But very little of it is suitable for tillage. At one time it contained several families, but now has none. It formed a part of the town of Goshen until 1854.

It was annexed to Plainfield in 1874. It was embraced in the Yorkist town of Truro, and its highest mountain, which is called from that circumstance Mt. Truro, was measured by the writer, and found to be 2,229 feet above Plainfield station, or about 2,984 feet above the sea.

Winooski river flows about 1½ mile through the north-western corner of the town. Soon after it passes the line into Plainfield, it runs through and over a ledge of rocks, making an excellent mill privilege, around which has grown up the village of Plainfield.

By the canal survey of 1826, this stream at the west line of Plainfield was 152 feet above Montpelier, 546 above Lake Champlain, and 636 feet above the ocean. By the railroad survey, the station at Plainfield is 264 feet above the meadow near the mill-pond at Montpelier, or about 755 feet above the ocean.

The Great Brook rises in the eastern part of the town, and in Harris Gore, passes into Orange and returns, flowing northerly through the town, and enters the Winooski in Plainfield village. Gunner's Brook is a small stream, that rises in the southern part of the town, and empties into Stevens' Branch in Barre village.

In the southern part of the town on the banks of the Great Brook, is a medicinal spring, which is very efficacious in the cure of cutaneous and other diseases. Its vir-

tues are largely owing to the presence of sulphuretted hydrogen gas.

The town of Truro, which was chartered by New York, contained 22,000 acres. Its form resembled a carpenter's square, each limb being a little over 3 miles wide, and on its outer or longest side, nearly 6 miles long. The northern part of what is now Barre formed the southern limb. The eastern part of Plainfield, with a corner of Orange, the eastern or northern limb. The western part of Plainfield, with Montpelier and East Montpelier, was embraced in the town of Kingsboro, and contained 30,000 acres, and was chartered to John Morin Scott.

In 1773, Samuel Gale commenced the survey of one or both of these townships, and this was the first party of white men known to have passed through Plainfield. [For a biography of Gale see Hall's History of Eastern Vermont, p. 643.] In Ira Allen's History of Vermont he says: "In the summer of 1773, Ira Allen, learning that the land jobbers of New York were engaged in surveying near the head of Onion River, started with a party from Colchester in pursuit of them. He passed through Middlesex, Kingsboro and Moretown to Haverhill, when learning of the whereabouts of the surveyor, he returned and found his lines, which he followed to near the north-east corner of Montpelier, where he found the surveyor had just decamped, having been warned, he supposed, by a hunter Allen had met. According to Allen's field book the surveyor's camp was on a meadow near the north-east corner of the old town of Montpelier. Kingsboro was the Yorkist name for Washington. Moretown, or Moortown, is now Bradford, and not the present town of that name.

Allen then passed through Barre and Washington to Bradford, and returning with a knowledge of where the surveyor was to be found, passed through Plainfield on his return. As the line between Truro and Kingsboro passed nearly through the center of Plainfield, a large part of Gale's surveys must have been in this town. John Morin Scott, the grantee of Kingsboro, was a member of the New York

90

Legislature in the Revolution, and on account of his ownership of this town, was made a member of the New York council of safety, to represent this section of Vermont. He received $49.91 of the $30,000 which was paid by Vermont to New York to indemnify the New York claimants.

In Aug. 1788, James Whitelaw, of Ryegate, James Savage, of New York, and William Coit, of Burlington, caused the tract of land lying between Barre and Marshfield, Montpelier and Goshen Gore, to be measured and the bounds marked, and at that time or before, it received the name of St. Andrew's Gore.

They also measured a gore near Cambridge, of 10,000 acres, one near Caldersburg, now Morgan, of 1,500 acres, some islands in Lake Champlain, containing 1,500 acres, also islands in Otter Creek, containing 30 acres, making 23,030 acres, or about the usual size of a township, St. Andrew's Gore being reckoned at 10,000 acres. These tracts were never incorporated into a town: like Goshen, which was composed of widely separated portions. The different parts of Whitelaw's grant, as it was called, had no connection with each other.

The charter of these lands was granted Oct. 23, 1788. In 1788, '90 and '92, Whitelaw, Savage and Coit deeded their claims to Ira Allen, of Colchester, brother of Ethan, and to Gamaliel Painter, of Middlebury, the chief founder of Middlebury College. Allen and Painter gave a verbal agency to Col. Jacob Davis, of Montpelier, who, upon this authority, in May, 1793, began giving warrantee deeds of these lands in his own name. The following letter is recorded in the Plainfield land records:

MIDDLEBURY, Apr. 5, 1795.
Sir:—On my return from your home, I called on General Allen. He seems to think that it would be altogether guesswork to divide the land without seeing of it, but agreed that I might sell adjoining to the land sold sufficient to make up my part reckoning of it in quantity and quality. And I wish you to sell to any person that wants to purchase and make good pay. You know my want in regard to pay better than I can write, and for your trouble in the matter, I will make you satisfaction.
I am, sir, Your most obedient,
Humble servant,
GAMA. PAINTER.

This letter proves that Allen and Painter then recognized Davis as their agent to sell and to convey; for no deeds had then been given by Allen or Painter to any one, under their own signature and seal. One of the old settlers claimed that once when Ira Allen was in Plainfield, he asked him to give him a deed of a lot that he had bargained for of Davis, and that Allen said, "Let Davis give the deed, he has the rest."

At last differences arose between Davis and Allen, and in 1799, Davis ceased to act as their agent, and sued Allen before the county court at Danville, and in 1804, recovered $2,500 on this suit, and a part of the town was set off to him on this execution, and Davis from Burlington jail-yard conveyed it over again to those to whom he had previously given deeds. About the same time the University of Vermont recovered $15,000 of Ira Allen, and the remainder of the town was set off to them. To strengthen their title, Davis and the settlers twice allowed nearly all of the town to be sold for taxes, once on a State tax, and once on a U. S. tax, each man bidding off his own farm.

In 1802, Ira Allen quit-claimed his rights in this town to Heman Allen, of Colchester. This was some 2 years before the lands were set off to Davis and the University on executions against Ira Allen. Davis and the settlers held their own against Heman Allen until Aug. 31, 1807, when Allen purchased the claim of the University, and five days after, deeded the whole to James Savage, of Plattsburg, N. Y. Three days after this, Savage gave Allen a power of attorney to dispose of these lands. This gave Allen, in the name of Savage, an opportunity to commence suits of ejectment against the settlers before the U. S. Courts at Windsor and Rutland. For, by the constitution, citizens of one state may sue citizens of another in the U. S. Courts. Probably the transfer to Savage of this claim was a sham, to enable Allen to bring his suits where the court, and especially the jury, would not have so much sympathy for the settlers as they would in the county where they resided. This trick, if trick it was, decided the contest. In 1808, Allen, in the name of Savage, got a decision of the circuit court in his favor. By a law of 1785, a person making improvements on lands to which he supposed he had good title, had a claim for his betterments, and for one-half of the rise in value of the property while in his possession, that there would have been had there been no improvements. The settlers, therefore, did not have to pay very much more for their lands the second than the first time of purchase; often not more than one-fourth of its value at that time. The price paid to Davis for land from 1793 to 1799 averaged about $1.25 per acre. The price paid to Allen in 1808, for the second purchase, averaged a little less than $3 per acre.

Davis died within the limits of Burlington jail-yard in 1814, having been sent there for debt about the year 1802. As this was several years before the Plainfield suits were decided, it could not have been on account of them that he was sent there.

It is the opinion of Hon. C. H. Heath and others who have investigated the matter, that as the laws are now administered, the settlers would have saved their lands by a suit in chancery; but at that time very little was done in this court, the powers of which have now grown to be so extensive.

It is a singular coincidence, perhaps an example of retributive justice, that in the same year that Jacob Davis died in the jail-yard at Burlington, Ira Allen died in poverty at Philadelphia, where he had gone to escape being imprisoned for debt in the same jail.

In the autumn of 1791, Seth Freeman, of Weldon, N. H., and Isaac Washburn, of the adjoining town of Croydon, came into town by the way of the East Hill in Montpelier. When they came to what is now the Four Corners near L. Cheney

Batchelder's house, Washburn decided that there should be his pitch. They camped for the night by the side of a hemlock log in the hollow between the south district school-house and Lewis Durfee's. Freeman chose this location. The next year they returned and made these pitches. When a man made a clearing before the land was surveyed, it was usual when the lines were run to survey him out a farm that would include all of his clearing without regard to the regular lot lines, and such a piece of land was called a "pitch."

Before the town was surveyed by Jacob Davis in the spring of 1793, there were five such pitches made. They were Hezekiah Davis' pitch, 304 rods long, 31 wide, which adjoined his farm in Montpelier. Joseph Batchelder's pitch of 650 acres, mostly lying in the S. W. corner of the town, Theodore Perkins' pitch of 100 acres, Isaac Washburn's pitch, 320 acres, Seth Freeman's pitch, 300 acres.

There was also a gore between Freeman's pitch and the 5th range of lots, 34 to 40 rods wide. They all lay in the S. W. corner of the town. The clearings of 1792 were made by men living in shanties, who abandoned the town in the fall. In 1793 they returned, and perhaps some of them brought their families; but they all removed in the fall excepting the family of Theodore Perkins, and Alden Freeman, a widower, who boarded with them.

Theodore Perkins and his wife, Martha Conant, were from Bridgewater, Mass. They removed to Pomfret, Vt., and from there to Plainfield, Mar. 10, 1793, on to a clearing said to have been begun by Benjamin Nash. The town being surveyed soon after, this clearing received the name of Perkins' pitch. July 8, Perkins built a log-barn; but his house seems to have been built before he moved into town. In Dec. 1793, Alfred Perkins was born— the first birth in town. The last that was known of him he was living in the State of New York.

In the spring of 1794, Isaac Washburn's family moved into town, bringing with them Polly Reed, who afterwards married Benjamin Niles, and was grandmother to the present Geo. Niles   She went over to Perkins' house, and was the first woman Mrs. Perkins had seen for several months. Whatever scandalous stories may have been told by or of the fair sex of Plainfield since that time, that winter it was certainly free from gossiping and tattling. Nov. 1794, Perkins sold his claim to Joshua Lawrence, who procured a deed of it from Jacob Davis. Perkins removed to Montpelier, and in 1798 went to Kentucky to look after a tract of several thousand acres of land that had fallen to him. He wrote home that his title was good, and that he was coming after his family. Nothing more was ever heard from him. His friends think he was murdered. His widow removed to Lyme, N. H., in 1800.

Theodore Perkins left four sons and one daughter: Thomas, who died at Lyme, N. H., in 1871; Martin P., who lived at Shipton, Canada; Elinas P., lived in Scituate, Mass.—one of his sons, Thomas Henry, is a broker in Boston. The wife of Rev. A. S. Swift, formerly in charge of the Congregational church in Plainfield, was Theodore Perkins' grandaughter.

The Perkins house was on the flat, east of the Joshua Lawrence house, and south of the present road.

Seth Freeman made a pitch of 300 acres, and purchased lot No. 1, in the fourth range, which made him a farm of 430 acres. This he divided among his brothers, apparently as he thought they needed and deserved. He was one of the two men who purchased their land of Davis, who did not have to buy it again of Allen, having gained it by possession, and was for a time called rich, but became poor and moved away before his death.

He was not the oldest of the family, but like Abraham was the head of it. Unlike that patriarch, however, he cannot be the founder of a nation, for he left no children. His father, Ebenezer, lived with him.

Alden Freeman was the oldest of the family. He married for his second wife, Precilla, daughter of Isaac Washburn, which was the first marriage in town. He lived at first on the Courtland Perry place, (lot 1, range 4,) but removed to the N.

W. corner of Freeman's pitch, where he built the Thompson house, now in ruins and owned by Alonzo Batchelder.

He had a large family; Sally, widow of Thompson and of Larabee, of Barre, and Lucy, widow of Lawson, of Barre, and mother of George Lawson, were his daughters.

Ebenezer Freeman Jr. lived on the Courtland Perry farm. In his barn was kept one of the first schools in town,—perhaps quite the first. He was the father of the late Mrs. Freeman Landers.

Edmund Freeman lived on the S. W. corner of Freeman's pitch,—the farm now owned by his son Edmund.

Isaac Freeman built the house now owned by Elias Gladding, in 1806. It is on the N. W. corner of the Freeman lot (No. 1, range 4). He taught the first school in town. Mrs. Daniel A. Perry is his daughter. He died in 1813, and his widow married his brother Nathan, who owned the S. E. corner of Freeman's pitch, next to Barre line, and to J. Wesley Batchelder's farm. Isaac Freeman, Mrs. N. W. Keith, and Mrs. Carrol Flood are his children.

The Batchelder brothers, Joseph, Moulton and Nathaniel, came from Lyndeboro, N. H. Nathaniel lived and died in Barre, and was the grandfather of the late J. Wesley Batchelder, of Plainfield. Lieut. Joseph Batchelder, then 42 years of age, commenced his clearing in the S. W. corner of the town, in 1792, and moved his family permanently on to it in 1794.

Nathaniel Clark had commenced a clearing in Montpelier, on the farm lately owned by his son George. Neither knew of the neighborhood of the other until Clark one day, hearing the sound of chopping, started toward it, and found Batchelder with a company of stalwart boys, who had already made a large slash.

Lieut. Joseph Batchelder had two daughters, of whom Mary or Polly was born in Plainfield, July 26, 1795, and was the first girl and the second child born in town. She married Henry Parker, of Elmore. The other daughter, Nabby or Abigail, married Joseph Glidden, of Barre.

The Lieutenant's sons were : Nathaniel, Isaac, Joseph, Jr., Alpheus, William and Josiah. Of these Nathaniel lived for a time on Batchelder's pitch, near the Four Corners, next to Montpelier. He afterwards lived on the spruce flats in East Montpelier, but died at Seneca Falls, N. Y., in 1843. The late Mark Batchelder and Mrs. Sally McClure were his children.

Alpheus lived near his father. Ambrose Batchelder, now of Barre, is his grandson.

Isaac also lived on Batchelder's pitch for a time, and had a son, Josiah, 2d, who was the father of the late Harvey Batchelder, of Plainfield.

William forged a note, intending to take it up before it became due, but failed to do so. He was arrested, and when the officers were taking him to Barre, cut his throat at Joseph Glidden's, and only lived a few days after. I should not have mentioned this, had not the family been so numerous that the disgrace if divided among them will not be much for each one to carry.

Josiah is said to have been the first man in Plainfield who paid taxes on interest money. He got thoroughly rid of that incumbrance, however. He was the "Siah" Batchelder who lived and died at Daniel Lampson's.

Joseph Batchelder, Jr., lived for a time on that part of Batchelder's pitch afterwards owned by Abram Mann. His children were : Alice, wife of Stephen, and mother of H. Quincy Perry ; Joseph Batchelder, the 3d ; Nancy, wife of Levi Bartlett ; Fanny, wife of Jonathan Blaisdell, of Albany ; Abigail, wife of Asa Foster, of Marshfield ; Judith, wife of Wm. B. Foss, and Elijah A. Joseph, the 3d, was killed by his horse running away on the Lampson Hill, in 1841. He was living at that time on the Ebenezer Freeman place. His children were : Elvira (Mrs. Arouette Gunnison), Charles T., L. Cheney, Erastus B., Adeline (Mrs. K. P. Kidder, of Burlington), Sewell, killed by accident in 1856, near the place where his father was, Alpheus, Harriet (Mrs. Ira Nichols), and Wheeler J.

The Lieutenant's brother, Moulton Batchelder, about the year 1795 settled upon that portion of Batchelder's pitch now owned by the family of Wm. B. Foss. He began work upon it in 1794, his family living in the Wheaton district in Barre, and he, passing to and fro by the guidance of marked trees. His children were : Nathaniel, called the Captain ; James, born in Barre, but at his death the oldest resident, but not the oldest person in Plainfield : Jeremiah, called Jerry, of Barre ; Jonathan M., called Jack, who died on the old farm ; Olena, wife of Sewell Sturtevant, the veteran schoolmaster of Plainfield and Barre.

Capt. Nathaniel had three children, now residents of Plainfield : Alonzo J., Elvira (Mrs. Mack), and Bridgman.

James had 3 children : James Merrill, Daniel, and Mariam, (Mrs. Boyce, of Waitsfield.)

Jonathan's children were : Ira, Harrison, Adeline (Mrs. Levi Martin), Susan (Mrs. Arthur Colburn), Mary (Mrs. Wheeler), and Moulton, now of Lowell, Mass.

Isaac Washburn had one daughter, Precilla, and 4 sons : Isaac, Jr., Miles, Asa and Ephraim.

Isaac, Jr., lived with his father, and opened the first tavern in town. It stood at the Four Corners, near L. C. Batchelder's present residence, and was a large, two-story house, never entirely finished.

Asa lived north of his father's, at the top of the hill, on the place now owned by Nathan Skinner. It was the northern part of the Washburn pitch. He married Polly, daughter of Esek Howland.

Miles first settled on lands of his own in 1798, when he bought of Esek Howland the southern part of lot 3, range 2, where he built the first blacksmith shop in town. It stood near the angle of the road that now leads from Willard Harris' to the Barre road. In 1803, he sold this farm and built a house and shop in the village, on the north bank of the Great Brook, near the present tannery. This was the first shop in the village. Gamaliel Washburn, of Montpelier, was his son. Miles died at New Bedford in 1823. He was for many years constable of the town.

Ephraim built a barn west of his father's, towards East Montpelier. He was engaged to be married to a daughter of Esek Howland. To get money to build a house, he went to sea, and the ship was never heard from. It was supposed to have been wrecked, and that all on board perished.

The Washburns were not able to pay for their lands twice, perhaps not once, and in 1812, Isaac, Jr., and his father sold their farm and went to Lisle, N. Y., and from thence to Indiana, but never again possessed much property. Asa Washburn followed them soon after. Of the four families who commenced the settlement of the town, Perkins soon moved away; but some member or members of each of the others came to be a public charge.

Elijah Perry, of Middleboro, Mass., bought 100 acres of Batchelder's pitch next to lot 1, range 3. June, 1823, his daughter, Sally, committed suicide by hanging, the only suicide ever committed in town. He was a brother of Elder James Perry. His son Daniel was the father of John Perry, of Rosette, wife of Charles T. Batchelder, and Harriet, wife of Daniel Batchelder.

The five pitches of the town all lie in its south-western corner. The remainder of the town was divided by the survey of 1793 into 9 ranges—the first range lying next to Montpelier. Each range is 160 rods wide excepting the 9th, which is next to Goshen Gore, and is about 90 rods wide. The first four ranges being shortened by the pitches, contain but 6 lots each, lots No. 1 in these ranges lying next to the pitches, their south-western lines are irregular. No two lots in town whose number is one, are of the same size. In range 5 they commence to narrow, until in the 9th they come to a point at the corner of the town. All the lots adjoining Marshfield are 110 rods wide.

THE ORIGINAL SETTLERS

upon each lot in town; also the present owner of a part of the same, not with the same, bounds then as now, for the farm of

Allen Martin was the last one in town, sold before 1800, that preserved its boundaries unchanged.

Lots in Range 1.—No. 1 was first owned by SAMUEL NYE, of Falmouth, who sold the southern portion to HEZEKIAH DAVIS. It is now owned by Nathaniel M. Clark, whose wife is a grand-daughter of Davis.

ELIJAH NYE, of Falmouth, Ms,, settled upon No. 2. He sold to John Chapman in 1808 and moved to Calais. His daughter Nabby, born Sept. 28, 1796, was the 3d child born in town. This lot was divided into the Thomas Whittrege or Dennis Vincent farm, and the Holmes or Dix farm.

Lot No. 3 was purchased by JOHN CHAPMAN, of Montpelier. When St. Andrew's Gore was incorporated into a town, he gave a set of record books to the town to have the name changed to Plainfield. He was originally from a town of that name. The northern part of this lot he sold to Benjamin Niles, Jr., father of Albert, and grandfather of George Niles.

The southern part Chapman sold to Levi Willey, of Deerfield, Mass. This is the lower, or old Ozias Dix farm.

About 1811, Willey, after a visit to Montreal, was taken sick with the small pox, of which he died. His attendants buried him near the top of the hill, close to a large stone near Montpelier line ; then killed his dog, and the alarm in time abated.

The southern part of No. 4. now owned by Ira Grey, was cleared by BENJAMIN WHIPPLE. He was town representative, and held other offices in town, and was much respected. He removed to Middlesex, Vt.

JOHN MELLEN cleared portions of lots 4, 5 and 6, including the meadow now owned by Prentiss Shepard ; but he lived on the eastern part of these lots, where Willard S. Martin now lives. The late John Mellen was his son.

Benjamin Lyon settled in the corner of the town, on portions of lots 5 and 6, which is now called W. S. Martin's Enoch Cate place.

Range 2—lot 1 was nearly obliterated by Washburn's pitch, and was never by itself a farm. Its form is like a Carpenter's square, each limb being about 30 rods wide and half a mile long.

Lot 2, now owned by Mrs. Bridgman Batchelder, was settled by Thomas Vincent, of New Bedford, in 1796. He was a prominent business man, was the 1st town clerk, 4 years representative, and became the richest man in town. He was a very zealous member of the Methodist church. He died in 1848, aged 79.

Lot 3. The southern part was settled by Esek Howland, in 1797, who built a log-house, but was unable to pay for it, and sold the next year to Miles Washburn. When Harvey Bancroft was fatally injured, Howland was with him, and carried him on his back 100 rods to the house. Mrs. William C. Bartlett is his granddaughter. The northern part was settled in 1801, by EBENEZER BENNETT. He established the first tannery in town, between the Ezekiel Skinner house and the little rivulet, now often dry, just north of it.

Lot 4 clearing was begun by ASA COBURN, who sold to JOHN and THOMAS VINCENT, and removed to Cabot, but had to pay Allen for it in 1808. John was a less active business man than his brother, but was much respected, and was 3 years representative. His children were : John, Dennis, Stephen, of Chelsea, and Desire (Mrs. Coolidge Taylor.)

Lot 5. The south-western part was first owned by Chester House, then by Benjamin P. Lampson, who built what is now S. B. Gale's farm-house. Charles McCloud settled upon what was recently Allen Martin's farm. His house was in the pasture north of Martin's house. This is the north-western part of lots 5 and 6.

ROBERT MELLEN was a brother of the first John Mellen. He owned the eastern part of lot 6; also lot 6 in the 3d range, and in fact nearly all of what is now Plainfield village. In Sept. 1805, as he was riding home from North Montpelier, he fell from his horse, near the present residence of Alvin Cate, badly injuring his ankle. As they were carrying him home on a litter made of a straw bed, he said, "You will have to bring me back in a few days," and they did so, burying him in the graveyard there. The Mellens were from the old town of Derry, N. H., and they were one of the Scotch Irish families who came from Londonderry, in Ireland. Robert Mellen's house was where the Methodist parsonage now is, and his log-house was the first house built in the village.

Range 3—lot 1 was first owned by Lieut. JOSEPH BATCHELDER, but was first settled upon by JONATHAN WHITE, of Montpelier, who afterwards lived in various parts of the town. It is now owned by Nathan Skinner.

Lot 2 was first settled by CORNELIUS YOUNG, near where Willard Harris now lives. His father, Ebenezer Young, broke into a store at North Montpelier, and was sent to the state prison at Windsor.

At the time of the Plattsburg invasion, Cornelius borrowed a famous fleet horse of Willard Shepard, Esq., and passing everything on the road, was present at the battle. When the British retreated, he followed after, and seeing three of them leave their horses, he dashed in among them, pistols in hand, and compelled the whole three to surrender to him alone. At least one of them was an officer, and his sword, brought home by Young, is now in the possession of Dudley Perkins. His last days were less glorious. He was appointed a custom house officer, and had various encounters with smugglers, in one of which at Cabot, vitriol was thrown upon him, spoiling his clothes, but not injuring his person. His ignorance of the law caused him to commit some illegal acts in the discharge of his duties, and the resulting lawsuits ruined him pecuniarily and morally. He removed to the State of New York, and for some felony was sent to Clinton prison.

Lot 3. The south part was first purchased by JOSIAH FREEMAN, and is now owned by Elijah A. Batchelder. The north part was first leased by James Perry ; now by Daniel Batchelder.

Lot 4 was settled by Dea. NEHEMIAH MACK, whose house was in Ira F. Page's pasture, east of his house now occupied by his son Dan. Page. Russell Young, brother of Cornelius, owned 45 acres next to Lampson's. He went to New York, and was drowned in North river when trying to escape from the police.

Lot 5. The western part was settled by JOSEPH LAMPSON, who was for many years constable of the town. He was a weaver, a large part of the cotton cloth used in town being woven by him. Daniel and Benjamin P. were his sons; Mrs. James Batchelder and Mrs. Jeremiah Batchelder his daughters. His farm is now owned by Charles Bancroft.

Lot 6 is in the village, and was purchased of Robert Mellen by CHARLES McCLOUD, 2d, and mills erected in 1798, which were burned the same year, and rebuilt by McCloud. The first framed house in the village was built by him, where the Methodist church now stands, and is the old house back of it now owned by Wm. Bartlett.

The first store was a small one, opened by JOSEPH KILBURN, in 1803 or '4, on the Silas Willis place, near the Great Brook. The building was owned by ELIAS KINGSLEY, the miller, and when sold to Ira Day, of Barre, in 1807, there was a kiln for making earthen ware between that and the brook. The next store was opened by Philip Sparrow about 1804, upon the place where Andrew Wheatley built the large brick store on the north side of the Methodist church common.

SILAS WILLIAMS built and opened the first tavern in the village, which is now the southern part of S. B. Gale's house.

SHUBAEL WALES, from Randolph, father of George C. Wales, built the first clothing works, below the mills, in 1805 or '6.

AMASA BANCROFT, in 1809, built the first trip-hammer, south of the Great Brook and just above the present tannery. He was a son of Lieut. John Bancroft, an officer in the Revolution.

There have been three distilleries in the village—one on School street, in Mrs. Chamberlain's garden, one on High street, in Wm. Park's garden, and one east of S. B. Gale's house.

The cemetery in the village was at first just S. W. of the railroad station. Among those buried there was Parnel, daughter of Joseph Lampson. She was the betrothed of Geo. Rich, who disliked the place, and gave the land for the present cemetery, and those interred in the old one were removed in 1814.

Range 4—lot 1, was settled by the Freemans, as mentioned.

Lot 2. Clearing began by John Nye, of Falmouth, but first settled upon by Richard Kendrick. The eastern part is now owned by H. Q. Perry; the western by Hartwell Skinner and Enos P. Colby's estate.

Lot 3. The southern part was settled by David Kinney, and is now owned by Edward Bartlett. The northern part at a later date was settled by Jonathan White, and is now occupied by Solomon Bartlett.

Lot 4, now owned by Curtis Bartlett, was settled by WILLARD SHEPARD, of Sharon, about 1796. The first spring he had a yoke of oxen and was out of hay. He took his oxen and sled, went to the Four Corners near Freeman's, thence to Montpelier, and up Worcester Branch 2 miles, where he got a load of Col. Davis. By the time he got home nearly one-half of it had been shaken and pulled off by the bushes, which so disgusted him with that business that during his long life he never after bought a load of hay.

He had a small flock of sheep which he kept near the house for safety. One night he heard the wolves howling, and in the morning found they had killed every sheep.

He took a prominent part in town affairs, and did a large part of the business of justice of the peace. He removed to the farm partly in East Montpelier, now owned by his son Prentice, where he died.

Lot 5 is divided by the Great Brook. The eastern portion was settled by Nathan Jones. The lot is now partly owned by N. C. Page and George Huntoon.

Lot 6, now owned by Orrin Cree, was cleared by John Chase, who, unable to pay for it the second time, went West, but returned and died in Calais.

Range 5—lots 1 and 2, were settled by Judge BRADFORD KINNE, about 1795. The northern part he deeded to Philoman and Stephen Perkins in 1803, but they oc-cupied it in 1801. This part is now owned by A. Gunnison; the southern by J. Batch-elder. Judge Kinne was born in Preston, Conn., but moved here from Royalton, Vt. He was the most prominent man in town, and with good advantages might have become a distinguished lawyer. The story is well known of his defending Fisher in the suit of Cairnes *v.* Fisher, for assault, at the Caledonia County Court, where he directed his client to cry, when he himself did. Kinne made a pathetic appeal to the jury in favor of his client, who was a poor man, assuring them that "every dollar they took from him, they took from the mouths of babes and sucklings," at which dismal prospect Kinne burst into tears, and was followed by such a tremendous boo-hoo from Fisher, that the damages were assessed at a trifling sum, although the assault was a severe one. He re-moved on to the Washburn pitch in 1812, where he died in 1828, aged 64. Brad-ford Kinne Pierce, the distinguished Meth-odist clergyman, is his grandson.

Lot 3 was settled by James Perry. He was one of the first deacons of the Con-gregational church, but became a Metho-dist preacher. His farm is now owned by his grandson, Daniel A. Perry. The northern part of this lot was settled by Ja-cob Perkins, about 1799. It is now owned by Emmons Taft, who married his daugh-ter.

Capt. JONATHAN KINNE was born in Preston, Conn., where he married, and mov-ed to Bethel, Vt. He lived there 10 years. In 1793, he commenced clearing lot No. 4, living in a shanty through the week and going to Seth Freeman's on Sundays. He lived thus for two summers, and built a framed house in 1794, the first in town, which stood nearly opposite to H. Q. Perry's present residence. He moved his family here in Feb., 1795. The death of their little boy, Justus, Mar. 6, 1796, was the first death in town. He was the first minister in town, and preached for the Congregational church many years. He died at Berlin, in 1838. His son, Dea. Justus Kinney, lives upon this farm.

No. 5, is lease land. The southern 50 acres was leased by Dea. GEORGE AYERS, who was the progenitor of all of that fami-ly in this town. This place is now occu-pied by Ira Stone. The middle 50 acres of this lot was first leased by Elder James Perry's son, Elijah. The northern 50 acres was leased by Aaron Whittlesey. The last two portions are now leased by Levi Bartlett's estate.

Lot 6 is lease land. The eastern por-tion was first leased by John Moore, now by Hiram G. Moore. The western portion was first leased by Levi Bartlett, now in part by Lee Batchelder.

The southern 100 acres of lot 7 was settled by Asa Bancroft, of Warmouth, Mass., about 1797. About the year 1801, as he and his wife were coming home, one evening, from Jeremy Stone's the wolves began to assemble in their rear. His wife was on a horse carrying their infant son, Tyler. They hurried on as fast as possi-ble, but the wolves came so near, that they abandoned to them a piece of fresh meat that Mrs. Stone had given them, and reached home safely, the wolves howling about the house as soon as they entered it. Mr. Bancroft was frequently elected to town offices, and died in 1856, aged 87. His children were, Tyler, William, John, Eunice (Mrs. Ira F. Page) and Mrs. Reu-ben Huntoon. When it began to be ru-mored that the settlers' titles were not good, he went to Jacob Davis', who gave him security on other property, and sent word by him to the other settlers, that if they were frightened he would secure them. This quieted their fears, and only one or two went.

No. 8 was settled by JOHN MOORE. His son, Heman Allen Moore, born here, was elected a representative to congress from Ohio, in 1844, but died the next year. Wm. Huntoon now owns this farm.

Range 6, lots 1, 2 and 3, were settled by JOSEPH NYE, of Falmouth, Mass. Several members of this family settled in Plainfield, or owned land in it. They were of Welch descent, and when they first came to Falmouth wrote their name Noye. Joseph Nye was representative 5 years, justice of the peace a long time, &c. His son, Vinal, died many years since, leaving several children, Irving, George, Alanson, and Mary, wife of Edward Bartlett. Joseph's daughter, Sally, married Nathaniel Townshend, Cynthia, Daniel Gunnison, Augusta, Elijah A. Batchelder. Lots 1 and 2 are mostly owned by Dudley B. Smith. Seth F. Page lives upon No. 3.

No. 4 was settled by Elder James Perry's son Stephen, in 1818, who built the plastered house standing upon it, now owned by Alba F. Martyn.

No. 5, the southern part now owned by A. F. Martyn, was settled by Joseph F. Ayers, who moved to Thetford, and thence to Manchester, N. H. The northern part, now owned by Nathaniel Townsend, was settled by Gideon Huntington, father of Amasa, and of Mrs. Leonard Moore, and uncle to David and Samuel Huntington, of Marshfield.

No. 6 was settled by Frank Crane and Joseph Deering. It is now mostly owned by N. Townsend.

HARVEY BANCROFT, from Ware, now Auburn, Mass., settled upon lot 7, in the 6th range, part of lot 7 in the 7th range, and a part of lot 6 in the 8th range, next to the Bancroft pond. He was clerk under the attempted organization of St. Andrews Gore as a town. His house was opposite to the burying-ground near Newcomb Kinney's. While clearing some land, about 20 rods easterly of Benjamin F. Moor's present residence, he fell a tree upon a small one, which fell across another. The small one flew up striking him on the chest. He died July 8, 1797, a few days after the injury, aged 27. He left a wife and two small children. One died young, the other was Dr. Nathaniel Bancroft. His widow, Polly Carrol, married Sanford Kinne, a brother of Jonathan and of Bradford Kinne. Sanford purchased nearly all the land formerly owned by Harvey Bancroft, but upon the death of his wife, in 1814, he went West, and his fate is unknown. Newcomb Kinney is his son.

No. 8 was settled by Ezra Bancroft, father of Horace Bancroft, now of Barre, but it was first owned by his brother,

Aaron, of Boston. It is now occupied by Duron Norcross.

Range 7, lots 1, 2, 3 and 4, were purchased of Davis by Enos Colby, of Hawk, N. H. He made a clearing and built a house in 1800, some fourth of a mile west of the Great Brook, on land now owned by C. H. Heath. He stayed in it one night, and then went back to N. H., leaving it in care of Moulton Batchelder. One Currier without leave moved into the house, and was sued off by Heman Allen, who found when too late that Currier was not holding under Colby, who thereby got it by possession against Allen. Lots 1 and 2 are now mostly owned by his grandson, Moses Colby. No. 1 is only 20 rods wide; 3 and 4 are partly owned by Henry Camp, whose wife is Colby's granddaughter.

Lot 5 is mostly lease land, and portions of it were rented to Eli Boyd, Isaac Perry, James Perry, Jr., and the N. E. corner next to Moses Bancroft's was sold to Patrick Reed. It is now leased to Nathan Hill, Seneca S. Bemis and Lyman Moore.

No. 6 was probably first owned by Harvey Bancroft. It was on the northeast corner of this lot that he was at work when fatally injured. It is now owned by Joel Sherburn, Baxter Bancroft and Henry Moore.

No. 7 was first owned by Harvey Bancroft and Charles Bancroft. Lee Martin's farm is a part of it.

No. 8 was settled by ZOPHER STURTEVANT, of Worcester, Mass. He was persuaded by his friend Harvey Bancroft to come up and buy a farm next to him. He returned to Mass. to earn money to pay for it, and while there heard of Bancroft's death. Sewell Sturtevant was his son. It is now occupied by Newcomb Kinney.

Range 8—lots 1 and 2, were purchased and settled by STEPHEN PERKINS, who built a saw-mill in 1812-'13. He also had one set of mill-stones. In the summer of 1857, the banks by the side of the dam gave way, and the pond of about 7 acres was discharged in a short time, carrying off every bridge on the Great Brook. It was repaired, but gave way again before the pond was quite filled. It was again repaired more thoroughly, and held until a heavy rain in the spring of 1869 carried off the new dam and all the bridges below. It was repaired, and when the pond was about half filled it burst through the quicksands under the dam, and no more efforts to repair it were made. R. L. Martin then put in a steam-mill, which was burned in 1871, and he removed the remains of it to Harris Gore. Dudley Perkins and Silas Worthen occupy portions of these lots.

No. 3 was settled by Ralph Chamberlain, of Hanover, N. H., and is now owned by his grandson, Jeremy Stone Chamberlain. Plainfield Sulphur Springs are on this lot.

No. 4 was settled by David Benedict, of Randolph, who sold the southern part, now owned by Scott and Smith, to Amasa Bancroft, and the northern part, now owned by Goodrich, to Robert Carson. Feb. 29, 1816, an old house on this lot, occupied by Moses Reed, and used for a school-house, caught fire, and a little son of Reed was burned to death. David, Patrick and Woodman Reed were his sons; Joanna (Mrs. William Parks) his daughter.

No. 5 was settled by Charles R. Woolson, who sold the northern part to his wife's father, Moses Bancroft, of Ward, Mass., in Nov. 1796. Woolson was not able or willing to pay for his land the second time, and removed to New York, where he became rich. His son Ephraim getting homesick, returned, and bought back the old farm, on which he died. It is now owned by Erastus Batchelder. Mary, wife of S. O. Goodrich, and Sarah, wife of Joseph Lane, are Ephraim's daughters.

Moses Bancroft had 4 sons: John, Charles, Chester and Baxter. John had 2 sons: Lewis, of Calais, and Preston, of Marshfield. Charles had a son Charles, and Mrs. Wm. Skinner and Mrs. Lewis Wood are his daughters. Baxter had but one child, Moses.

Baxter has resided in Plainfield longer than any other person—84 years. He says that as late as Oct. 1804, neither his father

nor any of the neighbors had chimneys to their houses. Stones were laid up into some form of a chimney for a few feet, and the smoke allowed to go out, if it would, through a hole in the roof. The roof for years was made of large pieces of elm bark, tied on with strings of the same. Sometimes a storm in the night would blow off these pieces, and his father would get up and tie them on again. It would often get on fire, and once the house burned down.

One summer they had nothing to eat but milk for a long time, until Willard Shephard gave them a bushel of rye very badly sprouted, but some of this ground and cooked tasted the best of anything he ever ate.

The senior Moses had a brother, Lieut. John Bancroft, a Revolutionary soldier, who began a clearing on Prentice Shephard's farm (lot 5, range 1), but soon removed to the village. Amasa Bancroft was his son. C. Watrous and Carlos Bancroft, of Montpelier, were his sons.

No. 6 contains the Bancroft Pond, and was purchased by Harvey Bancroft.

No. 7 was settled by Charles Bancroft, and is now owned by Gardner Heath.

No. 8 is mostly a swamp.

Range 9. Lot 1 is 110 rods long, and 7 rods wide at one end, and a point at the other. It was never sold by the original proprietors.

No. 2 was a part of Stephen Perkins' purchase, and is now owned by his grandson, Emory F. Perkins.

No. 3 was settled by David Reed, of Hanover, N. H., in 1809, and is now owned by David Perkins.

David Reed and Ralph Chamberlain married sisters of Israel Goodwin, who lived many years in this town, but removed to East Montpelier. T. Goodwin Reed is David's son.

No. 4, now owned by Erastus Batchelder, was settled in 1796, by James Boutwell, of Barre, a relative of Col. Levi Boutwell, of Montpelier.

Oct. 9, 1804, snow fell to a great depth, some 3 or 4 feet. One Richardson, of Orange, started a bear out of his cornfield, and followed it to Capt. Boutwell's and returned. Boutwell, Robert Carson, and Jeremy Stone, pursued it to the round mountain, north or east of Pigeon pond, where they treed her. Boutwell fired, wounding it in the neck, it ran by Carson who fired and missed. Stone followed after with an ax, having no gun, setting on the dogs. Stone soon saw the bear returning, perhaps to defend her cubs, and got upon a rock, and when the bear attempted to get on, tried to split its head open with the ax, but the bear instantly knocked it from his hand, mounted the rock, pushed Stone off from it into the snow, and then over on to his back, getting top of him. Stone put up his hand to push its head away from his, when his little finger went into the bear's mouth, which began to chew it. At this moment, Boutwell, who had reloaded and come up, fired, the bear's head being only a few inches from Stone's, and bruin fell dead.

Another time Boutwell went up on to the high, round topped hill north-east of his house, after partridges. He found a bear up a tree. His gun was loaded with shot and he had no ball. He drawed the shot and whittled a beach plug, with the end pointed, and loaded with this. The first shot had no effect, but the second killed the bear.

He was captain of the first militia company in town; was one of the selectmen from 1799, until his death, in 1813, of typhoid fever, at that time very prevalent and fatal. He was a man whose character was almost above reproach; but his dog was even more strict in his faith and practice than his master. The dog had learned to observe the Sabbath, as intelligent dogs in Christian families often do, and never attempted to follow his master on that day. Once when Boutwell was on his way to church, he met a party in pursuit of a bear, and they wished for the dog, which was a famous hunter. Boutwell went back with them to the house, and ordered the dog to follow them, but it refused. He called it to follow him, but it would not. He then took off his Sunday clothes and put a gun on his shoulder, when the dog, probably thinking that it was not Sunday after all, followed. Boutwell was justly punished for his duplicity by not getting the bear. The dog afterward followed a deer into the woods, and was never seen again.

Lot 5 was first purchased of Heman Allen by Eathan Powers, who hired men to cut and burn wood for the ashes. Sylvester Grinnel, a quaker, first resided upon it.

Lot 6 was settled by Moses Bancroft's son, John. Charles Morse owns a portion of it.

No. 7 was settled by JEREMY STONE, of Ward, Mass., in 1796. He chose this place because he expected it would be near a good road. The legislature, in 1797, appointed a committee to work a road from Chelsea court house to Danville court house. This committee reported to the county court at Chelsea, in 1799, that they had built the road through Washington and Orange. A little work was done on it in Goshen gore, near Plainfield line, and the work abandoned. Ira Stone, Rev. Jesse Stone of Maine, and Jeremy Stone are his sons; Mrs. Hial P. Chamberlain and Mrs. Marian Stone Tarbell, his daughters. His farm is now owned by Ira Robinson.   -

Lot 8 was settled by Daniel Rice, of Barre, in 1825. Dudley Marshall now resides upon it.

According to Thompson's Gazetteer, the town was organized Apr. 4, 1796, under the name of St. Andrew's gore, and Harvey Bancroft elected town clerk. This is probably true, but it was illegal, a gore not having the power to form a town organization. Nov. 6, 1797, the gore was incorporated into a town by the name of Plainfield, and the town meeting held at James Perry's, in Mar., 1798, is the first of which there is now any record, but was not the first, because called by Joshua Lawrence, James Perry, Moulton Batchelder, as selectmen of Plainfield. At this meeting, Thomas Vincent was elected town clerk. Town meetings after this were held at Capt. Jonathan Kinne's until 1823, when they were held in the village.

In 1798, '99 and 1800, the road tax voted was 4 days work for each poll. In 1798, the General Assembly, at the request of the town, voted a tax of one cent per acre, which was to be used to build roads. In 1807, another of three cents per acre was laid upon Plainfield. At that time, improved lands were listed at $1.75 per acre, unimproved not at all. Polls at $20, a yoke of oxen $10, houses worth less than $1000, 2 per cent, over $1000, 3 per cent. Interest money 6 per cent.

The first road in town was worked from Seth Freeman's north westerly to Hezekiah Davis' in Montpelier, as early as 1794, but no highways were laid out until June, 1799, when this and several others were laid.

In 1798 and 99, the town sent no representative, probably because a town with a grand list of less than $3,200 was not " doomed" to pay a state tax, if it sent no representative.

Thomas Vincent was a federalist. All the other representatives were republicans, until the reorganization of the parties under Jackson and Adams. After that they were all democrats except John Vincent, antimason, until the formation of the antislavery party, which elected D. A. Perry. Frank Hall was the only whig.

In Sept. 1801, Isaac Tichenor received 10 votes for governor—all that were cast. In 1802, Isaac Tichenor had 25, Jonas Galusha 23, which was the largest vote cast for several years.

PHYSICIANS.

The first physician in town was AMHERST SIMONS, from Windham, Ct. He studied with Dr. Glysson, of Williamstown, and came to Plainfield in 1801. For many of the last years of his life he was blind.

Dr. EBENEZER CONANT studied with Dr. Robert Paddock, of Barre, and came to Plainfield in 1809. In 1832 he removed into Marshfield, about 2 miles from Plainfield village, near Perkins' mill, but returned to Plainfield after a few years, where he died.

Dr. NATHANIEL BANCROFT was brought to Plainfield by his father, Harvey Bancroft, from Ward, Mass., when an infant. When 12 years old he went to Montpelier, where he attended school, and at last studied medicine with Dr. Lamb. About 1822, he came to Plainfield to practice, where he remained until 1851, when he went to Ohio, where he stayed 2 years, thence to Belvidere, Ill. His pungent and witty sayings are still often quoted by his old friends in Plainfield.

Dr. DANIEL KELLOGG came to Plainfield in 1834, and built the brick house east of the hotel. His health failing he removed to Berlin in 1836, where he soon died.

Dr. JARED BASSETT came to Plainfield in 1839, and removed to Northfield in 1843, and thence to Chicago.

Dr. DANIEL BATES was here from 1845 to 1851.

Dr. STEPHEN BENNETT from 1851 to 1856, when he removed to Ohio.

DR. PHINEAS KELLOGG, of Brookfield, commenced practice here in 1851. He died of diphtheria Apr. 10, 1862, age 39.

Dr. WALTER S. VINCENT, of Chelsea, now of Burlington, had his residence here for several years, but a large part of the time he was surgeon in the Union army in the war of the rebellion.

Dr. DUDLEY B. SMITH, of Williamstown, came to Plainfield in 1856, and Dr. W. F. LAZELL, of Brookfield, came in the fall of 1867. They remain here now.

LAWYERS.

The first lawyer in town was CHARLES ROBY, who came about the year 1812— not long after the result of the Allen lawsuit had put a mortgage on nearly every farm in town. Probably the people had no desire or money for any more lawsuits at that time, as he left soon.

In 1828, AZEL SPALDING, of Montpelier, now of Kansas, was here one year.

In 1833, SYLVESTER EATON, of Calais, came and stayed until 1838.

STILLMAN H. CURTIS was here from 1838 to 1843.

J. A. WING was here from 1836 to 1852, when he went on to his farm on Maple Hill, in Marshfield, where he stayed about

3 years, then moved to Plainfield, and from here to Montpelier in 1857.

In 1843 LEWIS CHAMBERLAIN came. He died in Aug. 1863, of dysentery, which was very prevalent and fatal at that time, there being 18 deaths from that disease, 16 of which were within or near the village.

CHARLES H. HEATH came here in 1859, and removed to Montpelier in 1872.

S. C. SHURTLEFF commenced the practice of law here in 1864, and removed to Montpelier in 1877.

O. L. HOYT came here in 1873, and still remains.

THE FIRST CHURCH

was organized Nov. 13, 1799, at Jonathan Kinne's, under the name of

THE CHURCH OF CHRIST IN PLAINFIELD.

The council called to organize this church was composed of Rev. Richard Ransom of Woodstock, Rev. John Ransom of Rochester, Rev. James Hobart of Berlin, Dea. William Wood of Woodstock, Capt. Peter Salter of Orange. Dea. Judah Willey, Henry Taft and Joseph Sterling, of Barre, were invited to join the council. The members embodied into a church were only six : Capt. Jonathan Kinne, James Perry, James Boutwell, Mrs. Esther Perry, Deborah Boutwell, Judith Batchelder. Others joined soon after. In June, 1801, they passed this vote :

" Whereas some members of the church are dissatisfied with the articles of faith, Therefore, Voted that the aggrieved members have liberty to select such articles as they are satisfied with, which when selected shall be considered the church articles of faith, not to prevent any from believing them as they now are."

This compromise did not prevent the Methodist portion of the church from seceding in June, 1802, and forming another church. Those who left to join the Methodist were, Dea. James Perry, Esther Perry, Bradford Kinne, Ebenezer Freeman, Esther Freeman, John Chase, and Richard Kendrick. Those who remained with the original church were, Dea. Nehemiah Mack, Moses Bancroft, Sally Bancroft, James Boutwell, Deborah Boutwell, Jonathan Kinne, Lydia Kinne, Sanford Kinne, Polly Kinne, Zopher Sturtevant, Polly Sturtevant, David Bancroft.

The same year Charles R. Woolson was unanimously expelled from the church for " neglect of family prayer, and public worship on Sunday and church meetings." Moulton Batchelder having joined the Methodists, on Sunday, Jan. 22, 1816, the following sentence of excommunication was read before the assembled congregation :

" Whereas our brother, Moulton Batchelder, has violated his solemn covenant obligations by neglecting the stated meetings of the church on the Sabbath and at other times, and going after, as we think, false teachers, and embracing dangerous errors and sentiments, derogatory to the character of an infinitely wise and holy God, We now, under the pressing obligation of duty we owe to our Lord and Savior Jesus Christ, have undertaken this painful and bitter labor, and we hope in faithfulness and prayer, but without success. Therefore, according to the rule of Christ's family, we are under the painful necessity of saying unto you, and that in this public manner, that for these reasons, the door of our fellowship and communion is closed against you, and you are no longer to be considered of this church and body ; but as an unprofitable branch, and therefore are now severed from this body. It is our humble prayer, that God will bless this our unpleasant, but plain duty to you, and open your understanding that you may see your error, and give you repentance, that you may enjoy his favor at last, and be gathered with all of the redeemed from among men, to inhabit the new Jerusalem, where Jesus Christ is the joy and the light thereof."

I do not give these facts to increase the self-complacency of those at the present time, who are inclined to plume themselves upon their own superior liberality, and tolerance of differences of opinions. Such should consider, that people who thought their peculiar tenets of such vital importance, that they incurred the dangers and hardships of a settlement in New England to establish them, could not be expected to see the result of their labors impaired or destroyed, with indifference or equanimity.

Jonathan Kinne preached to the church until 1826 ; but was not ordained because he disbelieved in infant baptism.

Nathaniel Hurd was the acting pastor in 1826. [For his biography see Tinmouth, vol. III.] He was succeeded by John F. Stone.

In 1829, Joseph Thatcher became the first settled minister. He removed to Barre in 1834, and was succeeded by Mr. Hadley in 1836, by John Orr in 1839, Samuel Marsh in 1842, Calvin Granger in 1846, and A. S. Swift in 1849,—none of whom were settled ministers, however.

Rev. Joel Fisk was settled as pastor in May, 1855, and died Dec. 16, 1856. Soon after Rev. Horace Herrick became acting pastor, who was succeeded in 1861, by Rev. C. M. Winch, who remained until Nov., 1868, when he was succeeded by Horace Pratt, who removed in 1871.

After an interval of nearly 2 years, Charles Redfield became acting pastor, and in 1877, C. E. Ferrin was settled, and remained until his death, in 1881.

The deacons have been James Perry, Nehemiah Mack, George Ayers, Dan. Storrs, Justus Kinney, Emmons Taft.

Their first meeting-house was built in 1819, the second, on the same site, in 1854. Until the building of a church their meetings were usually held at the dwelling house of Jonathan Kinne.

THE METHODIST CHURCH has no early records in Plainfield, and I am obliged to glean this account from various sources. The first Methodist sermon preached in Plainfield was by the Rev. Nicholas Sneathen— or "Suethen," as his family write it—a very able man, who was chaplain of Congress in 1812. He came to Seth Freeman's, made known his name and occupation, and succeeded in attaching nearly all of the people in the southern part of the town to the Methodist church, including Dea. James Perry, who afterwards became a Methodist preacher, the first probably that resided in town.

A church was organized in 1801, or '2. It formed a part of Barre circuit. The first Methodist minister stationed at Plainfield that I can learn of was David Kilburn, who was here in 1812 and 1825.

Rev. Thomas C. Pierce, who was married to Judge Kinne's daughter, Sally,

lived upon the Asa Washburn place in 1820. This, with 15 acres of land, was given to the Methodist church for a parsonage by Judge Kinne. It was afterwards sold and the parsonage in the village bought.

Rev. John Lord was stationed here in 1823; —— Harvey in 1827, '28; R. H. Deming, '30, '31; John Nason, '33, '34; N. Stone, '35; David Wilcox, '36, '37; Jacob Boyce, '38; Daniel Field, '39; J. L. Slason, '40; John W. Wheeler, '41; Richard Newell, '42, '43; Otis M. Legate, '44; H. P. Cushing, '45, '46; J. W. Perkins, '47, '48; Homer T. Jones, '49, '50; Mulfred Bullard, '51; Peter Merrill, '52, '53; Alonzo Hitchcock, '54, '55, '62, '63; W. J. Kidder, '56, '57; Edmund Copeland, '58, '59, '69, '70; P. P. Ray, '60, '61; Joshua Gill, '64, '65; S. B. Currier, '66, '67; Andes T. Bullard, '68; Thomas Trevillian, '71; Joseph Hamilton, '72, '73, '74; Joseph O. Sherburn, '75, '76; W. H. Dean, '77, '78; Elihu Snow, '79, '80, '81.

Before the erection of a church their meetings were usually held at Elder James Perry's, or at Lieut. Joseph Batchelder's. In 1819 a house was built for the Methodist society in the village, with an agreement that when they had no preacher, "any other Christian denomination, such as Calvinists, Anti-Baptists, Freewill Baptists, Friends, so called, Universalists, etc., who had a preacher, might occupy it."

The following is a list of the contributors to the building of this church:

Thomas Vincent, $100; Moulton Batchelder, $100; Harvey Pitkin, $75; John Vincent, $60; Seth Cook, $50; Bradford Kinne, $50; Amherst Simons, $50; Seth Freeman, $50; Asa Bancroft, $30; Eben Dodge, Jr., $25; John Moors, $25; Ebenezer Lyon, $25; Matthew Jack, $25; Nathan Freeman, $25; Benjamin F. Lampson, $25; Laomi Cree, $25; Enoch Cate, $25; Ebenezer Freeman, $20; Samuel Wilson, Jr., $20; Benjamin Whipple, $20; Earl Cate, $15; James Batchelder, $15; Joseph P. Page, $12; William Moors, $10; Friend M. Morse, $10; Solomon Bartlett, $10; Duron Whittlesey, $10; Andrew Jack, $10; Nehemiah Mack, Jr., $5; Charles

Patterson, $5; Allen Martin, $5; Eben Martin, $5; Richard Kendrick, $3; Elisha Mack, $2; total, $947. $100 was paid for the site, leaving the cost of the house about $850.

In 1852, this was sold to the Baptists and removed, and another built at a cost of a little less than $1,600.

The Vermont Annual Conference was held at Plainfield in 1855, Bishop Edward R. Ames presiding.

The present number in full membership, 132; probationers, 14.

FROM REV. J. R. BARTLETT, OF BARRE.

Rev. Nicholas Snethen, who is mentioned as the first Methodist preacher who visited Plainfield, was the pioneer Methodist preacher in this State. His appointment to Vermont was in 1796, and as he labored in this State but one year, it must have been at that time that he appeared in Plainfield. The records of "Vershire circuit," which was the name of the appointment in the earliest days, are probably not now in existence; but those of "Barre circuit," formed in 1804, are still preserved, and state that the first "quarterly meeting" for Barre circuit was held in Plainfield, Aug. 4th and 5th, 1864, and in Plainfield a little later. The records give Bradford Kinne, Richard Kendrick and Ebenezer Freeman as leaders, 17, 16 and 11 members, respectively, and four "on trial." Mr. Kinne was also a local preacher, and a very active man in the church, and the Rev. Bradford Kinne Pierce, D. D., now the editor of Zion's Herald, published in Boston, was named for him, being the son of Rev. Thomas C. Pierce, and therefore the grandson of Mr. Kinne, who is mentioned in the foregoing sketch as "Judge" Kinne.

This town was included in Barre circuit until 1838, and hence was visited by the appointees to that circuit at stated intervals as a regular preaching place. The names given in the foregoing sketch as Methodist preachers stationed here, are, in several instances at least, of appointees to Barre circuit, there being each year two or three such appointees, and one of them usually resident at Plainfield. On and after the conference of 1838, this station lost its identity with Barre circuit, and the preachers were appointed directly to Plainfield. The complete list of Methodist preachers on Vershire circuit to 1804, and on Barre circuit from that time to 1838, may be found in the history of Barre. The condition of this church has been particularly prosperous during the last three years, about one-third of its present membership having been added during that time.

Barre, Feb. 3, 1882.

THE BAPTIST CHURCH

was organized Oct. 17, 1809, at the schoolhouse near Dea. James Perry's (South district.) The members were: James Boutwell and wife, who withdrew from the Congregationalist church for that purpose, Jacob Perkins, Stephen Perkins and his wife Nancy, John Bancroft and his wife Phœbe. Elder Jabez Cottle and Elder Elijah Huntington were the clergymen present.

At the next meeting Philip Wheeler made a profession of religion, and joined the church. He became pastor afterwards, living near the center of Montpelier, but in 1826, sold his farm, and a house was built for him near the Plainfield Springs. In a few years after this, Stephen Perkins refused to commune, for the reason that Elder Wheeler had said that "he would not baptize a person that he knew intended to join another church." Soon after this, he and his brother Jonathan withdrew from the church. The result of this dissension was, that Elder Wheeler soon closed his pastoral labor with this church, and removed into Marshfield, one half mile east of Plainfield village, where he died.

After Elder Wheeler's dismissal, they were supplied at intervals by different clergymen, none of them living in town except Rev. Friend Blood.

In 1852, the Baptist churches in Plainfield and Marshfield united, and Abraham Bedel became their pastor, residing in Plainfield. The Methodist church was purchased, removed and repaired. Mr.

Bedel was succeeded in 1858 by Mr. Kelton, he in 1859 by S. A. Blake, and he in 1860 by N. W. Smith, who removed in 1862. After that they had only occasional preaching, and in 1871 their church was sold and converted into stores.

THE RESTORATIONIST SOCIETY
was organized in 1820, but had only occasional preaching until in 1840, Rev. L. H. Tabor came to Plainfield, and a church was erected costing $1,770 above the foundations, exclusive of furniture and the bell, the whole amounting to about $2,300.

Mr. Tabor remained 3 years only. The pulpit was afterwards supplied a part of the time by Mark M. Powers, of Washington, and Rufus S. Sanborn, of Barre. They were succeeded in 1854 by William Sias, who remained one or two years.

Rev. Joseph Sargent resided here in 1858 and 1859, Rev. Thomas Walton in 1860 and 1861, after which they had no stated preaching until in 1872, Rev. Lester Warren commenced to preach one half of the time. He was succeeded by Rev. George Forbes the next year. In 1876 L. S. Crossly removed here, and remained one year, since which they have been supplied a part of the time by non-resident preachers.

SCHOOLS.
In 1787, the General Assembly enacted a school law that authorized towns and school districts to build school-houses and support schools by a tax on the grand list. A majority of a town might do this, but it required a two-thirds vote of a school district, and neither a town or school district could tax the property of non-residents for this purpose. This law provided that schools might be supported by subscription, and the district collector had the same power and duties in collecting a subscription that he had in collecting a tax.

In 1803, Plainfield was divided into 5 school districts. The town never voted a tax for schools, and probably none of the districts did for several years. The northwest, or village, district schools were supported by subscription until 1809. They commenced to build a school-house in 1803, finishing it in 1804. It stood just

east of the present hotel, in James Martin's garden. This was the first built in town, and was paid for by a tax, one-third payable in money and two-thirds in wheat. This house having been burned in the winter of 1806-7, another was built in 1807, over by the present residence of Geo. C. Wales, near the railroad bridge. In 1826, this district formed a unison with an adjoining district in Marshfield, and a school-house was built near Marshfield line north of the river. In 1866, this district built another school-house near the old one, at a cost of $6,000, exclusive of the site.

The South, or Freeman, district did not have the first school-house in town; but they had the first school-house quarrel. It had been decided to build a school-house at the Four Corners, east of Seth Freeman's, to which the Freemans were opposed. The boys of Elder James Perry and of Philemon Perkins, and others, made arrangements to raise it secretly at midnight. The Freemans learned of the plot, and appeared to help uninvited; but they spelled the word raze. The result was, nothing was done at that time, but afterwards, in the fall of 1805, the house was built there.

Plainfield village is at the extreme northern part of the town, and as incorporated in 1867, includes a portion of the town of Marshfield. In 1812, it contained about a dozen families, in 1881 about 80.

The first mills were burned the same year they were built. The village suffered no more serious loss by fire until May 16, 1877, when the saw and grist-mills, 4 dwelling-houses, 2 shops and 4 barns were burned. James Richards was convicted of being the incendiary, and is now in prison.

The great freshet of Oct. 1869, carried off the saw and grist-mills, the clothing-works, machine-shop, blacksmith-shop, etc.

Railroad trains commenced to run from Montpelier to Plainfield for traffic, Sept. 17, 1873; to Wells River, Nov. 24, 1873.

It is said that a mail route was established from Montpelier to Danville, via Plainfield, in 1808, and a post-office was probably established at Plainfield at that time; but so little did it affect the daily life of the people, that no one knows who was the first postmaster.

As late as 1823, the fees of the postmaster at Plainfield were only $10.76; at Marshfield, $3.48: Cabot, $6.81: at Montpelier, $138.81. As postage was then very high, and the fees of the small offices about one-half of the gross income, the amount of mail matter must have been small. The mail was carried on horseback until 1827, then in a wagon until 1830, when a coach was put on, which was almost as much an object of curiosity and pride as was the advent of the cars in 1873.

TOWN REPRESENTATIVES.

Bradford Kinne, 1800, '2, '3, '4, '5, '7, '8, '9, '10, '11, '12, '13, '16, '21: Thomas Vincent, 1801, '22, '25, '26; Jonathan Kinne, 1806; Joseph Nye, 1814, '15, '17, '18, '24; Benjamin Whipple, 1819, '20, '23; Jeremy Stone, 1827, '28; Israel Goodwin, 1829, '30, 31: John Vincent, 1832, '33, '34; Baxter Bancroft, 1835, '36; James Palmer, 1837, '38, '41; Harvey Bancroft, 1839, '40: Mark M. Page, 1842; Ezra Kidder, 1843, '44, '50, '60, '61; Nathaniel Townsend, 1845, '46; Reuben Huntoon, 1847; Daniel A. Perry, 1848, '55; Francis Hall, 1849; Lewis Chamberlain, 1851, '52; John Mellen, 1853, '54; E. Madison Perry, 1856, '57; Dennis Lane, 1858, 59; Sullivan B. Gale, 1862, '63; Willard S. Martin, 1864, '65; Levi Bartlett, 1866; Julius M. Richards, 1867; Justus Kinney, 1868; Channing Hazeltine, 1869; Joseph Lane (biennial), 1870; L. Cheney Batchelder, 1872; Stephen C. Shurtleff, 1874; Nathaniel Townsend, Jr., 1876; Frank A. Dwinell, 1878; Dudley B. Smith, 1880.

DELEGATES TO CONSTITUTIONAL CONVENTIONS.

Lovel Kelton, 1814; John Vincent, 1822; Nathaniel Bancroft, 1828; James Palmer, 1836; Nath'l. Sherman, 1843, '50; Reuben Huntoon, 1870.

STATE SENATORS.

Nathaniel Bancroft, 1847, '48; Charles H. Heath, 1868, '69, '70.

JUDGES OF COUNTY COURT.

Bradford Kinne, 1811, '12, '13; Israel Goodwin, 1834, '35; Lewis Chamberlain,

1855, '56; Willard S. Martin, 1874, '75, '76, '77.

TOWN CLERKS.

Thomas Vincent, 1798, '99, 1800; '1, '2, '3, '9, '10, '11, '12, '14; Bradford Kinne, 1804, '5, '6, '7, '8, '13, '15, '16; Silas Williams, 1817 to '33; James Palmer, 1834 to '41; Ezra Kidder, 1842 to '51; Mark M. Page, 1852 to '60: Phineas Kellogg, 1861, '62; Walter B. Page, 1863 to '76; Mason W. Page, 1877; Frank A. Dwinell, 1878.

TREASURERS.

Moulton Batchelder, 1798, '99, 1800; Thomas Vincent, 1801, '08, '09, '10, '11, '12, '14; Ebenezer Freeman, 1802; Bradford Kinne, 1803, '04, '05, '06, '07, '13, '15, '16; Silas Williams, 1817 to '33: James Palmer, 1834 to '41; Ezra Kidder, 1842 to '51; Mark M. Page, 1852 to '60; S. B. Gale, 1861 to '70; Ira F. Page, 1871 to '74; Dudley B. Smith, 1875; F. A. Dwinell, 1877 to '81.

1ST SELECTMEN.

Joshua Lawrence, 1797; Thomas Vincent, 1798, '99, 1800, '01, '02, '03. '10, '11, '12, '14, '18; James Boutwell, 1804, '05, '06, '07, '08, '09; B. Kinne, 1813; Asa Bancroft, 1815, '16, '17; Willard Shephard, 1819; John Vincent, 1820; Benjamin Whipple, 1821, '22, '23, '24, '25; Jeremy Stone, 1826, '35, '36; Andrew Wheatley, 1827, '28, '29; Jabez L. Carpenter, 1830; Elijah Perry, 1831, '32, '33; Baxter Bancroft, 1834; Mark M. Page, 1837 to '41; James Palmer, 1842, '43; Levi Bartlett, 1844; Nathaniel Sherman, 1845; Nathaniel Townsend, 1846, '58; E. Madison Perry, 1847, '48, '49; Daniel A. Perry, 1850; Amherst Perkins, 1851; Joel Sherburn, 1852, '53; Dudley Perkins, 1854; Allen Martin, 1855; Ira Stone, 1856; Harrison Ketchum, 1859, '60; Charles T. Batchelder, 1861: L. Cheney Batchelder, 1862, 81: Joseph Lane, 1863, '64, '65, '75 to '79; Willard S. Martin, 1866, '71, '72; Heman A. Powers, 1867; Orrin W. Cree, 1857, '68, '70; Thomas P. Bartlett, 1869; Jeremy S. Chamberlain, 1873, '74, '80.

OLD PEOPLE

Who have died in Plainfield.

Mrs. Joseph Lampson, 95; Mrs. Isaac Mann, 94; Moses Bancroft, 87; Mrs. M.

Bancroft, 92; Jonathan Perkins, 89; Spencer Lawrence, 81; Mrs. Spencer Lawrence, 89; Asa Bancroft, 88; Jane (Carns) Hatch, 88; Mrs. Jacob Perkins, 89; Lydia (Carns) Perkins (Mrs. Jonathan), 83; Chauncy Bartlett, 86; Mrs. C. Bartlett, 85; Edmund Freeman, Charles Bancroft, 84; Mrs. N, Townsend, 83; Levi Bartlett, 80; Benjamin Niles, 84; Nathaniel Sherman, 80; Mrs. N. Sherman, 81; Eliza (Carns) White, 80; David Reed, 82; Mrs. D. Reed, 81; James Allen, 84; Roderic Taylor, 83; John P. Ayers, 82; James Batchelder, 81; Allen Martin, 82; Isabella (Nash) Powers, 80; Coolige Taylor, 83; C. W. Alvord, 82; Asa Fletcher, 82; Mrs. A. Fletcher, 85; Daniel Lampson, 80; James Perry, 80; Isaac Mann, Nathan Hill, 82.

OLD PEOPLE LIVING.

Daniel Spencer, 91; Susan Collins, 88; Baxter Bancroft, 87; Mrs. B. Bancroft, 82; Mrs. John P. Ayers, 86; Eben Martin, 85; Mrs. Nathan Parker, 85; Justus Kinney, 83; Mrs. J. Kinney, 80; Susan Corliss, 82; Mrs. Roderic Taylor, 81; William Parks, 81; Benjamin F. Moore, 81; Alex Woodman, 80; Mrs. Levi Bartlett, 80; Nathan Hill, 82.

MASONIC.

RURAL LODGE.—The records of this Lodge having been lost or destroyed, no extended history can be written of it or of its early members. The only authentic papers belonging to it are the original by-laws in manuscript form, from which we learn that a charter was granted by the Grand Lodge at its annual session in Montpelier, Oct. 12. 1825.

Charter Members.—Horace Pitkin, Marshfield; Alden Palmer, Montpelier; Jabez L. Carpenter, Plainfield; Stephen Pitkin, William Martin, Marshfield; William Billings, Nathaniel C. King, Montpelier; Charles Clark, Calais; Nathaniel Bancroft, Silas Williams, Jr., A—— Simons, Plainfield; Merrill Williams, Montpelier; Harvey Pitkin, Edwin Pitkin, James Pitkin, Daniel Spencer, Marshfield; Nathaniel Davis, Robert Nesmith, Montpelier; James English, Marshfield.

The organization of the Lodge was kept up, and some work done, until the annual session of the Grand Lodge in 1830, when they are supposed to have surrendered their charter. Only two of the charter members are known to be living, Daniel Spencer of Plainfield, at the advanced age of 91 years, and Nathaniel C. King, of Montpelier.

WYOMING LODGE, NO. 80.—Wyoming Lodge, F. & A. M., No. 80, was chartered by the Most Worshipful Grand Lodge of Vermont, June 11, A. D. 1868.

Charter Members.—Charles H. Heath, Leroy H. Hooker, Stephen C. Shurtleff, Nathan Skinner, Dudley B. Smith, Jas. M. Perry, Channing Hazeltine, J. M. Richards, William Armstrong, A. H. Whitcomb, Walter B. Page, Mark M. Page, R. H. Christy, Byron Goodwin, Fitch E. Willard, W. S. Little, Ezekiel Skinner, Samuel Simpson, Martin V. B. Hollister, D. M. Perkins, Samuel Wilson, Horace Hill, Reuben Huntoon, Lewis H. Cunningham, N. Davis, Jr., Mason T. Page, Silas E. Willis, Willard Harris, James Pitkin, Luther G. Town, Solomon L. Gilman, Nathaniel Sherman, Daniel Spencer, Nathaniel Davis, Horace H. Hollister, Nathaniel C. Page, C. W. H. Dwinell, E. O. Hammond, Eben D. Stevens.

First officers: Charles H. Heath, W. M.; Loren H. Hooker, S. W.; Stephen C. Shurtleff, J. W.

Officers for 1881-2: W. R. Gove, W. M.; John W. Fowler, S. W,; Dan. W. Moses, J. W.

REV. C. E. FERRIN, D. D.

Abridged from a sketch in the *Vermont Chronicle* by Rev. A. D. BARBER.

CLARK E. FERRIN was born in Holland, Vt., July 20, 1818. He grew up there on the farm with his father till he was of age, teaching a common school in the winter from the time he was 17, and aiding his father in the support of the family. In the fall after he had attained his majority he went to Brownington Academy, of which Rev. A. C. Twilight was preceptor, and began fitting for college. At Brownington he not only set his face collegeward but heavenward, experiencing that change of which our Lord said to Nicodemus, "Except a man be born again he cannot see the kingdom of God." Remaining at Browington about a year, he went to Derby, finished his preparation and entered the University at Burlington in the class of 1841. Though at a disadvantage by lack of early opportunities, by diligent application he gained upon the class during the course, and graduated in 1845, with the last third. The fall after he taught the Academy at Marshfield, and from thence went to Macon, Ga., where he taught for 2 years. From Macon he went to the theological seminary at Andover, Mass., completing the course in the class of 1850. The spring before he graduated at Andover he visited Barton, Vt., preaching there, and receiving a call to the pastorate of the Congregational church. Accepting this call, he was ordained and installed at Barton, in 1857, Rev. O. T. Lamphear, a college classmate, then at Derby, preaching the installation sermon from Exodus IV : 14, "I know that he can speak well." Another, a seminary classmate, Rev. Mr. Dean, gave the charge to the people. Zealous and faithful at Barton, he was after nearly 3 years attacked with that facial neuralgia, which rendered his after life one of almost continued pain, and often for months and years at a time one of intense suffering. His enemy compelled him to suspend his ministry at Barton and seek dismission from his charge. This was granted by council. Dismissed, he sought for a time renewed health and strength in farm labors. As soon as health permitted, he took up the ministry again, received a call, and was installed pastor of the Congregational church in Hinesburgh in 1855. At this second installation, another of his classmates, Rev. N. G. Clark, then professor in the University at Burlington, preached the sermon, and another classmate, Rev. A. D. Barber, of Williston, gave the Right Hand of Fellowship. Here, after no very long time, he began to suffer again from the assaults of his adversary, neuralgia, but for long years, though in real suffering and much of the time in keen distress by day and by night, he persisted in doing a manly work, building with one hand for Christ and his church, and resisting the enemy of his peace and strength with the other. Here, indeed, he fought a good fight, yielding only after many years. In the winter of 1874 he went to Philadelphia, and submitted to the severe surgical operation of removing a part of the facial nerve. This gave only partial relief. In the fall of 1875 he took a voyage to Europe, visiting London and Paris, seeking aid, but finding little. Having failed now for some time in strength, but not in heart to labor, he resigned his pastorate. His resignation was after long waiting and hope of the church and parish for his recovery, accepted, and he was dismissed, having been pastor about 24 years. Remaining in the parsonage at Hinesburgh, and experiencing some relief with returning strength, he was able at length to take up again the work he loved so well. This he did at Plainfield, where he was installed pastor Feb. 13, 1878, Rev. W. S. Hazen, of Northfield, preaching the sermon, from I. Cor. 1 : 23, "We preach Christ and Him crucified," one of his classmates, again a member of the Council, presided and offered the installing prayer. In this his third and last pastorate, our brother labored continuously and successfully, though his old enemy still pursued him. He ceased his labors and entered into rest, after a sickness entirely prostrating him of about 5 weeks, June, 1881. His experience during this last trial was full of the peace of God. "I am surprised," he wrote, telling us the result of the first council of physicians called to consider his case. "The fullness with which I can say, 'Thy will, not mine,' surprises, almost troubles me."

Mr. Ferrin left a wife, 3 sons and 2 daughters; all fitted for usefulness, and of fine promise; all were present at the time of his death. His oldest son, reaching home but a few days before, is Professor William Ferrin, of Pacific University, at Forest Grove, Oregon. The oldest daughter is the wife of Rev. John Cowan, of Essex.

At the funeral, ten neighboring ministers

were present, the deacons of the church from Williston and Montpelier, and a good delegation from Hinesburgh and other towns. His children conducted the services at the house, Prof. Ferrin reading select passages of Scripture, Rev. Mr. Cowan offering prayer, and all the family uniting in singing the hymn, "Rock of ages cleft for me." The service was beautiful, tender and touching. The casket was borne by his brother ministers. At the church, Rev. C. S. Smith read the Scripture, Rev. J. H. Hincks offered prayer, his two classmates, Rev. J. G. Hale and A. D. Barber, spoke; Mr. Hale, of Mr. Ferrin as a man, of his place in college and in the ministry, and Mr. Barber of him as a Christian pastor.

Mr. Ferrin, besides his work as minister, was a most respected and highly useful citizen. He represented the town of Hinesburgh in the legislature one or two sessions, was a faithful and influential member of the corporation of the University for more than 20 years. He received the honorary degree of Doctor of Divinity from Middlebury College at the commencement, a year ago, and was a man such that the family, the church and the State can alike trust.

[Mr. Ferrin compiled from the papers of the venerable Erastus Bostwick the history of Hinesburgh for Vol. I. in this work, and in Vol. III. wrote the biographical sketch of the Rev. O. T. Lamphear in the history of Orleans County.]

SOLDIERS ENLISTED FOR PLAINFIELD IN THE WAR OF THE REBELLION.

Names.	Reg. Co.	Mustered.	Term.	Remarks.
Ayers, George A.	2 F	June 20 61	3 y	
Ball, Henry L. C.	9 I	July 9 62	3 y	Deserted Dec. 25, 62.
Blaisdell, George,	4 G	Sept 20 61	3 y	Died Nov. 29, 61.
Bradford, Amos C.	2 F	do	3 y	
Bradford, John M.	do	do	3 y	Discharged Aug. 26, 63.
Buxton, Chas. B.	4 A	Dec 31 62	3 y	Pris. June 23, 64; died at Andersonville, Ga., Oct. 6, 64.
Bell, Joel	Cav H	Aug 29 64	1 y	Enlisted for Barre, Aug. 26, 61.
Bartlett, Mark	12 D	Oct 62	9 m	
Boles, David	4 G	Jan 20 65	1 y	
Cummins, John D.	do	Sept 20 61	3 y	Discharged Apr. 17, 62. [Church.
Cole, Parker	Cav C	Dec 25 63	3 y	Killed in action May 5, 64, at Craig's
Carr, Jason	12 D	Oct 4 62	9 m	
do	2 Bat	Aug 27 64	1 y	Died June 13, 65.
Clark, Nathaniel	12 D	Oct 4 62	9 m	
Dolan, Bernard	4 B	Feb 15 65	1 y	
Duke, Edward V.	4 G	Feb 25 65	1 y	
Downs, John H.	9 I	July 9 62	3 y	
Edmons, Douglass	Cav F	Sept 26 62	3 y	Promoted corporal.
Fraqua, Peter		Nov 25 63	3 y	Deserted Nov. 1, 63.
Farrar, D. W.	2 Bat	Aug 13 64	1 y	
Farr, Benjamin A.	4 E	Feb 14 65	1 y	
Gale, Sullivan F.	13 C	Oct 10 62	9 m	Sergeant.
Gunnerson, Daniel	12 D	Oct 4 62	9 m	
Haywood, Wm. H.	Cav F	Sept 26 62	3 y	Deserted Feb. 29, 64.
Hill, David	9 I	July 11 62	3 y	Discharged May 9, 63.
Lapieu, Louis	2 D	Apr 22 62	3 y	Discharged Sept. 62.
Lupien, Lewis	Cav K	Dec 3 63	3 y	Promoted corporal.
Leazer, Buzzell	3 H	July 16 61	3 y	Re-enlisted 3d Battery.
Leazer, Joseph	9 I	July 11 62	3 y	Deserted Sept. 28, 62.
Lemwin, Peter	1 Bat	Feb 28 62	3 y	Mustered out Oct. 10, 64.
Ladd, Andrew J.	Cav C	Dec 25 63	3 y	Discharged April 19, 64.
Lease, Joseph N.	4 D	Dec 31 63	3 y	Died July 8, 64, of wounds received in action June 23, 64, Welden Railroad.
Lease, Julian C.	do	do	3 y	Died June, 64.
Lease, Rufus	do	do	3 y	Died at Burlington, Mar. 7, 64.
Lemwin, Rock	17 E	Mar 3 64	3 y	Died at Andersonville, Sept. 3, 64.
Lupien, O. Liva	Cav K	Dec 31 63	3 y	

Names.	Reg, Co.	Mustered.	Term.	Remarks.
Mann, John C.	4 G	Sept 20 61	3 y	Discharged Apr. 21, 62.
Mears, Horace B.	Cav D	Sept 26 62	3 y	Discharged Sept. 18, 63.
Morse, Marshal C.	12 D	Oct 4 62	9 m	
Nye, Ervin	4 A	Dec 31 63	3 y	Discharged May 12, 65.
Nasmith, K. R.	4 G	Jan 20 65	1 y	
Paronto, Gideon	2 A	Apr 12 62	3 y	Died June 17, 62.
Perry, Edwin R.	4 G	Sept 61	3 y	Discharged Oct. 8, 62.
Perry, Willard M.	do	do	3 y	Re-enlisted Dec. 15, 63.
Paronto, Napoleon	Cav K	Dec 31 63	3 y	Deserted Sept. 19, 64.
Porter, Geo. W.	10 I	Jan 5 64	3 y	Prisoner July 9, 64; died March, 65.
Rollins, Charles	2 Bat	Aug 27 64	1 y	
Rollins, Orvis	do	Aug 13 64	1 y	
Reed, Clark	12 D	Oct 4 62	9 m	
Reed, Roswell	do	do	9 m	Sergeant.
Richards, Linus	do	do	9 m	Died May 2, 63.
Rathbury, Ira P.	4 F	Feb 14 65	1 y	.
Spencer, Ira D.	4 G	Jan 20 65	1 y	
Scott, George		Sept 22 62	3 y	Discharged Oct. 21, 62.
Scott, Orange	2 H	June 20 61	3 y	Died Nov. 4, 61.
Shepherd, Dennison	7 K	Feb 21 62	3 y	Re-enlisted.
Shepherd, John	4 G	Sept 20 61	3 y	Discharged April 21, 62.
Shorey, Joseph	2 F	Sept 22 62	3 y	
Simons, Louis	4 G	Sept 61	3 y	Re-enlisted.
Skinner, Ezekiel	do	Sept 20 61	3 y	Discharged Sept. 63,
Stearns, James E.	4 A	Jan 6 64	3 y	Promoted corporal.
Stearns, Lowell	4 K	July 17 63	3 y	Wounded; ambulance train captured; never heard from afterwards.
Taylor, Stephen	2 F	June 20 61	3 y	Re-enlisted Jan. 64.
Valley, Felix	13 C	Oct 10 62	9 m	
Wilson, Calvin O.	9 G	July 9 62	3 y	Died Feb. 23, 65.
Woodcock, C. A.	2 F	Sept 22 62	3 y	
Webster, Nathan L.	4 A	Dec 31 63	3 y	Prisoner June 23, 64; died Dec. 23, 64, soon after being exchanged.
Willey, Geo. W.	2 S S E	Jan 5 64	3 y	Died Feb. 14, 64.
Whicher, Geo.	2 Bat	Aug 19 64	1 y	

Total, 68, of whom there were 5 deserted, 1 killed in action, 2 died of wounds, 11 died of disease, 12 discharged before enlistment expired, 37 served their term, or were discharged at the close of the war.

Furnished under draft—Paid commutation, Solomon Bartlett, Jacob Batchelder, Martin B. Bemis, John D. Cummings, Lucius M. Harris, Jirah S. Lawrence, Alba F. Martyn, Erasmus McCrillis, Philander Moore, Charles Morse.

Procured substitute—Edwin B. Lane.

Revolutionary soldiers—Lieut. Joshua Lawrence, John Bancroft, Solomon Bartlett, Moses Reed.

FUNERAL HYMN FOR GARFIELD.
BY MRS. E. E. YAW.
(Written for the memorial services at Plainfield, Sept. 21, 1881.)

Years a-gone, a cry of woe
Rose to Heaven an April day,
As beneath a murderer's hand
Our martyred Lincoln bleeding lay.
Revive the story of that crime,
How all nations mourned with us,
Bowing with uncovered heads,
Weeping o'er his honored dust.
. . . . .
And to-day, in grief again—
Lord of nations, Lord of might—
We come to thee with cries of pain;
Shine upon our dreary night.
Ah, our tears they fall like rain
That the honor nobly gave,
Placing Garfield at the nation's head,
Led so close beside a grave.

. . . . .
Lay him softly in his narrow bed,
Cover him with garlands fair,
Gentle zephyrs, requiems sing;
Angels watch—leave him there.

The services were in charge of the pastor. Remarks were made by O. L. Hoyt, E. N. Morse, Dr. D. B. Smith, Godwin Reed, Ira Stone, Joseph Bartlett, Allan Ferrin and H. O. Perry.

Mary E. Davis, also, born in this town, has published a book of verse, of which, had a volume been placed at our command, in time, we should have given a review.

ROXBURY.

BY MRS. SARAH BRIGHAM MANSFIELD.

Located in the south part of Washington County, 17 miles south-westerly from Montpelier; bounded N. by Northfield, E. by Brookfield, S. by Braintree and Granville, and W. by Warren; was granted Nov. 6, 1780, and chartered to Hon. Benjamin Emmonds and others August 6, 1781; 23,040 acres, situated on the height of the land between Winooski and White rivers. The village is at the summit, the highest point of land on the Central Vt. R. R. There are no large streams. Three branches of Dog river flow north into the Winooski; one rising on the East Hill, flows south, passing a branch of Dog river at the Summit, one running north, the other south, the latter into White river.

Many years ago, one Capt. Ford, who owned a manufacturing establishment at Randolph, and wished a greater supply of water, came to the Summit, and turned the course of the stream going north into the one flowing south, deriving great benefit therefrom, but of short duration. The trick was detected by mill-owners north, and he was obliged to undo his work, and let the river take its natural course.

There are two natural ponds in town, one just south of the village and one on East Hill. Both have at one time been homes for the "beaver," where they built dams and carried on business beaver style; but long ago they deserted their old haunts, and the pond that once reached to where the village now is, is fast disappearing, and a few years hence will no doubt be *terra firma*.

The surface is uneven, but the soil is fertile. There are some fine dairy farms along the river, and the hill farms are well adapted to wheat raising. The timber is mostly hard wood, with some spruce, hemlock and fir. Rocks, argillaceous slate, soapstone and marble.

There were three divisions of land in this township; the 1st div., the north half of that portion of the town lying east of this valley; the 2d div., the south half; the 3d div., the western side of the town.

The 1st and 2d contain 100 acres; the 3d, 136.

The first road laid in town was in 1799, from Warren line down to the first branch of White River, to the north line of Kingston (now Granville). Next, on the hill west of said branch, from Kingston, until it joins the branch road toward Warren. The third road led from Samuel Richardson's house by John Stafford's and Wilcox's to Warren; Samson Nichols surveyor. In 1802, the road through the middle of the town, from Northfield to Brookfield, was laid out, 6 rods wide. A road was surveyed from Northfield to Brookfield through the east part of the town, in 1802. In 1806, the road was laid from Samuel Smith's on East Hill, by Wm. Gold's to east part of the town. These are a few of the first roads surveyed in town.

The first town meeting was held at the house of Jedediah Huntington; the warning was dated at Williamstown, Mar. 12, 1796, signed by Joseph Crane, justice of the peace, and the meeting was held Mar. 25, 1796; when following the town officers were elected in Roxbury: Joseph Crane, moderator; Thomas Huntington, clerk: Samuel Richardson, Isaac Lewis, Jedediah Huntington, selectmen; David Cram, treasurer: Jonathan Huntington, constable; David Cram and Thomas Huntington, listers; Samuel Richardson and Christopher Huntington, highway surveyors. The sum total of the grand list at this time was £165 and 15s. Zebediah Butler was first town representative; he resided south of what is known as E. K. Young's place.

The first warning for freeman's meeting was in 1797.

Record of the meeting: The freemen of Roxbury, all to a man, met at the house of Jedediah Huntington, in said town, according to warning, when the freeman's oath was duly administered by the town clerk to the following men: Christopher Huntington, Roswell Adams, Isaac Lewis, David Cram, John Stafford, Benoni Webster, Jedediah Huntington, Perus Huntington, Benjamin Hunter, Jr., Daniel Corbin, Chester Batchelder.

The freemen voted as follows: For Gov.,

Isaac Tichenor 9, Nathaniel Niles 4, Paul Brigham 1; Lieut. Gov., Paul Brigham 10, Nathaniel Niles 3; Treas., Samuel Mattocks 14; for counsellors, Elisha Allen 11, Cornelius Lynde 10, Elias Stevens 9, Jonas Galusha 2, Joel Marsh 9, Reuben Hatch 2, Martin Chittenden 2, Joseph Hubbard 1, Ebenezer Walbridge 4, John French 6.

Thomas Huntington, town clerk.

Freeman's oath had previously been administered to Samuel Richardson, Thomas and Jonathan Huntington. There were just 14 voters in town, at that time. In Mar., 1799, voted that from Apr. 1 to May 20, it shall not be lawful for sheep or swine to run at large on the commons or highways, and if willfuly or negligently allowed to run, the owners thereof shall pay double damages. When there were neither highways or commons, even passable for swine or sheep! They also voted, at the same time, that Joseph Newton should have approbation to retail liquors to travellers the ensuing year. For all their privations or hard struggles, these early settlers seemed to have a vein of drollery and fun underlying all. In 1802, they called a meeting to see if the town would vote to *set the small pox* in town. Not wanting it, voted to dissolve the meeting. Sept. 12, 1803, called a meeting to see if the town would vote to set up inoculation of small pox in town; did not want it, and dissolved the meeting. In 1806, voted to raise 7 mills on a dollar for the purpose of buying surveying implements. Chose Samuel Robertson surveyor for the town—to have the use of the instruments for doing the surveying for said town. A compass and chain was bought, a very good one for those times, and is still the property of the town. In 1811, voted to set off the east part of the town to Brookfield. Voted to petition the general assembly at their next session to be annexed to Jefferson Co., (now Washington). To be stingy and small with their neighbors did not seem to be a fault with them.

On record, Jan. 26, 1799, "I, Samuel Richardson, in consideration of the love and good will I bear to my well respected friend, Polly Corbin, gave her a deed of 20 acres of land."

First land tax in town: Petitioned to the legislature for a land tax in 1796. The legislature, then in session at Windsor, raised a tax of one cent on an acre of land in said town. The "delinquents" lands to be soid the 8th day of May, 1798, at David Cram's dwelling-house, by David Cram, constable.

July 31, '98, vendue sale of lands at Jedediah Huntington's, by Abel Lyman, collector.

First deed upon the land records: from Asa Huntington to Daniel Kingsbury, dated at Brookfield, Sept. 3, 1794, recorded Mar. 24, 1796.

In June, 1812, called a meeting to see if the town would provide arms, amunition and equipments for the soldiers who have this day volunteered in the service of their country as minute men. Voted that the monthly pay of each minute man should be raised three dollars per month, while in actual service, payable in grain or neat stock. Voted to deposit magazine and public arms at the dwelling-house of Elijah Ellis, the town having received gun powder and lead. In 1816, voted to set off 4 tiers of lots on east side of town, to form a separate town with part of Brookfield. Passed the same vote in 1827, and seems to have been dropped there, as there is no farther record of the matter.

Christopher Huntington was the first settler. He came to the east part of the town, and built the first house, where O. A. Thayer now lives. He came from Mansfield, Conn., where his children were born, but had resided in Norwich a short time before coming here. He also preached the first sermon in town, to a small but no doubt appreciative audience. He was a Universalist minister, and as the town became settled, preached in various places.

Mr. Huntington drew his goods into town on a hand-sled on bare ground, and with the other early settlers, endured privations hard to realize from the standpoint of to-day. His daughter, Lydia, died Jan. 23, 1792, at the age of 17, the first death in town. Mr. Huntington removed to Canada in 1804. The Mr. Huntington wbo recently died in Canada, bequeathing $25,000 to the State of Vermont, is said to be one of his sons. Another son was several years a Baptist preacher in Braintree.

SAMUEL RICHARDSON was the first to settle in the west part of the town. He was born in Stafford, Conn., June 13, 1750, and was a veteran of the Revolutionary War, having "been out" nearly half the war. His wife, Susanna Pinney, was born July, 1749. After their marriage, they came to Randolph and settled. When the Indians burned Royalton, they passed through Randolph and burned the house next to theirs, but it being somewhat retired, they probably did not discern it. Mr. R. came to this town in 1790, and built a small log-house near where the watch factory now stands, and returned home to come back again in the early spring with his son, Uriah, whom tradition has it, brought a five-pail iron-kettle on his back through the deep snow, with marked trees for roads. A niece of his has injured the story, by declaring her ancestor to have been a brave lad and a willing one, but that he was not a Hercules, and it was really a seven-pail brass-kettle. Well, even that seems almost incredible, considering the distance, and roads. After the sugar-making was well begun, Mr. Richardson returned to Randolph, leaving his son alone in the wilderness for 6 weeks. No one to speak to, no daily or weekly paper; but the solemn hoot of the owl, the lonesome winds through the trees, the howling of the hungry wolves about his cabin, as he said, made weird music, not exactly conducive to sleep. But his father came with the rest of the family as soon as snow was gone. There are said to have been several reasons why Mr. Richardson moved into this wilderness. One, he was greatly averse to his children marrying, and his sons were becoming sturdy young men, and his daughters tall and handsome. And he was not the only one who seemed to realize the fact. Beaux would drop in of an evening; the little by-play on the old settle by the fireplace—naming the rosy-cheeked apples, and comparing them to the not less rosy cheeks of the maidens, going on under *pater familias'* eye, not unnoticed; no sympathetic chord in his heart vibrating to the echo of "long ago," when he leaned

over the gate, and made love to the fair Susanna after escorting her home from spelling-school, away down in old Connecticut. To keep the necks of his offspring out of the "noose," he reflected the surest way was to get them where beaux and belles were not, and removed his family to the wilderness; but even there, four of them out-generalled him at last. His eldest daughter, Sarah, and Chester Batch-elder, Jan. 27, 1799, by Israel Converse, justice of the peace, were made one, and this was the first marriage in town. Hannah, taking courage from the example of her elder sister, married Peter S. P. Staples. Lydia married Charles Cotton, hesitatingly, not swiftly, as lovely maidens should be expected to wed—her lithe form had lost some of its willowy grace, her cheek its first youthful bloom; she was a bride of 45 summers. Samuel married Sally Ellis. Half his children were gone, but by the care and admonitions of this tender sire, half his family were still preserved, four perpetually saved from marriage fate.

That the "females" of this unmated half of the Richardson family were able to care for themselves, and give a helping hand to the weak of the stronger sex, the following proveth : "Tim" Emmerson had a large amount of grain to be harvested, and no help to be had at any price; it was already over-ripe; Susan and Mary Richardson, who were noted for thrift, and disliked to see anything go to waste, offered, if their brother would accompany them, to give the poor man a lift. The men folk smiled as the resolute damsels came into the field, but as the golden grain fell before their gleaming sickles, and was dexterously bound and placed in stooks by their deft hands, the men hung their diminished heads, and the perspiration coursed down their brown cheeks as they vainly strove to keep pace with their fair reapers. Before night tradition saith each masculine had fallen meekly to the rear. Mary and Susan sheared their own sheep, and if occasion required, could chop off a 2 foot log as soon as most men.

Susan Richardson was once going home from "squire" Robertson's, through the

93

woods. She heard a strange cry as of some one in distress. It was growing dusk, the sound came nearer and nearer: she could see it was gaining upon her at every step. She was a very courageous person, not easily scared, but as those quick, sharp screams fell upon her ears, the grass didn't grow under her feet until she reached the clearing; but, once out of the woods, she gathered her sheep into a place of safety before she sought shelter for herself. It was found, the next day, a catamount had followed her; his tracks were plainly visible in the soft earth. It had followed her to the edge of the woods, which reached nearly to her house. At another time, she, with a friend who was visiting her, went to a neighbor's for an "afternoon tea." It was late before they got started for home, and all the way through the woods. They heard the dismal howling of wolves. Susan knew the sound very well, but her friend, unused to pioneer life, had no idea, and wondered, as Susan took her babe from her arms and hurried rapidly forward. When they reached the clearing, and Susan had gathered in her sheep, and they were safe in the house, she told her friend it was wolves they had heard, and they would surely have got her baby had they not quickened their pace.

A grand-daughter of Mrs. Richardson's told me another little incident that occurred when she was a child of twelve. Herself and a younger brother were in the woods gathering flowers, they had wandered some ways farther than they were aware, the sister was wakened to a realizing sense of it when she spied, but a few feet from them, a large white-faced bear, erect on his hind paws, coming towards them. Not wishing to frighten her brother, who was very timid, and fearing he would be overcome with terror, she took him by the hand and strove to hurry him away; but no, just a few more flowers, he said. He was determined not to go home. "See there," said she, pointing to the bear, who stood contemplating the situation. The boy beheld, and gave so terrific a scream, that the bear turned and fled as fast as his clumsy limbs could carry him, preferring to go without his supper to making it off a boy who could scream so loud.

Another reason given (to return to Mr. Richardson's reasons for coming to this town), was that when the bass viol was carried into church at Randolph, it was more than his orthodox nerves could stand, and he preferred the primeval forest, "God's own temple," with the birds to sing anthems of praise, and no profane, new-fangled instrument, made by the hand of man, with which to worship God for him. He was a Congregationalist deacon, and his wife was a member of the Baptist church. They lived in their log-house only about a year, and then moved farther up, where they built the first framed house in town—where Julius Kent now lives—many years afterwards sold to Jonathan Burroughs, and moved near the village, and is the frame of Mrs. Martell's house.

Mr. Richardson built a saw and gristmill above where Mr. Kent now lives, and a larger house leading to the S. E. Spaulding place. A grand-daughter of theirs, who is now 79 years of age, and who spent much of her childhood with them, tells me Mr. Pinney, the father of her grandmother Richardson, was high in the esteem of King George, and was commissioned by him to attend to a great deal of business for His Majesty in New England.

GEORGE the Third, by the Grace of GOD of *Great Britain*, *France* and *Ireland*, KING, Defender of the Faith, &c.

To all to whom these Presents shall come, GREETING.

KNOW YE, That We have assigned, constituted and appointed, and by these Presents do assign, constitute and appoint Our trusty and well beloved Subject, Isaac Pinney, Esq., to be Judge of Our Court of Probate, to be holden within the District of Stafford, in our Colony of *Connecticut*, in *New England*, with the Assistance of a Clerk, to hold our said Court of Probate of Wills, granting of Administration, appointing and allowing of Guardians, with full Power to act in all Matters proper for a prerogative Court.

In Testimony whereof, We have caused the Seal of Our said Colony to be hereunto affixed. *Witness*, Jonathan Trumbull, Esq., Governor of our said Colony of *Connecticut*, and with the Consent of the

General Assembly of the same in Hartford, this first Day of June, in the 13th Year of Our Reign, *Annoque Domini*, One Thousand Seven Hundred and Seventy-three. By His Honor's Command,

JON'A. TRUMBULL, *Gov.*
GEORGE WYLLYS, *Sec'y.*

At one time he received important messages from the King, and although he had six clerks, he took his daughter, afterward Mrs. R., from school as his private secretary. His daughters were all taught the science of medicine, and Mrs. R. attended to the sick in this town before other physicians came in, and some afterwards, going about on horseback, with a heavy riding dress for unpleasant weather. She never shrank where duty called, and not expecting other recompense than the gratitude of those she served; for in those primitive days the few inhabitants were not burdened with riches, and were neighborly to each other.

One fall, seeing the destitution around them, Mr. R. took a yoke of oxen to Williamstown, exchanged them for potatoes, and divided them among the destitute, taking his pay in work as they could do it. Mrs. Richardson at this time gave her family two meals per day, with a cup of milk for supper, giving what they saved by so doing to the needy ones.

Living on the road that crossed the mountain to Warren, the glimmer of light from their windows was often a most welcome sight to the benighted traveler. A man overtaken by night, with intense cold and darkness, crawled on his hands and knees for miles, fearing he should lose the track that led to their house, knowing if he did he must perish. Large, warm hearts these people had, with a hand ever out reached to help any poorer than themselves. Their noble charities, their exemplary Christian characters amid all the struggles and hardships of pioneer life, are most worthy of imitation. They, with their children, all of whom reached maturity, now rest in the old burying-ground, near the residence of O. A. Staples.

DAVID CRAM,

one of the next to come into town, was from Lyndsboro, N. H. His son, Philip,

born Mar. 18, 1795, was the first male child born in town. Lydia Huntington, daughter of Jedediah H., got four days start of him, so the honor of being the first child born in town rests upon her. Whether she is living, I am unable to say; but Philip Cram married Abigail Heath, of Randolph, and is now living in Brookfield.

Daniel Corbin came from Randolph about this time, and Isaac Lewis, David, Robert and Jonathan Cram located on farms now owned by Messrs. Chatterton, Bowman and Orra Boyce.

Benoni Webster came, in 1798, I think, from Connecticut, and located on the place now occupied by James Steele. Mr. Webster came from Connecticut with an ox-team, rather a slow mode of conveyance for the distance, but "patience and perseverance" were household words in those days. The "blue laws" did not allow people to be moving on Sunday in the old state, and Mr. Webster was stopped in a small village to give an account of himself. He declared it was against his principles to be traveling on the Sabbath, but his wife had been exposed to the small pox, and he was in great haste to get to his journey's end. He was allowed to pass on. His oldest son, Charles, born in Connecticut, married Eleanor P. Ryder, and settled in the east part of this town, where his second son, Aaron, now resides, and is the only one of the family in the State.

Charles Webster was killed by being thrown from his carriage in 1834. Benoni Webster, the youngest of the family, is still living, at an advanced age, in Northfield. He was born in a barn, not a modern affair, but an old log-barn. Whether he was cradled in a manger, tradition saith not. One of the children being so ill he could endure no noise, to secure him the quiet needed to save his life, the rest of the family moved into the barn, with the exception of one to nurse the sick child, and there they remained until he was restored to health, which was over a year.

JOEL HILDRETH

came to this township in the autumn of 1797, from Cornish, N. H., and boarded with a family who lived on the farm now owned by G. L. Walbridge, while he built his log-house on the place now owned by Mr. George Williams, who purchased of Mr. Hildreth's grand-son, Samuel A. Hildreth, a few years since. One morning soon after Mr. Hildreth was settled in his cabin, he heard a rooster crow to the eastward, and as the ringing notes came across the wooded valley, it fell upon his ears like music. He followed that "crow" for four or five miles, and at last found his new neighbors in Northfield, near where William Winch now resides.

Mr. Hildreth, with his trusty rifle, was a terror to the denizens of the forest, having, to use his own words, "unbuttoned many a bear's shirt collar." Upon one occasion returning late in the evening from his day's work, he heard a bear clambering down a tree close at hand. He could hear his claws clinging in the bark, and could just discern in the darkness the dim outlines of his unwieldy figure. He was alone in the forest, a great ways from home; thoughts of the dear ones there awaiting him nerved his arm. He dealt the bear a powerful blow with his ax, and fled. Returning next morning to the "scene of carnage," they found he had decapitated a huge hedge-hog, and pinned him to the tree with his ax. Mr. Hildreth resided on the place he had cleared up until his death in 1844.

WILLIAM GOLD,

known as Deacon Gold, came to town with Samuel Robertson, and after working for him one year, bought a piece of land, a mile east of Dog river, and built a log-cabin. This is where he had a famous bear fight. The bears had been making havoc with the Deacon's cornfield, and he swore a "pious oath" [made a pious resolve would be better for a deacon], the thieves should be captured. A trap was devised that none but a very wise bear would fail of walking straight into, for a taste of the tempting bait. The bear that came was not a wise one, for when the

Deacon appeared on the ground next morning, bright and early, sure enough there was a great surly fellow, with one of his hind paws fast in the trap. The Deacon seized a club and rushed forward, old bruin equally ready and delighted with an interview, striking the club from his hand like a flash, cordially clasped the Deacon in his furry arms, and had about squeezed the life out of him, when the hired man, Paddleford, came to the rescue with an axe. "Don't cut the hide!" gasped the Deacon, as bruin clasped him in a still more fervid embrace. The hide was cut in several places before the poor Deacon was released, who, though "pure grit," came out of the combat in a sadly demolished condition, and carried the marks of bear teeth and claws to his grave.

From John Gregory's History of Northfield.

DEA. WILLIAM GOLD,

born in Springfield, Mass., Oct. 30, 1780; came to Roxbury in 1801, and settled upon one of the highest mountains in that town. He was a deacon of the Baptist church. Any one at this day looking the mountain land over where he located, can see under what discouraging circumstances this early settler was placed.

In 1847, he removed to Northfield. He married Annevera Dewey, who was born in 1780; had 7 children: Annevera, William, Sherman, Buel, Joseph, Mary, Sophia, all born in Roxbury. Deacon Gold died in 1859; Mrs. Gold in 1856.

JOHN B. CRANDALL

moved into town in 1804; was eccentric, quite a pettifogger, and always called "Judge." One time, having a lawsuit, he became disgusted with his counsel, considered an able lawyer, paid him off and dismissed him before the suit was fairly commenced, plead his own case, and won it. Another time he went to Waitsfield to take charge of a lawsuit. Knowing his opponent, an attorney from Montpelier, to be extremely fastidious in his tastes and manner of dress, he chose the other extreme, an awfully shabby coat, and trowsers that suggested the idea that some time in an earlier stage of existence they had been the property of a Methodist preacher—they had certainly done a great deal of knee service—a dilapidated hat, a boot on one foot, an old shoe on the other, completed his outfit. The fine gentleman strutting back and forth in dignity, wondered why Mr. Crandall did not arrive, when some one turning to Mr. C., introduced them. The Montpelier attorney looked at Mr. C., surprise and contempt expressed in every feature. "What, *that creature!*" he at last blurted out; "why, he don't know enough to say boo to a goose." The "Judge" drew his grotesque figure to its full height, made a low bow, and said "boo!" very emphatically in the face of the offended lawyer, which brought down the house, and the sleek gentleman was yet more discomfited when he lost his case, and the "Judge" won the laurels he had anticipated.

Mr. Crandall's widow married Jonathan Lamson, of Fayston, where she died a few years since, at the advanced age of 108. (See History of Fayston.)

LEWIS CHATFIELD

came to town in 1810, and settled on the farm now occupied by his son, Lewis. He was a man of peculiarities, but sterling worth. He, like many of the early settlers, had a hard struggle to feed and clothe his family. One winter he fortunately captured a huge bear, whose meat and lard kept grim want from the door till spring. He made a business of hop raising the last 40 years, and through industry and frugality, acquired a competence. He died in 1880, aged 94.

BILLA WOODARD

came from Tolland, Conn., in 1802; settled on East Hill, and was for many years engaged in the manufacture of saddle-trees, and the only one in New England for a long time in that business.

HON. CHARLES SAMSON

came here in 1810. Z. S. Stanton, in his Historical Centennial Address, thus speaks of him:

He accompanied his father, Benjamin Franklin, who was a veteran of the Revolution, and participated in the battle of Lexington and Bunker Hill.

Mr. Samson bought the place where L. A. Rood now lives. The previous occupant was Dr. Stafford, who kept a tavern, and the first in town. Charles Samson settled where Mr. Wetmore lives. He has been closely identified with the affairs of this town ever since, and is still permitted to be with us. He has represented the town in the legislature of the State for 13 sessions, and has held many other important positions in the town and county. It was owing to his exertions that Roxbury was transferred from Orange to Washington County, in 1820. In those days the main road through the west part of the town, which was also the stage road, led from where A. J. Averill now lives past where the residences of W. I. Simonds and S. G. Stanton now are, and intercepted the mountain road near where Mrs. Brackett now lives, thence up where the present road is as far as the old mill above Royal Batchelder's house, and then past the present residence of O. A. Staples, down to the "Branch road," where Samuel Edwards now lives. From here it followed its present course. There was also a road through the eastern part of the town, and also the central part, where E. K. Young now resides. Elijah Ellis lived where Mrs. Brackett now does. He built the house at this place, and it was the first house built in town that was arranged for the use of stoves, I am informed. He had no fireplace or "stack of chimneys," as they were called, and people thought it a great departure from the old ways. He built the first clover-mill that was erected in this town, on the site now occupied by S. N. Miller's carriage-shop. He also erected a saw-mill at this place.

BENONI WEBSTER,
(BY A. WEBSTER.)

A native of Connecticut, brought his family to Roxbury in the spring of 1797. He had previously lived in Hartland, Vt., a few years.

He settled in the N. E. part of the town on lot No. 3, of the 1st range, now owned by James Steele, which he had bought in 1796, then an unbroken wilderness. His first house was logs, roofed with bark, and floored with split basswood, smoothed with an axe. In 1810, he built a large framed-house, making the rooms about 2 feet higher than it was usual to make them at that time, so that "Uncle Sam Metcalf (of Royalton), could stand up in them with his hat on." The doors were also made unusually high, so that his wife's tall relations could come in without stooping, as he said. He was the first to plant fruit trees in town, a large apple orchard, and pear and plum trees in the garden being among his earlier improvements.

It is said that at the time of the memorable great November snow-storm, the effects of which may still be seen in our forests in bent and distorted trees, while the family were at dinner, the young apple trees were discovered to be breaking down beneath the fast accumulating snow, and the boys left their bowls of "hominy and milk" to shake the apple trees, which were saved only by repeating the shaking at short intervals through the afternoon and evening.

In 1804, his entire stock of cattle, consisting of a yoke of 4-years-old oxen and of 2 cows, were bitten by a mad dog that came along, and all died and were buried in one hole together.

Mr. Webster died Jan. 8, 1823, aged 60 years, 9 months, 21 days, leaving a wife, who died in 1838, aged 66 years, and 6 sons and 4 daughters, all of whom lived to have families of their own. Of these but two, Edmund Webster, of Randolph, and Benoni Webster, of Northfield, are known to be now living; but the descendants of the third and fourth generations are widely scattered through the country from New Hampshire in the East to California in the West, and from Minnesota in the north to Texas in the South; but one family, that of the writer, being left in Roxbury.

CHARLES WEBSTER.

BY A. WEBSTER.

Charles, oldest son of Benoni and Sally Metcalf Webster, was born June 5, 1790, at Lebanon Parish, Conn., and came to Roxbury with his father when 7 years old, and was educated in the common schools of district No. 1 and the home college by his father's hearth, reading by the light of the open fire during the autumn and winter evenings. It was his custom to keep a supply of birch bark to furnish light when the usual fire was insufficient.

Being the oldest boy and large of his age, he was his father's chief assistant in clearing away the forest and making a cul-

tivated farm. One of his recreations at this time was fishing in the stream that runs through the valley half a mile north of his father's farm, where the brook trout were so abundant that he often hired one of the Adams boys to help him carry his fish up the hill, home.

The wolves made havoc with the sheep of the neighborhood, and he and the Gallup boys devised a plan to capture them. They built a conical pen of saplings, about 6 feet high, and placed in it a couple of lambs to entice the wolves into the trap, shrewdly calculating while it would be easy for the wolves to run up the inclined sides and leap down into the pen, it would not be so easy for them, after gorging with mutton, to leap out.

Sanguine of success, they visited the trap every morning, expecting to find a large pack of fierce wolves safely corraled and howling with rage. This for several mornings. At length, one morning when they came to inspect, beginning to wonder why the wolves were so slow in getting in; the trap seemed to be empty. No lambs appeared skipping around within, and after a close examination, there appeared only a few bones and shreds of wool. The wolves had doubtless climbed upon the shoulders of each other and got out. Their two lambs were gone for nought. Not to be foiled in this way, the boys immediately built a much stronger and higher pen, but the wolves were not heard from afterwards, and it was supposed they left the place in disgust.

He commenced teaching school when quite young, and followed it for fourteen winters, acquiring such a reputation as a teacher and disciplinarian that his services were often sought for in schools where other teachers had failed.

On one occasion, it is said that some large boys burned his ferule, and made other preparations for carrying him out, as they had a previous teacher. The game commenced promptly, but a leg hastily wrenched from a bench did such effective service that there was no further use for instruments of discipline during that term.

In Aug. 1823, he married Eleanor P. Ryder, and settled on his farm in East Roxbury, half a mile below the mills where his son, Aaron, now resides, where he lived till the next spring, when, having bought a part of the farm of his father's estate, he moved on to it, and lived there until the spring of 1830, when he returned to his first farm, where he lived until his death, Nov. 5, 1834.

About 1830, he raised from his famous "Wild Air" mare twin colts, of which he was proud; but one of which, a noble and powerful animal, but skittish and uncontrollable when frightened, was the occasion of his instantaneous death, by being thrown from his wagon in the night, near the Peck farm in Brookfield. He had often expressed a presentiment that he should die by accident, and was the last of three cousins, the oldest sons of three sisters, to be killed instantly by accident.

SPAULDING FAMILY.

Darius Spaulding was from Plainfield, Conn., married Hannah Ingraham from Providence, R. I. They had a number of children when they came here, in 1799. Mr. Spaulding came in the fall, slashed a piece, built a log-house, and moved his family the next spring. Nearly, and perhaps all the Spauldings in town at the present day, and they are very numerous, are descendants of Darius and Hannah Spaulding. They reared a family of 8 sons and 3 daughters.

Gilbert, the eldest, married Renda Mc Clure, moved to New York, and died at the ripe age of 90. He was a great chopper, even for those days, when all were supposed to know how to wield an ax. It is said 8 cords only made him a fair day's work, nothing at all to boast of.

Darius Jr. married Betsey Spaulding, and they lived and died at a good old age, in Roxbury. Two of their sons still live in town, Charles and Samuel.

John, the 3d son of Darius Sen., married Betsey McClure, of Stafford, Conn. They commenced keeping hotel in 1822, near where Julius Kent now lives. They had also a saw and grist-mill.

Mr. Burnham, merchant at Roxbury vil-lage, says, when a small boy, he went there with his grist, and Mrs. Spaulding who was an energetic little woman, took his grain, carried it into the mill, ground it and brought it back to him.

Mr. Spaulding built the Summit House in 1830, where he remained until a few years previous to his death, in 1864. His widow is still living, hale and happy, loved and respected. Her friends celebrated her 90th birth-day the 9th of last Sept. [1881.] She has had 5 children, all of whom are living, Erastus N. Billings, Mrs. P. Wiley, Mrs. Brackett and Mrs. A. N. Tilden. All living in their native town, clustered about their aged mother.

Philip married Polly Nichols, of Northfield, is now living in Hermon, N. Y., 84 years of age.

Erastus, the 4th son, built the house where Dea. Edwards now lives, and kept a hotel there several years. He married a widow, Whitcomb, by name, from Waitsfield. They removed to DeKalb, N. Y., where he died a short time since, at an advanced age.

Allen was their first child, born in this town in 1804, and married Hannah Samson in 1828; moved on to the Rood place, and kept a small store 3 years; then built a store in the village, which he occupied for 10 years, near the R. R. crossing, where Geo. Butterfield now resides. He represented the town 4 years. He enlisted, in '61, in Co. H, 6 Vt. Reg., as major; was appointed sergeant with captain's pay.

At one time during the war, he was ordered to take a small squad of men, and go in search of cattle for beef, as it had been a long time the regiment had subsisted on salt meat and "hard tack." They travelled till nearly night before they got track of what they were in quest of, and they found themselves 25 miles from camp in the enemy's territory. Being told a woman near by owned a fine flock of sheep, he took a couple of men and called on her. She with her two daughters sat on a rustic seat in a beautiful garden, surrounded with the appearances of wealth and luxury. He made known his errand, when out of her mouth poured a torrent of oaths and the coarsest invectives that he had ever heard a woman utter, abusing him and the Union army in general. A servant rode up on an elegant horse, and dismounting, asked his mistress " if she knew she was addressing Union officers?" She said she knew it very well. The Major informed her he came to buy her sheep, but as she had none to sell to " Union men," he should take them without if they suited him, and ordering one of his men to mount the horse her servant had just dismounted from, they rode off, amid the hysterical screams of the mother and daughters. They camped for the night on an old plantation, about 2 miles from there, but had pickets out to keep an eye on the movements of the enemy. After all was quiet at the plantation, 200 mounted darkies came, and attempted to retake the widow's property, but at the first crack of a rifle, they " skedaddled." The Major got back to camp with 25 head of fat cattle, and presented the beautiful pony to the Colonel.

At another time there were 100 men sick, and the surgeon said they would all die unless they had milk. The Major was ordered to take 10 men and go and buy milk for the sick. They went to a plantation where 100 cows were kept, just as they were coming off the ranche to be milked. They asked to buy milk for sick soldiers. The surly old fellow said he had " no milk to sell Union soldiers." The Major went back, got a permit from the Provost Marshal, and was there early the next morning; selected 10 fine cows, and in spite of the old gentleman's protesting, drove them to camp. The sick had milk freely, and when they were ordered to Florida, in 6 weeks from that time, every man but one was able to go. The Major turned over his dairy to the Provost Marshal, according to army regulations, and the surly old fellow who would not sell milk to sick soldiers, never recovered his lost kine.

So carefully did Major Spaulding look after the interests of the soldiers, he was called the father of the regiment. He is now living, hale and hearty, at the age of 77, and the oldest person living but one who was born in town, and has lived there the most part of his life.

SAMUEL ROBERTSON,
(BY OHAMEL RICHARDSON.)

Son of Patrick and Elizabeth Robertson, natives of Scotland, was born in New London, Ct., Aug. 18, 1775. He lost his father when quite young. His mother married again, and lived in Stafford, Ct., where he lived till he came to this town. Aug. 1801, he married Persis Richardson, of Tolland, Ct., and the next March they moved here, on to the place now owned by John Cumins, on East Hill. Their first business after getting settled was sugaring. They made 16 pounds, their stock of sugar for that year.

There were only five or six families in that part of the town. Mr. Samuel Richardson had a few years before begun a settlement in the extreme west part of the town, and that at this time was the "center" of civilization, and here Mr. Robertson taught a school during the winter of 1802 and '3. The school-house was the first framed building in town, and stood very nearly where the Royal Batchelder house now does. He had 68 scholars, and the room being small, they were packed like " herrings in a box," and came from five or six miles around in different directions. He lived some 3 miles distant, and walked to and from his school each day through the deep snows, with no track most of the way except what he made himself. He taught here two or three succeeding winters, and during the time moved into the school-house he had occupied, and lived there a few years, when he bought the land now owned by Hira G. Ellis, and made a permanent settlement, clearing up the forests and erecting comfortable buildings. His house was on the old road leading by where Dea. W. I. Simonds and S. G. Stanton now live. He moved his buildings, about 1834, down on to the county road, where they now stand. Here he lived until within 12 years of his death.

He possessed a vigorous mind, and was very fond of investigation and argument, especially on religious subjects. His house was known far and wide as the "minister's tavern," and ministers of all "evangelical sects" usually made it their home when in that vicinity, and nothing suited him better than to have some stiff Baptist or Calvinist stop over night. On all such occasions, as soon as supper was over, chores done and candles lighted, the gauntlet was sure to be thrown down, and then came the " tug of war"—generally the old clock in the "square room" struck twelve before the battle ceased, and then only from exhaustion, and never because either party considered themselves vanquished. He was a great reader, and never failed or feared to express his opinion on any subject up for public discussion, and never failed to cast his vote every year after he attained his majority until his death. He was once in the state of New York, teaching, when an election occurred, and altho' but a temporary resident of the state, so great was his interest in the election, he purchased a piece of land for the sole purpose of being qualified to vote (a property qualification being then necessary in that state).

He held many town offices in the early part of his life, but was rather too pronounced and positive in his opinions of men and measures to be "popular" in political circles. He took an active part in the first temperance movement which agitated New England. He had previous to that time been a temperate user of ardent spirits, but when the subject was presented to him, he at once gave it his unqualified support, and conferring "not with flesh and blood," he banished every drop from his house, and going farther, he abandoned the use of tobacco, breaking a habit of 30 years standing.

There is an anecdote about his using tobacco: Some 60 years ago, Moses Claflin, a simple man who lived in this town, who occasionally made his home with Mr. R., one evening sat by the fire in a "brown study," and Esq. Roberston sat opposite, quietly chewing, and now and then spitting into the broad fireplace. At last Moses looked up and asked, "Squire,

what did you learn to chew tobaker for?" Mr. Roberston replied, "Oh, so's to be a gentleman." Moses studied the matter a moment and with great gravity replied, "W'al, ye did'nt make out, did ye?"

Mrs. Roberston died Dec., 1859, after a married life of almost 60 years, during which she had borne her full share of the duties and cares of their lot.

Twice after they came to Vermont she made the journey to the home of her youth in Connecticut on horseback, a feat our lady equestrians of to-day would hardly care to undertake.

Ever after the death of his wife, Mr. R. seemed to lose his hold of things earthly, and to be quietly waiting for the realization of the faith which had been an anchor to him and his companion during their long pilgrimage together. He was a life-long Christian. He maintained his mental faculties to a remarkable degree up to within a few weeks of his death, and was during his latter years very cheerful, very grateful for kindnesses he received, and at last passed away as an infant sinks to slumber, beloved by all who knew him, Sept. 6, 1872, aged 97 years, 19 days.

SETH RICHARDSON came here in 1802; settled near Braintree, in the south part of the town; died May 25, 1829, and Sarah, his wife, died July 1, 1836. Their children were: Phila, Hannah, Joel, Alva.

JOSIAH SHAW came to town in 1800; lived in the East part, and was quite a prominent man. Henry Boyce, son of Dr. Boyce, was also a prominent man in the East part of the town. He died in 1860.

JONATHAN F. RUGGLES was a resident of the east part of the town, and perhaps no man enjoyed in a greater degree the confidence of his fellow-townsmen, there being no office of importance but he had at some time filled. He died in Northfield.

ALVIN BRIGHAM
came here when a young man, about the year 1823, from Fayston. He was born in Old Marlborough, Mass., and a brother of Elisha Brigham (for whose biographical sketch see Fayston, this vol.) Alvin Brigham married Flora Baxter, of

Fayston. They moved on to the present Wetmore place. He was a man scrupulously honest, a leader in the church, and for many years leader of the choir. They had 9 children.

The eldest son, Ozro, fell in the last war. Don, the youngest son, served through the rebellion, but died a short time after his return. Bravely like a true soldier he yielded up his young life without a murmur, when life was fairest; ere the clouds had dimmed the horizon of his sky, bade them all— his dear ones—a smiling "good-bye," and went out into the great "unknown."

Two other children died during an epidemic of fever—Flora Ann, 18, and Alphonso, 14 years of age. One son and three daughters now reside in Lowell, Mass., and the second son, William, lives in the edge of Northfield. Mr. Brigham was a great sufferer for several years before his death. When the summons came, and told he might live an hour, he said, "O! can I wait so long before I shall be with my Father?" He died in 1871; his wife survived him only a few months.

EBENEZER L. WATERMAN

is one of the early—not earliest—settlers. He came from Connecticut, as did most of them, but when he was very small. He has been a great musician in his day, and people are scarce in Central Vermont who have not heard of "Uncle Eb." Waterman and his violin. And even now, when he is between 80 and 90 years of age, the young people delight to gather in "Uncle Eb.'s" ample kitchen, and "trip the light fantastic toe," or listen to the still sweet strains of his old violin. At the age of 45 he married a wife of 18. They had 6 children.

BERT WATERMAN, leader of the Howard Opera House Orchestra at Burlington, is his only living son, and probably has not his peer in the State as violin player.

ORCUTT FAMILY.

Capt. Job came from Stafford, Conn., in 1803; was a carpenter by trade. He settled on the high lands then, and for many years, the centre of the town. He had 7 sons and 4 daughters.

Samuel M. Orcutt, with whom he spent his declining years, was one of the stirring business men of those times, holding various important offices from time to time. He was town clerk for 20 years, and town meetings were held at his house for a long time. At the time of the "invasion" at Plattsburgh in 1812, he went out as Captain of Roxbury Co. (said company including every man in town excepting Samuel Richardson, who much regretted that he was too aged, and Job Orcutt, a lame man.) Capt. Samuel Orcutt married Mary Buel, of Lebanon, Conn., and the bride came to her new home on horseback. They reared a family of 7 boys and 2 girls. The eldest daughter married Wm. Gold, of Northfield, where she now resides.

Samuel A. received an injury while assisting at a "raising," from a falling timber, from which he never recovered. He died in 1835.

Benjamin F. went to Michigan just previous to the Mexican war; enlisted and served through the war: returned to Kalamazoo, Mich., where he was elected county sheriff, and filled that office many years. When the rebellion broke out, he again enlisted, and went out as Lieut. Col. of the 25th Mich. Reg't., serving under Gen. Sherman until the war was over, when he returned to Kalamazoo, and was again elected high sheriff, and Dec. 12, 1867, was fatally shot, while on official duty, by a desperado who was trying to assist prisoners to escape from the jail. He died in the prime of a noble manhood, aged 53. James, 3d son, died when quite young.

Orrin has lived in town most of the time since his birth. He has been sheriff and deputy 25 years; postmaster 26 years, occupying that position at the present time.

Wm. B. has always resided in his native town; has 3 times represented the town in the legislature, and 2 years been county judge.

Stephen P. remained at the old family homestead many years, but now resides in Northfield. The aged mother spent her last days with him, dying, at the age of 96, in 1879. Jasper H. was the 7th son. He moved to Northfield.

SCHOOL DISTRICTS.

No. 1 district, in the east part of the town, was set off in 1801, then known as Daniel Kingsbury district, afterwards as Wales district, No. 1. In 1802 a district was set off in the N. W. part of the town, where Samuel Richardson now lives, known as N. West district, No. 2. In 1805, another district was formed in the S. E. part of the town, known as David Cram's district, No. 3. The same year it was voted all the inhabitants not in regular districts should form one district, No. 4. There have been alterations from year to year and new districts organized. There are now 11 districts and 10 good school-houses in town.

The number of scholars in 1807 were 108; 1811, 104; 1816, 157; 1831, 431; 1849, 418; 1850, 351; 1860, 336; 1880, 251; the average since 1816 to 1881, 340 scholars yearly.

EARLY TAVERNS AND LATER HOTELS.

The first tavern in town was where Conway now lives, what is known as the "Rood place," John Stafford, proprietor. The next was kept by Darius Spaulding, where Frank Snow now lives. John Spaulding kept the third hotel, opposite where Mr. Pearsons now lives, on the mountain road.

In East Roxbury, Stillman Ruggles, E. B. Pride, Samuel P. Wales, Shubael Wales, Alpheus Kendall, kept a public house on the Samuel Edwards place.

The Summit House, built in 1822, by John Spaulding, and occupied by him, has been kept by Stephen Fuller, Chester Clark, Page J. C. Rice, E. G. Sanborn, Van Ness Spaulding, Edwin Ferris, James P. Warner, Thomas Wilson, E. N. Spaulding, Spaulding & Colby, Spaulding & Nichols, Warner & Spaulding, Mrs. J. P. Warner, present proprietor, and D. A. Spaulding.

EARLY MERCHANTS.

The first in town was Asa Taylor, near where E. N. Spaulding's steam-mill stands.

The next was Robertson & Orcutt, who also had a potash run, and manufactured salts. Allen Spaulding, Orrin Orcutt, were the next in order among the first settlers. Partridge built the store where the post-office now is, and occupied it for several years. Then Brackett & Thorp, E. N. Spaulding, Benjamin Spear, Seth Holman and J. A. White. Union Store.

CEMETERIES.

In 1804, the town laid out three burying-grounds; one in the west part of the town, on Uriah Richardson's farm, near where O. A. Staples now lives; one in the east part of the town, on the road from Roxbury to Braintree, near where Mr. Bowman now lives, and one in the centre of the town, on the Billa Woodard farm. Some years later another was located on the Haynes farm—the lot given by the Haynes family, and the only one in use at the present time in the west part of the town. There was also one laid out in the east part of the town, near the Henry Boyce place, about the same time. Albert Averill has been sexton for many years.

EPIDEMICS.

This has ever been called a healthful locality; and with good reason,·yet at different times it has been visited by epidemics. The dysentery swept through the town, carrying off many victims, in 1823. The diphtheria has appeared at different times in epidemic form, and desolated many homes.

PHYSICIANS

who have lived here: John Stafford was the first. How well versed in the science of medicine he may have been there is no record; but there is no doubt but he dealt out "pills and potions" to the early settlers with a generous hand, to say nothing of cupping, blistering and bleeding.

Next came Dr. David McClure, from Stafford, Conn., the father of Mrs. John Spaulding, who remained in town during the rest of his life.

Dr. Hunter lived several years where E. L. Waterman now lives, and was considered a skilful physician, as was Dr. Boyce, of the East part, who practiced there at the same time.

For several years there was no physician in town. Dr. White came for a few months, in 1868, and Dr. S. N. Welch in 1870, and remained a few years, building the house where Mr. Frink now lives, and he had a very good practice.

Dr. George Maloy, of Montpelier, was the next. He was a student of Dr. Woodard, of Montpelier, but remained only a few months.

Dr. Ira H. Fiske came from Hardwick in 1878, and is the only physician in town at the present time, and is the only homœopathic physician that ever settled in town, and has been very successful.

MANUFACTORIES.

Samuel Richardson built the first saw and grist-mill in town, 1½ miles from the village, on the Warren road. He afterwards built another on the west branch of Dog River, about half a mile from the village. Elijah Ellis built a saw and clover-mill in 1818, where S. N. Miller's carriage shop now is. The clover-mill was swept away by freshet in 1830; the saw-mill had the same fate in 1832; latter was rebuilt.

John McNeal erected a frame for a saw-mill in the "four mile woods," on a branch of Dog River, in 1825. Samuel Orcutt finished it, and it done good business until 1830; it was swept away by a freshet, which seemed the common fate of mills of those days. David Wellington built a saw-mill in 1825, near where E. N. Spaulding's steam-mill now stands.

Charles Colton put a grist-mill into the same building shortly afterwards. Amos Wellington built a saw-mill on the West hill in 1839, now owned by Asahel Flint. Josiah Shaw built a clover-mill on east branch of Dog River, in the East part of the town.

John M. Spaulding, in 1822, built a saw-mill near the Richardson grist-mill, and another, several years afterwards, in the village, now owned by J. G. Hall.

John Prince built a saw-mill, in 1849, near where Spaulding's mill now stands, and also manufactured butter-tubs, now owned by E. P. Burnham for a clap-board mill.

Samuel Robertson and Leicester Davis

erected a building in 1820, on the farm where W. I. Simonds now lives, for the purpose of manufacturing wooden bowls and plates. But it did not prove a success and was given up in a few years. Jotham Ellis built a mill in 18— for manufacturing wooden boxes, clothes-pins, turning bedposts, &c. Later it was used by Siloam Spaulding for a carriage shop, and by Philander Wiley for turning, &c.

Stillman Ruggles built a carriage shop in the east part of the town in 1830, and carried on the carriage business until 1850. Samuel Ruggles and S. N. Miller carried on the same business there afterwards.

S. N. Miller commenced carriage-making near the Elijah Ellis saw-mill in 1860, and still continues at the business there.

Howard Warriner had a cabinet-shop in the south-east part of the town, and Mr. Wright built a saw-mill on the same stream west of Warriner's shop.

Luther and David Ellis built a saw-mill on the middle branch of Dog river in 1850; Laban Webster & F. A. Wiley on middle branch of Dog river in 1869; Ebenezer Brackett in the south part of the town in 1848; sold to Thomas Cushing, of Dover, N. H. A vast amount of bridge timber, plank and ties were sawed here for the Vt. Central when being built. E. N. Spaulding and Samuel R. Batchelder built a steam-mill in the south-west part of the town in 1849. Henry Smith built a saw-mill on "Tracy Hill" in 1823; burned in 1835; Joseph Wardner a saw and grist-mill in the east part of the town, now owned by Jacob Wardner, and Bezaleel Spaulding a saw-mill on his farm in 1848.

Benjamin H. Warriner built a shop near the "old Hutchinson place" in 1829, for the manufacture of sleighs, chairs and furniture of all kinds, and in 1835 put in machinery for manufacturing window-sash, blinds, etc.

James Cram built a saw-mill on the brook above the Hutchinson place in 1830.

Daniel Kingsley commenced wool carding in 1800, in the east part of the town.

Harrison and Charles Fields built a steam saw-mill about a mile below E. N. Spaulding's in ——, and after carrying on an extensive business for two years, moved it to Richmond.

E. N. Spaulding's steam saw-mill, built in 1866, has turned off yearly an average of 1,500,000 feet of lumber. He has also manufactured croquet to a considerable extent.

William Bruce & Sons built a steam-mill in the south part of the town in 1877. It was burned in 1880, and rebuilt. This mill, as well as E. N. Spaulding's, has furnished employment for a great many hands. Ira Williams & Victor Spear are now erecting a steam saw-mill in the south-east part of the town.

Dan Tarbell erected a steam saw-mill near the railroad crossing in the village in 1881, not yet thorougly completed.

Charles Samson owned a distillery and manufactured potato whisky on the west hill, near what is now called "Wetmore place."

Billa Woodard manufactured saddle-trees several years, and Eleazer Woodard later carried on the same business.

Ephraim Morris & Nathan Kendall owned a tannery at the foot of East Hill, on land now owned by Wm. B. Orcutt. They carried on the business only a few years.

In 1853, immense veins of

VERD ANTIQUE MARBLE

were discovered. A large building was erected, with steam power for working the marble. It was found to be very beautiful, and capable of receiving a high polish. Monuments, tables, mantels, etc., manufactured were extremely beautiful, but the company became involved in debt, and the property was sold in 1856, to pay liabilities. It was purchased by an association under the name of "Verd Antique Marble Company," for the amount previously expended. It was then managed by a joint stock company, but finally suspended business in 1857.

THE WATCH FACTORY

was built in 1867. It is located in a lovely and picturesque place, a short distance west from the depot. 12 hands are now employed there. Aug. 1, 1879, a partnership was formed, under the title, "J. G.

Hall Mfg. Co.," between J. G. Hall and his son, F. W. Hall, for the manufacture of watchmakers' tools, principally a "Staking Tool," the invention of J. G. Hall, which meets with a ready sale, owing to the very fine workmanship and correctness exercised in their manufacture, they being worthless unless exact. These tools are in use in nearly every State in the Union, and also in Canada, France and England. They also manufacture a variety of small tools for watch-repairers' use. The Co. had a sample of their tools on exhibition at the State Fair in 1880, receiving the only gold medal awarded in Mechanics' Hall.

THE FIRST MAIL ROUTE

through Roxbury was up the first branch of White river from W. Randolph, through Braintree and Kingston (now Granville), up the old road to John Spaulding's hotel, near the Royal Batchelder place. John Spaulding was postmaster. Guy Edson carried the first mail in 1826. It being known the mail was to arrive at such a time, there was a great gathering and rejoicing, and a little new rum as a matter of course. The route continued down the old road east to Elijah Ellis' (now Mrs. Brackett's), thence north by the old Joseph Hixon place, Samuel Robertson's, John Paine's, Nathan Haynes', and then on to the hill near where Clark Wiley now lives, to Northfield. The mail run that way until about 1830. In 1828, the county road from Northfield line to Granville, through Roxbury village, was surveyed by David M: Lane, county surveyor. In 1830, John Spaulding having built the Summit House, where the village now is, the mail commenced running on that road, with a daily stage of 4 or 6-horse coach for some years; then the stage and mail went from West Randolph through East Roxbury to Northfield, and the mail was carried to West Randolph and back with a horse and gig until the railroad was built in 1848. The cars came to Roxbury 40 days before the road was completed to Northfield, making it a very lively business place. Teams from as far as Burlington for freight, 6 and 8-horse teams, making it very profitable for inn-keepers those days.

OUR LARGE CATAMOUNT.

A large catamount was killed in town in 1823. Allen Spaulding gives this account. He had been calling on his sweetheart, who lived near the "Leonard place." The fair Hattie was the best of company, and he could hardly credit his senses when he started for home and saw the rosy morning peeping over the eastern hills. As he was making rapid strides on, he noticed the huge track of some animal in the new snow, and the track seemed a new one. He examined it closely, and came to the conclusion it was a bear track, and thought he would get help and capture him. Joseph Batchelder and himself followed the trail all day, but without once getting a glimpse of "the bear," and Batchelder gave it up in disgust. Spaulding, however, renewed the pursuit the next morning, accompanied by Capt. Young, who had quite an exalted opinion of his own prowess and skill in hunting, of bears, especially. They struck a new track in the light snow, and followed it to a ledge opposite the old steam-mill. Matters were becoming quite interesting, but "Capt. Sip." declared "by the gods he never was afraid of a bear, and if Spaulding would go one way he would go the other, and start him out," but he took another look at the huge track, and his ardor cooled a little. He concluded they had better keep together. They had not proceeded far when they heard a fierce growl and a bound, and saw the leaves flying in every direction, but by the time they had got around the ledge, the animal was out of sight, making 20 feet at a leap. Spaulding thought it could never be a bear, but "by the gods it *is*," persisted Capt. Sip., "and a regular old long fellow, too." They followed on till dusk, and gave up the chase for that day. The next morning tracks were seen near Billa Woodard's, on East Hill, and James McNeil, Charles Ellis, Ira Spaulding and Orrin Orcutt started in pursuit. Charles Ellis getting a glimpse of the hunted animal's tawny coat, declared, "the dog had a fox up a tree." They soon found they had a rather different foe to meet, and that without rifles. They had only shot-guns loaded with slugs to contend with a huge catamount, but they gave him a salute from two or three, breaking his shoulder, and down the fierce animal came, about 20 feet, caught on a limb, ran up again, turning on his pursuers with open mouth, preparing for a spring. One of the party gave him a charge of "chain-links" in the open mouth, when he turned and jumped the other way, tearing huge splinters from a fallen tree and the earth up around him in every direction in his death agonies. He was the largest catamount ever killed in the State previous to the one killed in Barnard the present season. They were of the same length and height, but the last killed was several pounds heavier. He was sold at auction to Orrin Orcutt, prepared for and kept on exhibition until every one had seen him in this vicinity, and then sold to Mr. Ralph, of Warren, a man in poor health and indigent circumstances, who made quite a fortune taking him about the country.

About this time there was also a moose killed near the old pond, the man who was so fortunate being very destitute. The meat (he was a large fellow), was a perfect "God-send" to his family.

CHURCH HISTORY

is very meagre here. There have been no records kept of the early churches. The Methodist and Calvinist Baptist seem to have been first organized. The first minister publicly ordained in town was

OPHIR SHIPMAN.

The charter of the town allowed the first ordained minister a lot of land, and Rev. Lyman Culver was privately ordained, and claimed the lot, it is said, but there was great dissatisfaction. Mr. O. Richardson says they came to his uncle, Samuel Robertson, in the night to let him know it, and he went to Northfield after 12 o'clock at night, and the next day Rev. Ophir Shipman was ordained.

BAPTISTS.

Rev. Lyman Culver was one of the earliest Baptist preachers (probably the first), and resided in town several years. Friend Blood and Jehial Claflin preached considerably from 1835 to '45. A good old Baptist lady was " churched " for communing with the Methodists, and she with several others joined the Congregationalists about this time.

There was a Calvinistic Baptist church in town many years, but I find no record of it now. Mrs. Woodard is the only member of the Baptist church left in town. A great revival was, brought about in that church in this manner. A little girl overheard her mother and a neighbor talking of the necessity for a Christian life, and the beauty and purity of a true Christian character, and was so deeply impressed that she went to praying earnestly in secret, and came out a shining light, leading others of her companions to do likewise, until it spread into the most extended revival ever in town.

METHODISTS IN ROXBURY.

As early as 1813, how much earlier I am unable to say, the Methodists held their meetings at Eleazer Woodard's and David Young's. Benjamin F. Hoyt preached in 1813, Joel Winch from 1820 to '30, E. J Scott in 1830, '33, John Smith, called Happy John, in 1834, and Hollis Kendall, a native of Roxbury, preached here several years. He moved to Maine, and died there a few years since. Ariel Fay and John Mason preached here at different times. None of these, with the exception of Hollis Kendall, lived in town. Those early Methodists are nearly all gone to their reward. Phineas Wiley, or " Father " Wiley, as he was called for years, died in 1881. I think he was the last member of the first Methodist church formed in town. The first meeting house was built in 1837, a union church.

CONGREGATIONALISTS.

Of the Congregationalist ministers who preached here in the early times were Rev. Mr. Hobart, of Berlin, Elijah Lyman, of Brookfield, Ammi Nichols, of Braintree, as early as 1814, and meetings were held at Samuel Robertson's and at the old school-house that stood north of where O. A. Staples now lives.

THE FREE CONGREGATIONALIST CHURCH was organized about 1837, by Rev. Ammi Nichols, of Braintree, and what remained of the Methodists and most of the Baptist church joined with them, but they never had a settled minister until 1865, when Rev. A. Ladd was ordained and installed pastor, and remained here until the autumn of 1879. They built a pleasant and convenient house of worship in 1871. Samuel Edwards and W. I. Simonds are the only deacons ever chosen, both of whom now officiate.

A CHRISTIAN CHURCH was organized in the east part of the town in 1868. Rev. Henry Howard is present pastor (1882).

Rev. EDWARD BROWN, Universalist, lived in town several years, where John Baird now resides, and preached a part of the time.

The different religious organizations of this town have been : Congregationalist, Methodist, Episcopal, Free Will Baptist, Calvinist Baptist, Christian, Universalist and Spiritualist.

GOLDEN WEDDINGS.—I learn of two having been celebrated in this town, that of Mr. and Mrs. James Wiley, in 1871, and Mr. and Mrs. Otis Batchelder in 1880.

ACCIDENTAL AND SUDDEN DEATHS AND SUICIDES.

BY ZED. S. STANTON, ESQ.

Joseph Batchelder drowned July 14, 1822.

Uriah Richardson died from injuries received while chopping, Jan. 21, 1831.

Alvah Henry, killed by the fall of a tree June 28, 1831.

Mrs. Belcher, suicide by hanging, about 1831.

Charles Webster, killed by being thrown from a wagon, Nov. 5, 1834.

Shubael Wales, suicide by shooting, Mar. 18, 1843.

David Dexter, supposed to have wandered away in a state of insanity and died of exposure, about 1843.

Royal Flint, frozen to death, Jan. 22, 1846.

A man named Jackson was killed by the premature discharge of a blast, at the time the Central Vermont Railroad was in process of construction, Jan. 25, 1846.

An Irishman, name unknown, died of exposure in the summer of 1847.

A young man, name unknown, was drowned in what is now known as Hall's Pond, about 1848.

Lewis Hutchinson, killed by the fall of a tree, Jan. 26, 1850.

Charles Green, suicide, by shooting, in 1854.

Lutheria Spaulding, aged 5 years, killed by falling beneath a loaded wagon, Aug. 5, 1854.

Joseph Paine,

Peter S. P. Staples, found dead in the woods, Sept. 27, 1856.

John Campbell, died by poison taken accidentally, Apr. 13, 1861.

Delia Green, found dead, Aug. 17, 1867.

A. E. Stockwell, a railroad brakeman, killed Nov. 12, 1870.

Peter Shinah, killed by cars June 29, 1870.

Isaac A. Flint, suicide by cutting his throat, about 1870.

Mrs. Plurinna Erskine, suicide by hanging, Sept. 8, 1872.

Buel Gold, suicide by hanging, Aug. 29, 1876.

Clarence Tracy, a child, death caused by scalding, Sept. 26, 1876.

A Central Vermont Railroad brakeman named Shárrow, killed by falling beneath the cars, Feb. 5, 1881.

A wood chopper named Fox, killed by a falling tree, Feb. 21, 1881.

OLD PEOPLE OF ROXBURY, LIVING 1882.

ROXBURY BOYS ABROAD.

Andrew Stanton, a graduate of Tufts College, is now "principal" in the academy at Stoughton, Mass. Will Snow graduated at Hanover, and is now a civil engineer in Montana.

There are a good many graduates of the Normal school in town, Will Simonds was one, who is now teaching near Chicago, Ill.

Lucius Jenney went from this town, about 20 years ago, to Middlesex, and from there to Omaha, Neb., and now occupies the position of R. R. Master on the Union Pacific R. R.

Benj. J. Ellis went from here when a very young man, enlisted and served through the Mexican war; after its close went to Chicago, Ill., and took up the profession of law. He has assisted in organizing and sustaining several mission schools, some of them now flourishing churches, and he often supplies the pulpit, as well as pleads at the Bar.

S. G. Stanton went to Nebraska in 1879, and is engaged in building a railroad on the Union Pacific. Mr. Stanton was an active business man.

Mr. O. Richardson moved to Bellingham, Mass., in '78. Is engaged in the mercantile business. He had been organist and leader of the choir at the Union church for 20 years when he left town. He was an adopted son of Samuel Richardson, with whom Mr. R. spent his declining years.

John Webster, of east part of town, went to California in '57, has been successful in business, and amassed quite a fortune. z. s. s.

Will R. Mansfield, at the age of 20, took his small valise in hand and started for the "far west." He stopped a few weeks in Nebraska as telegraph operator on the B. & M. R. R. He then accepted the position of baggage-master and telegraph operator on a new branch of the Atchison, Topeka & Sante Fe R. R., through New Mexico, and served 2 months, when he was invited to dine with an old Spaniard at Los Vegas, for whom he had done some slight service, and started to return to Grenada, Col. in the caboose that was sent ahead of President Hayes and his escort, on their way from California, to see that the road was clear. The party in the "caboose" had been "looking upon the wine when it was red," and when the "caboose" gave a great bound, and any sober person must have known there was some obstruction, they declared there was "nothing wrong," nor would they stop to see whether there was or not. So this Vermont boy turned the brake, caught a lantern and jumped off, and upon examination, several feet of rails were gone, and he had nothing to do there in the wilds of N. M. but wait for the train, and this was not a pleasant task as the coyotes began to gather from every direction. This was his first experience of the kind, and grim terror seized him, quick as a flash, he sprang up a telegraph-pole close at hand, and sitting astride the cross-bar, watched the howling pack, thinking all the while what an excellent mark he would be for an Indian, and it was far from being an agreeable thought. At last the train came up and he clambered down from his perch, gave a great shout at the wolves and swung his lantern to stop the train. The wolves scattered, and the train had to stop for repairs. For this act of faithfulness, he was

promoted at once to conductor, and has occupied that position until the present time. s. B. M.

ROXBURY'S MILITARY RECORD.

BY ZED S. STANTON, ESQ.

Among the early settlers of Roxbury were doubtless several who served during the Revolutionary War, but just what number it is impossible to determine. Samuel Richardson, the first settler in the westerly part of this town, was a veteran of that war, having served one-half the time during the entire contest. He came to Roxbury in 1790. Mr. Richardson was born at Stafford, Conn., June 15, 1750, and died at Roxbury, in 1822.

Capt. Benjamin Samson, who came here in 1810, was also a Revolutionary soldier, and participated in the battles of Lexington and Bunker Hill. He rang the church bell to arouse the minute men on Lexington green, on the memorable 19th of April, 1775.

BATTLE OF PLATTSBURG.

On the morning of Saturday, Sept. 10, 1814, a company, consisting of all the able-bodied men in town, under command of Capt. Samuel M. Orcutt, left Roxbury for the purpose of assisting in repelling the British invasion of our Northern borders. All the following Sunday those who were left at home heard the distant roar of cannon, and supposed that their loved ones were engaged in battle with the foreign foe. But the men of Roxbury did not arrive at Plattsburg until Monday evening, Sept. 12, and the fighting was then over. They returned to their homes Friday, Sept. 16, 1814.

ROXBURY COMPANY FOR PLATTSBURG.

Capt. Samuel M. Orcutt; Lieut. Gilbert R. Spalding; Ensign Billa Woodard; Sergeants Joel Hildreth, Enos Young, Jonathan Cram, Charles Samson; Corporals James Woolfe, Philip Cram, Dan Lord, John Paine; Drummer Jonathan Nutting; Fifer Bezalleel Spalding.

Privates Benj. Samson, Darius Spalding, Robert Cram, Samuel Ford, Alding Loomis, Ambrose Hutchinson, John Baldwin, Truman Peterson, John M. Spalding,

95

Gideon Flint, Peter S. P. Staples, Abraham Z. Haynes, John Wilcox, Timothy Emerson, Joseph Hixon, Samuel Robertson, Darius Spalding, Elisha Wilcox, Elijah Ellis.

There is on file in the Adjutant's General's office at Montpelier an affidavit made by the captain and ensign of said company, Mar. 6, 1850, stating the main facts in regard to the company going to Plattsburg, and also that parties from other towns joined their company, and that none of the officers or men of said company ever, to the knowledge of the said captain or ensign, received any compensation for their services on that occasion. Of this company of men only one is now living (Feb. 6, 1882), that one being Philip Cram, who resides in Brookfield.

ROXBURY SOLDIERS IN THE WAR OF '61.

Chauncey M. Allen, C, 1st Vt. Cavalry; mustered out Nov. 18, '64.

Corp. Frank O. Allen, B, 4th; must. out Apr. 12, '65.

Franklin Anos, H, 6th; dis. Mar 25, '65.

James Bailey, H, 6th; died Oct. 22, '62.

Henry M. Barrington, I, 9th, died Oct. 6, '62.

Byron A. Batchelder, K, 3d; died at Washington, D. C., May 30, '64.

Harrison Bean, I, 11th; mustered out June 24, '65.

Allen J. Bennett, C, 1st Vt. Cav.; dis. Nov. 21, 62.

John Benjamin, C, 1st Vt. Cav.: sick and absent from regt. Nov. 18, '64, is last report on Adjutant General's report.

Joseph Benjamin, H, 6th; dis. June 1, '63.

Beman H. Campbell, H, 6th; must. out May 22, '65.

Marshall Chaffee, H, 6th; dis. May 15, '63.

Frank Clukey, K, 7th: died July 22, '62.

Anson P. Coburn, I, 11th; mustered out June 24, '65.

Patrick Clukey, G, 8th; mustered out June 22, '64.

Andrew J. Cross, 1st S. S., F; trans. to invalid corps Sept. 1, '63.

Henry A. Cross, K, 7th; died at Carrolton, La., Nov. 30, '62.

Martin Cross, K, 3d; must. out July 27, '64.

Joseph Currier, G, 8th; mustered out June 28, '65.

Thomas Daniels, H, 6th; killed at battle of Lee's Mills, Apr. 16, '62.

Capt. David B. Davenport, H, 6th; died Sept. 20, '62.

Henry D. Davenport, H, 6th; dis. Nov. 30, '62.

Peter Deott, K, 4th; deserted Dec. 10, '62.

Lieut. Eri L. Ditty, H, 6th; mustered out June 26, '65.

John Q. A. Ditty, F, 2d; trans. to invalid corps July 30, '63.

Ralph Ditty, F, 2d; must. out June 29, '64.

John W. Dunton, K, 7th; dis. Feb. 25, '63.

David Ellis, E, 3d; must. out July 27, '64.

Lorenzo Ellis, I, 11th; mustered out June 24, '65.

Samuel R. Ellis, H, 6th; dis. July 7, '62.

John M. Ferris, B, 6th; must. out June 26, '65.

Lieut. Amasa W. Ferry, F, 2d; discharged Jan. 4, '65.

Gideon E. Fletcher, I, 9th; deserted July 20, '62.

Royal Flint, H, 6th; died June 15, '62.

Victor Goodrich, F, 2d; killed at battle of Bull Run, July 21, '61.

Dan. A. Grant, H, 6th; dis. Nov. 16, '62.

Willis Grant, H, 6th; transferred to invalid corps Dec. 1, '63.

James Hall, K, 7th; died July 24, '62.

Samuel A. Hayward, E, 1st Vt. Cav.; dis. July 24, '62.

Walter R. Hayward, E, 1st Vt. Cav; must. out Aug. 9, '65.

James C. Hutchinson, H, 2d; killed at Charlotte, Va., Aug. 16, '64.

Corp. Stearns S. Hutchinson, F, 2d; must. out June 29, '64.

Stephen H. Jones, G, 8th; mustered out June 28, '65.

Leland Kimball, K, 8th; died at New Orleans, La., Sept. 16, '62.

Mason Knapp, K, 7th; re-enlisted, is the last entry of Adjutant General's report.

Carlos Lafaty, K, 7th; dis. Sept. 27, '64.

Joseph Lavalle, H, 6th; mustered out June 26, '65.

Henry Lock, H, 6th; mustered out Aug. 2, '65.

Alexis Martell, I, 11th; mustered out June 24, '65.

Frank E. Martell, H, 6th; mustered out July 7, '65.

Corp. Samuel Maxham, 2d S. S., E; killed at battle of Wilderness, May 6, '64.

Henry Morfit, K, 7th; died at New Orleans, La., Nov. 16, '62.

Russell Morfit, K, 7th; died at Fort Pickens, Fla., May 5, '63.

Capt. Patrick Murphy, H, 6th; mustered out June 26, '65.

Lieut. Thomas Murphy, H, 6th; mustered out Oct. 28, '64.

William Murphy, H, 6th; died Oct. 25, '62.

Carlos Nedo, K, 7th; dis. Sept. 27, '64.

Langdon H. Nichols, C, 1st Vt. Cav; died July 27, '62.

Abial Patch, H, 6th; dis. Dec. 28, '63.

Calvin B. Phillips, E, 1st Vt. Cav.; discharged May 22, '62.

Edmund Pope, Jr., E, 1st Vt. Cav.; died Dec. 14, '64.

James Putney, H, 6th; mustered out June 26, '65.

William Quimby, K, 7th; died at New Orleans, Oct. 16, '62.

Felix Quinn, I, 9th; must. out June 13, '65.

Eli Rich, K, 3d; died Nov. 1, '62.

John E. Rich, K, 7th; died July 18, '62.

Geo. C. Richardson, H, 6th; died at Frederick City, Md., Dec. 9, '62.

Harrison A. E. Richardson, H, 6th; must. out Oct. 28, '64.

Lafayette Richardson, H, 6th; discharged Nov. 24, '62.

Samuel Richardson, H, 6th; died at Roxbury, Jan. 15, '63.

Corp. Ira Royce, E, 1st Vt. Cav.; dis. Nov. 22, '62.

Thomas P. Rundlett, E, 1st Vt. Cav; dis. May 22, '62.

Joseph Shiney, H, 6th; mustered out June 26, '65.

Joseph Simonds, H, 6th; des. July 24, '65.

John Slocum, H, 6th; mustered out June 26, '65.

Corp. Emery L. Smith, G, 6th; dis. Oct. 31, '64.

Otis Snow, K, 3d; died Aug. 19, '62.

Lieut. Allen Spalding, K, 6th; resigned July 13, '64.

Sergeant Dennison F. Spalding, K, 6th; must. out May 18, '65.

Israel Steele, K, 7th; dis. Oct. 20, '62.

Stillman S. Stephens, K, 7th; died July 17, '62.

Sergeant Edward F. Stevens, F, 1st S. S.; mustered out Sept. 13, '64.

Benjamin F. Stone, I, 9th; discharged June 27, '65.

Joseph Veo, G, 6th; mustered out Oct. 28, '64.

Lucius W. Wales, H, 6th; killed at Lee's Mills, Apr. 16, '62.

Samuel Wales, Jr., K, 3d; trans. to invalid corps Sept. 1, '63.

Ezekiel D. Waterman, K, 3d; killed at battle of Lee's Mills, Apr. 16, '62.

Henry Waterman, C, 1st. Vt. Cav.; died at Washington, D. C., Aug. 9, '65.

Stillman Waterman, H, 6th; discharged March 31, '62.

Stillman Waterman, I, 9th; discharged Jan. 15, '63.

Joseph White, H, 6th; died Oct. 22, '62.

Loren J. Wiley, K, 7th; must. out May '65.

Wallace Wolcott, H, 6th; dis. Mar. 25,'63.

Augustus Bresette, 3d Vt. Bat.; must. out June 13, '65.

Volunteers that re-enlisted.—Paul Burke, Carlos Lafaty, Henry Locke, Frank E. Martell, Carlos Nedo, Edmond Pope, Jr., Dennison Spalding.

Veteran Reserve Corps.—John W. Dunton.

Also two men were credited to Roxbury, but not by name.

Furnished under draft and paid commutation.—Edwin W. Ellis, Edwin Ferris, A. H. Fisk, Lemuel A. Rood, Luther Tracy, Rodney Wiley.

Procured Substitute.—Nathan W. Cady.

Entered Service.—Samuel A. Richardson, H, 6th; dis. Aug. 2, '65.

Besides the above-named soldiers, there were several other residents of Roxbury who enlisted, credited to other towns, viz.: George R. Waterman, F, 1st; must. out Aug. 15, '65; Franklin Knowles, C. 15th; Charles A. Fisk, F, 17th; Orza Boyce, B, 4th; George H. Pearsons, D, 9th; Samuel Shepherd, I, 56th Mass. Vols. ; died June

27, '64; Francis F. Young, Mass. Vols.; Sergeant Jones W. Ferris, K, 3d; severely wounded at the battle ot Lee's Mills, Apr. 16, '62, and discharged Aug. 1, '62.

When the war closed, Roxbury had a surplus of 23 men in excess of all calls for troops that had been made, a much larger number in proportion to the population than any other town in the State.

ROXBURY LONGEVITY.

Persons 70 years of age and over, who have died in Roxbury,

1855	Mary Spaulding	100
2846	Benjamin Samson	90
1819	Moses Woodward	74
1813	David McClure	80
1822	Samuel Richardson	71
1868	Thompson Jenney	85
1832	Jane Hixon	75
1872	Samuel Robertson	97
1879	Persis Robertson	76
1855	Dorcas Prescott	72
1835	Darius Spaulding	74
1844	Joel Hildreth	77
1864	Polly Hildreth	94
1872	Arathusa Hildreth	79
1862	Samuel Edwards	84
1869	Lydia Edwards	85
1869	Benga Edwards	87
1859	Betsey Edwards	75
1850	Henry Lcck	75
1856	Obedience Lock	71
1842	Elijah Ellis	79
1852	Mary Ellis	88
1861	Gideon Ellis	89
1878	Mehitable Ellis	87
1880	Sally Allen	89
1841	Mrs. Samuel Richardson	91
1869	Silas Spalding	88
1865	John M. Spaulding	76
1850	Ruth Sargent	86
1856	Nathan Haynes	78
1857	Hannah Haynes	86
1864	Abraham J. Haynes	76
1872	Daniel Haynes	88
1859	Polly Paine	72
1861	Asa S. Simonds	71
1860	Hannah Simonds	70
1876	Charles Samson	86
1865	Sally Samson	76
1858	Benjamin Samson	77
1879	Roxana A. Batty	77
1873	Anna Gray Stanton	80
1873	Hannah Merrill	75
1870	Alvin L. Brigham	71
1875	Eleanor Spaulding	84
1862	Samuel Richardson	79
1865	Lucy Richardson	76
1875	Barton Tracy	72
1880	Enos K. Young	72

1861	Silas B. Spaulding	81
1848	Samuel Ford	76
1866	Sarah Batchelder	86
1866	Lydia Beckwith	86
1866	Hannah Staples	77
1825	Capt. Job Orcutt	75
1825	Mary Orcutt	74
1851	Samuel M. Orcutt	74
1878	Mary B. Orcutt	95
1845	Billa Woodward	72
—	Mary Woodward	69
1850	Borga Wiley	87
1879	James Wiley	83
1881	Phineas Wiley	91
1879	David Wiley	82
1873	Hannah Wiley	76
1866	John Williams	72
1876	Mabel Williams	75
1880	Otis Batchelder	91
1877	Alva Richardson	76
1868	Dennis Crimims	80
1842	Chester Batchelder	69
1864	Eunice Williams	72
1876	Elias Rich	87
1874	James Butterfield	76
1865	Susannah Richardson	84
1863	Sarah Batchelder	87
1871	Betsey Spalding	82
1865	Jemima Silver	75
1852	Phineas Flint	82
1859	Seth Richardson	70
1836	Sarah Richardson	73
1873	William Knowles	94
1878	Burton Skilleger	78
1869	Nabby Ford	85
1859	Arny Wilson	81
1859	Samson Bates	70
1860	Anna Hatch	80
1861	Mary Bealey	76
1861	Darius Hatch	81
1861	Hepsobath Cady	81
1862	Lurinda Flint	81
1863	William Hutchinson	89
1864	Aaron Webster	85
1865	Abigail Cram	80
1169	Francis Clukey	70
1869	Jemima Webster	88
1870	William B. Tyler	78
1873	Fanny Jones	78
1874	Phila Darling	76
1874	Calvin Cady	74
1875	Daniel C. Rich	71
1875	Lamos McGregor	78
1876	Louis Loomis	75
1867	Aaron Spencer	84
1861	Polly Lyndes (colored,)	81
1863	Stephen Rumney	75
1877	Sally Wardner	78
1877	Margaret Martin	90
1878	Eunice Kent	80
1878	Samuel Steele	83
1878	Joel Wardner	83
1838	John B. Crandall	70
1865	Enos Young	80

O. W. ORCUTT.

TOWN MEETINGS.

Held at Jedediah Huntington's dwelling-house in 1796, '97, '98. At Samuel Richardson's, 1799, 1802. At Christopher Huntington's 1800, 1801. At David McClure's, 1803, '5, '6. At Samuel Robertson's, 1804. At Leonard Smith's, 1807, '8, '9, '10. At Billa Woodward's, 1811, '12, '13, '14, '15, '16. At Samuel M. Orcutt's 1817, '18, '19, '20, '21, '22, '23, '24, '25, '26, '27, '28, '26, '30, '31, '32, '33, '34, '35, '36, '37, '38, '39, '40, '41. At Luther Ainsworth's, Mar., 1842. At John M. Spaulding's, Sept., '42, '43, '44, '45, '46, '47, '48, '49. At Union Meeting House, 1850, 51, '52, '53, '54. Sept., '54, at new town house, 1854 to 1881.

MODERATORS.

Joseph Crane, 1796; Thomas Huntington, 1797; Samuel Richardson, 1798, 1801, '2, '3, '5, '7, '8, '9, '13; Jedediah Huntington, 1799; Isaac Lewis, 1800; Darius Spaulding, Job Orcutt, 1809; Zeb. Butler,

1804; Rodolphus Willard, 1810; Samuel Robinson, 1811, '12, '17, '18, '19, '20, '21, '23, 24; J. F. Ruggles, '18, '14, '15, '16, '22, '25, '26, '28, '30; Charles Sampson, 1827; Shubael Wales, 1829, '31, '34, '35, '36; Joel Hildreth, 1832; Nathan Morse, 1833; Stillman Ruggles, 1837, '38, '40; Allen Spaulding, 1839, '41, '42, '51, '52, '53, '54, '57, '58; Henry S. Boyce, 1843, '44, '46, '47, '48, '55, '56, '59, '60; O. Richardson, 1861–'68; Wm. B. Orcutt, 1868; Billings Spaulding, 1869; Samuel G. Stanton, 1870, '74, '75, '77, '78; Oramel Richardson, 1871, '72, '73, '76; Zed S. Stanton, 1879, '80, '81.

TOWN CLERKS, 1796–1881.

Thomas Huntington, 1796, '97, '98, '99, 1800, '1. Darius Spalding, 1802, '3, '14, '15. Samuel Robertson, 1804, '5, '6, '7. James Bancroft, 1808, '9, '10, '11, '12. Samuel M. Orcutt, 1813, '17, '18, '19, '20, '21, '22, '24, '25, '26, '27, '28. '29, '30, '31, '32, '33, '34, '35, '36, '37, '38. John F. Persons, 1816. Jehial Allen, '39, '40, '41, '42. Allen Spalding, 1843, '44, '45, '46, '47, '48. Allen K. Jeney, 1849, '50, '51, '52, '53, '55. (Jeney died in Aug., '55.) A. N. Tilden, 1854. Ormal Richardson, 1855. A. N. Tilden, 1856 to 1881.

SELECTMEN.

Samuel Richardson, 1796 to 1803, '7, '8; Isaac Lewis, 1796, 1800; Jedediah Huntington, 1796, 98, 99; Christopher Huntington, 1797; David Cram, 1797; Roswell Adams, 1798, 1800, '1, '3, '4, '5; John Stafford, 1799, 1806; Darius Spalding, 1801 to 1806, '9, '10; Perez Huntington, 1802; Lemuel Smith, 1803 to '8; Jonathan F. Ruggles, 1806, '7, '8, '19, '20, '21; Samuel Richardson, 1808; Joel Hildreth, 1809 to '13, '14, '15, '25, '26; Robert Cram, 1809 to '13, '14, '24, '25; Samuel M. Orcutt, 1811 to '15, '21, '22, '23, '25, '26, '27, '29, '30, '33 to '38; Isaih Shaw, 1813, '15, '18, '26, '27, '28, '36, '37, '47; Uriah Richardson, 1813; John Paine, 1815, '16, '17, '22; Nathan Morse, 1816, '17, '22, '23, '28, '29, '30, '33, '34, '35; Charles Sampson, 1816, '17, '20, '21, '27, '28, '29, '38, '47, '48; Samuel Robertson, 1818, '19, '23; Elijah Ellis, 1818, '19, '20; Billa Wood-

ward, 1824; David Young, 1824, '31, '32;
James Burnham, 1830; Amos Wardner,
1831, '32; Daniel Loomis, 1831; Henry
Smith, 1832; Jonathan Wiley, 1833, '34;
Bezaleel Spalding, 1835; Jared Hildreth,
1836, '37; Robert Cram, 1838, '39; John
Cross, 1838, '39, '40, '41; Darius Hatch,
1839; Thomas R. Shaw, 1840 to '44, '46;
Enos K. Young, 1840, '41, '42; Jehial
Allen, 1842; Wm. W. Woodward, 1843,
'44; Benjamin Edwards, Jr., 1843, '44,
'45, '56, '57, '58: H. S. Boyce, 1844, '49,
'50; Wm. P. Royce, 1845, '59, '60, '64,
'65; Samuel Edwards, Jr., 1846, '50, '52,
'53, '61, '62; Alvin Braley, 1846, '47, '48,
'61; Stephen Pierce, 1848; Dexter Sampson, 1849, '51, '54, '61, '62, '63; Wm. B.
Orcutt, 1849, '50 '55; Elijah Winch, 1851,
'58, '60; S. M. Hildreth, 1851, '58, '63,
'66, '67, '71; Geo. M. Sampson, 1852, '53;
Edmond Pope, 1852, '53, '55, '29, '61, '62,
'64, '66; S. G. Stanton' 1869; C. H. Merrill, 1854; Stillman Ruggles, 1854; Wm.
B. Orcutt, 1855; Charles B. Fiske, 1855,
'66, '67, '68; Clark Wiley, 1856, '57. '58,
'72, !77; James Cram, 1856, '57; E. N.
Spalding, 1860; C. Richardson, 1864, '65,
'68; S. P. Orcutt, 1865; Cyrus Howard.
1868, '69, '81; S. G. Stanton, 1869 to '74,
'78; Enos K. Yonng, 1869, '70; Isaac A.
Flint, 1870, '71; Storrs S. Clough, 1872,
'75 to '79; Geo. L. Walbridge, 1873, '74;
Charles Adams, 1873, '74; Billings Spaulding, 1874, '81; A. J. Averill, 1875, '76;
D. L. Nichols, 1875; Charles N. Eaton,
1876; Gideon Edwards, 1879; D. R.
Stanton, 1878, '79; C. M. Adams, 1879;
C. H. Eaton, 1879; Wm. B. Orcutt, Arza
Boyce, L. J. Wiley, 1880; L. J. Wiley,
J. B. Spaulding, 1880.

TOWN TREASURERS.

David Cram, 1796; Isaac Lewis, 1797.
'98, '99; Thomas Huntington, 1800, '01;
Darius Spalding, 1802, '15; Samuel Robertson, 1803 to 1808, '28; James Bancroft,
1808 to '13; Samuel M. Orcutt, 1813, '14,
'17 to '28, '29; John T. Pearsons, 1816;
Asa S. Simonds, 1830 to '61; Billings
Spanlding, 1861 to '68, '69, to '74; Wm.
B. Orcutt, 1868; A. N. Tilden, 1874 to
1881.

OVERSEERS OF POOR.

Selectmen in 1808; Jonathan F. Ruggles, Elijah Ellis, Samuel Robertson overseers, 1813; Robert Cram, Billa Woodward, Isaiah Shaw, 1820, 37; Robert
Cram, 1821; selectmen overseers of poor,
1822, 23, 24; Samuel Robertson, 1825,
26; Samuel M. Orcutt and Nathan Morse,
1827; Billa Woodward, 1830; Nathan
Morse, 1828, 29, 35, 36; Allen Spalding,
1835, 41, 42, 44, 45, 51, 58; Darius Hatch,
1843, 40, 46, 39, 38; Silas Braley, 1833,
32, 47, 31; Allen Spalding, 1848, 49, 50;
Asaph Silsbury, 1851; H. M. Nichols, 1853,
55, 52; Edmond Pope, 1856; Edmond
Lack, 1857; Benj. Edwards, Jr., 1860, 54;
Wm. B. Roys, 1861, 62; E. P. Burnham,
1863, 64, 65, 66; Sylvester Ellis, 1867, 68;
Alphonso Ladd, 1869, 70, 71, 72; Orza
Boyce, 1873, 74, 75; C. L. Ellis, 1876, 77;
Charles Adams, 1878, 79, 81; Salmon
Williams, 1880.

CONSTABLES AND COLLECTORS OF TAXES.

Jeduthan Huntington, 1796; David
Cram, 1797, '98, 1817 to 20; Isaac Lewis,
1799; Perus Huntington, 1800; Benjamin
Huntington, 1801; David McClure, 1802;
Chester Morris, 1803 to 1808; Roswell
Walter, 1808; Rhodolphus Willard, 1809;
Darius Houghton, 1810; Ezra Child,
1811; John B. Crandall, 1812; Charles
Bancroft, 1813; Joel Hildreth, 1814, '15;
Charles Sampson, 1816; John Paine,
1820: Henry Boyce, 1821 to 1830; Allen
Spalding, 2830, '33; Erastus Spaulding,
1831, '32; Amos Wardner, 1834 to 1837;
Henry S. Boyce, 1838 to 1841; Dexter
Sampson, 1841, '42; Elijah Winch, 1843;
E. B. Pride, 1844, '45; Samuel Ruggles,
1846 to 1850, '55; Ebenz. Ainsworth,
1861; S. P. Orcutt, 1852, '53 '59; Daniel
D. Hackett, 1855; Orin W. Orcutt, 1856,
'76, '78; Benjamin Edwards, 1857, '58;
W. J. Simonds, 1860, '62, '63; Langdon
R. Nichols, 1861; H. G. Ellis, 1864 to
1870; Charles Spalding, 1870, '71; Samuel M. Hildreth, 1872; Zed. S. Stanton,
1873, '74, '75, '77; Azro J. Boyce, 1879,
'80, '81.

LISTERS.

David Cram, 1796, 1806; Thomas Huntington, 1796, '98; Jedediah Huntington,

ROXBURY. 759

Samuel Richardson, 1797; Isaac Lewis, 1797, '98; John Stafford, 1798, '99, 1808; Chester Batchelder, 1799: Perus Huntington, 1799, 1802; Uriah Richardson, 1800, 1807, '12. '17; Joseph Adams, Darius Spaulding, 1800; David McClure, Benjamin Huntington, Daniel Freeman, 1801; David Nutting, Joseph Converse, 1802: Samuel Smith, 1803, '5; Clark Stone, Charles Fitts, 1803; Joel Hildreth, 1804, '5, '6; Charles Stone, 1804; Zeb. Butler, 1804; Jonathan F. Ruggles, 1805, '9, '10, '16, '17, '22, '24, '27, '30; Samuel Robinson, 1806, '21, '22, '24, '27; Samuel M. Orcutt, 1807, '12, '17, '18, '19, '34, '38; Robert Cram, 1807, '8; Lorin Green, 1808; Charles Bancroft, 1809; Ephraim Morris, 1809; Salmon Cross, 1810; James Bancroft, 1810, '11, '12; Gilbert R. Spaulding, 1811, '15; Anson Adams, 1812; Enos Youngs, Bezalel Spaulding, 1813, '15; Darius Hatch, 1813, '14, '15; John Paine, 1814, '19, '20, '26, '30; Thomas Davis, 1814; Billa Woodward, 1815, '20, '23, '28; Ira Hunter, 1818; Henry Boyce, 1818, '23; Amos Wardner, 1819; Charles Samson, 1822, '23, '30, '32, '33, '36, '37, '38, '47, '48, '51; Nathan Morse, 1826, '27, '28, '32, '36, '37, '42, '43; James Burnham, 1825, '26, '29; Elijah Ellis, 1827; Silas C. Briggs, 1828; Daniel Flint, Shubael Wales, 1829; Erastus Spaulding, Henry S. Boyce, 1831, '55, '56; Silas Hall, 1830; Isaiah Shaw, 1832, '37, '42, '43; David Withington, William Ruggles, 1833; John Walbridge, 1834; Stillman Ruggles, 1834, '36, '40, '54; Alvin Braley, 1838, '43, '44, '46, '48, '59, '61; Benj. Edwards, Jr., 1838, '49, '50, '53, '54, '59; Samuel M. Hildreth, 1839, '40, '41, '51, '71; Eleazar Woodward, Consider Hyland, 1839; Wm. Woodward, 1840; Philip Cram, 1841, '48, '49: Benoni Webster, 1841, '47; Samuel Edwards, Jr., 1841, '57, '60: Allen Spaulding, 1842, '46, '47, '60; Luther Ainsworth, 1844; Thomas R. Shaw, 1844, '45, '46, '49: Hibbard A. Perry, 1850: Wm. W. Woodward, 1850; Edmond Pope, 1851, '52, '56, '65; Elijah Winch, 1845, '57, '62, '63; Stephen Pierce, 1845; Asaph Silsbury, 1851; Alvin L. Brigham, 1852; Stillman Ruggles, 1853; Wilson I. Simonds, 1854, '66, '81; Seth M. Bailey, 1855; E, P. Burnham, 1855, '56. '61, '62; Clark Wiley, 1858; R. S. Glidden, Dexter Samson, 1858; Wm. 1807, '12. B. Orcutt, 1859, '64, '65; Joseph B. Edwards, 1859; Alphonso Ladd, 1862; Philander Wiley, 1862, '63, '72, '73; Azro A. Simonds, 1863; Buel Gold, 1865, '67, '74, '75; A. A. Smith, 1864, '65; C. B. Williams, Cyrus Howard, 1866; Samuel G. Stanton, 1867; Jason W. Powers, 1868; Ralph W. Rood, Aaron Webster, 1868; Charles Spaulding, 1869, 70; Billings Spalding, 1869; Isaac A. Flint, 1869; Clark Wiley, 1870, 71; Storrs S. Clough, 1870, 71; Frank T. Snow, 1872; Arza Boyce, 1872, '78, '81; J. E. D. Hildreth, 1873, '74; David B. Adams, 1873; David H. Stanton, 1873, '75; J. P. Warner, 1875; Horace A Thayer, 1876; Zed. S. Stanton, 1876, '77; Henry M. Spalding, 1876; Charles Adams, D. L. Nichols, 1877, '78; Clark Flint, 1879, '80, '81: E. C. Bowman, J. E. D. Colby, 1879; Geo. W. Williams, James Steel, 1880.

TITHINGMEN, 1805-'40.

Silas Spalding, Job Orcutt, Chester Batchelder, Caleb Stowe, Waterman Spalding, David G. Nutting, Enos Young, Roswell Adams, Elijah Ellis, Jas. Y. Wolf, John Baldwin, Wm. Gold, Jacob Wardner, Sam'l. Richardson, Willard Smith, John M. Spalding, Asahel Blake, Darius Houghton, Uriah Richardson, Sam'l. Wright, Benoni Webster, Jacob Loomis, Silas Braley, Nathan Morse, Adin Smith, H. M. Nichols, Eleazer Woodward, Benjamin Edwards, Stillman Ruggles, Alvin L. Brigham, Daniel Flint, James Pike, Samuel Ford, Alva Richardson, Cyrus Flint, Nathan Emerson.

TOWN AGENTS.

John B. Crandall, 1815, 1816; Henry Boyce, 1817; Charles Samson, 1829; Amos Wardner, 1833; Nathan Morse, 1834; Silas Braley, 1842, '44; Allen Spalding, 1841, '47, '49, '54, '60, '61; Alvin Braley, 1844, '46, '48, '50, '51, '52, '53, '55, '56, '59, '62, '63; Edmond Pope, 1864; Dexter Samson, 1867, '68; James P. Warner, 1872; Samuel G. Stanton, 1875; William B. Orcutt, 1869, '76; Erastus N.

Spalding, '77, '71, '70, '58, '57; Samuel G. Stanton, '78, '65; S. S. Clough, '79, '73, '74; Orrin W. Orcutt, '80, '81.

SCHOOL SUPERINTENDENTS.

Joseph Silsbury, 1851, '52, '48; Aaron Webster, '50, '52; Stephen Pierce, '46, '47, '49; Allen W. Jenny, '55; Hira G. Ellis, '56; Samuel G. Stanton, '57; F. V. Randall, '58, '57; Aaron Webster, '58; O. Richardson, '59; Austin A. Smith, '60, '61; Jas. F. Button, '48; Buel Gold, '62; H. G. Ellis, '63; Aldin Ladd, '64, '65; S. G. Stanton, '66, '67, '70, '71, '72; Wm. L. White, '68, '67; Andrew Stanton, '73: D. L. Nichols, '74, '75, '76, '78; Zed S. Stanton, '77, '79, '80, '81.

JUSTICES OF THE PEACE.

Charles Samson, 1850, '51, '52, '53, '54, '38, '40, '44, '45, '47, '27, '31, '33, 49 ,4,1, 39, 20, 28, 25, 26, 24, 22. 23, 48, 33, 34, 30, 55, 46, 21; Byer Edwards, 1850, 51, 52, 53, 54, 58, 61, 62, 40, 43, 44, 45, 47, 41, 46, 49, 48; Philip Cram, 1850, 51, 48, 49, 46; Buel Gold, 1850, 51, 64, 65, 66, 67, 68, 74, 75; Elijah Winch, 1850, 51, 52, 53, 57, 58, 62, 44; Stephen Pierce, 1851, 52, 44, 45, 47, 49, 48, 46; Hiram Walbridge, 1852, 53, 54, 55, 69, 70, 74, 75; Asaph Silsbnry, 1852, 53, 49; Alvin Braley, 1853, 54, 44, 45, 47, 49, 46; Stillman Ruggles, 1854, 55, 44, 47, 49, 48, 37, 35, 46; Wm. B. Orcutt, 1855, 56; Calvin Murray, 1855, 56; E. P. Burnham, 1855, 56, 59, 60, 61, 63; A. B. Hutchinson, 1855, 56; Edmond Pope, 1856, 61, 62, 63; Sewell Hutchinson, 1856, 57; I. M. Hildreth, 1842, 43, 44, 45, 47, 57, 49, 48; W. I. Simonds, 1857, 58; Solomon Ferry, 1857, 58; Sylvester Moffit, 1857, 58; O. W. Orcutt, 1859, 60, 61; Samuel P. Wales, 1859, 60; Austin A. Smith, 1859, 60, 61; Cyrus Howard, 1859, 60, 64, 65, 66, 67, 68; Horace M. Nichols, 1861, 62, 63, 64, 65, 66, 40, 43, 44, 45, 47, 41, 46, 48, 39, 49; Clark Wiley, 1860, 61; James Steele, 1862, 63, 64; Samuel G. Stanton, 1862, 64, 65, 66, 67, 68; Dexter Samson, 1862, 63; Jehial Allen, 1839, 40, 41, 42; E. Brackett, 1840, 41, 42; Wm. Ruggles, 1838, 40, 47, 39, 49, 48; Wm. W. Wood-

ward, 1838, 45, 47, 49, 48, 35; E. B. Pride, 1840, 47; Robert Cram, 1838, 43, 45, 47, 39, 23, 25, 24, 26, 22; John Cross, 1838, 39, 41, 35, 49; H. S. Boyce, 1838, 42, 43, 44, 45, 47, 41, 49, 39, 46, 48; Allen Spalding, 1842, 43, 44, 45, 47, 41, 49, 40, 48, 35; Darius Hatch, 1838, 39, 40, 42, 43, 44, 45, 47, 49, 41, 48, 46; Samuel M. Orcutt, 1822, 39, 38, 40, 44, 27, 28, 31, 33, 34, 41, 49, 32, 35, 36, 24, 26, 46, 20, 22, 30, 33, 34, 35, 23, 25, 26, 28, 21; Luther Ainsworth, 1842, 43, 45, 47, 49, 48, 46; Samuel Ruggles, 1840, 44, 49; Jared Hildreth. 1838, 42; A. P. Walcott, 1842, 43; Jared Keith, 1841, 42, 43, 44; Thomas R. Shaw, 1848, 42, 49; Isaiah Shaw, 1834, 41, 42, 43, 20, 30, 28, 24, 25, 23, 22; Jonathan F. Ruggles, 1827, 31, 33, 34, 13, 28, 16, 20, 30, 35, 22, 23, 24, 25, 26, 28, 9, 10, 11, 12, 14, 15, 17, 18, 19, 21; Daniel Loomis, 1849; Henry Smith, 1833, 34; James Cram, 1849; Amos Wardner, 1834, 35; Daniel Kingsbury, 1827; Uriah Richardson, 1817, 20, 27, 26, 22, 23, 24, 25, 28, 18, 19, 21; Nathan Morse, 1831, 33, 28, 30; H. G. Ellis, 1863, 64; W. S. Roys, 1863, 64; Ralph W. Rood, 1866, 67, 68; Emery P. Cram, 1866; Asahmel Flint, 1866, 67, 68, 72, 73, 80, 81; Oramel Richardson, 1868; Salmon Williams, 1868, 72, 73, 78, 79, 74, 75; Erastus N. Spalding, 1870; Storrs S. Clough, 1870, 74, 75; Charles Spalding, 1870; John F. Roys, 1870; Charles I. Holden, 1870; Gideon Edwards, 1870; J. F. Pearsons, 1871; Jothan Ellis, 1876, 77, 74, 75; Azro A. Simonds, 1871; A. J. Averill, 1873; Orza Boyce, 1873; C. L. Ellis, 1873, 76, 77; James Burnham, 1831, 32; Aaron Webster, 1876, 77; Luther G. Tracy, 1876, 77; Hira G. Ellis, 1876, 77, 78, 79; C. H. Eaton, 1878, 79; E. E. Bowman, 1878, 79; George B. Hall, 1878, 79, 80, 81; Alphonso Ladd, 1880, 81; A. L. Nichols, 1880, 81; L. F. Wiley, 1880, 81; Darius Spalding, 1804, 5, 14, 15, 16, 13, 9, 10, 11, 12, 14, 17, 18, 19; James Pike, 1839; Samuel Robertson, 1820, 9, 10, 16; Benoni Webster, 1846, 48, 49; Zeb. Butler, 1803, 4; Roswell Adams, 1803, 4; Rhodolphus Willard, 1810, 11, 12, 13; John Freeman, 1795.

TOWN REPRESENTATIVES.

Rhodolphus Willard, 1809, '10, '11, '12; Darius Spalding, 1813, '15, '16; Jonathan F, Ruggles, 1817; Charles Samson, 1818, '19, '20, '21, '24, '25, '28, '37, '38, '39, '41; Robert Cram, 1822, '23; Isaiah Shaw, 1826, '27, '31, '32, '33, '40; Nathan Morse, 1829, '34, '35, '36; Allen Spalding, 1842, '43, '52, '53; Thomas R. Shaw, 1846; Benjamin Edwards, Jr., 1847; Dexter Samson, 1849, '50; Henry S. Boyce, 1851; Elijah Winch, 1854; Alvin Braley, 1855, '56; Edward Pope, 1857; F. V. Randall, 1858; Wm. B. Orcutt, 1859, '60; Seth M. Bailey, 1861; Chester Clark, 1862; Seth M. Bailey, 1863; Edmond Pope, 1864, '65; Austin A. Smith, 1866; Samuel G. Stanton, 1867, '68, '69; Erastus N. Spalding, 1870, '71; 1872, no elections; Enos K. Young, 1874, '75; A. N. Tilden, 1876, '77; Wm. B. Orcutt, 1878-'81.

ASSISTANT JUDGES OF COUNTY COURT.

Charles Samson, 1842, '43; Nathan Morse, Alvin Braley, 1858, '59. Wm. B. Orcutt, 1874, '75;

Sheriff,—O. W. Orcutt, 1865, '66.

DELEGATES TO CONSTITUTIONL CONVENTIONS.

Darius Spaulding, 1814; Jonathan P. Ruggles, 1822; Nathan Morse, 1828, '35; Henry S. Boyce, 1842; Thomas R. Shaw, 1849; Samuel U. Hildreth, 1870.

POSTMASTERS.

First postmaster, John M. Spaulding, from 1826 to '49; O. W. Orcutt, 1849 to '53; Billings Spaulding and A. N. Tilden, 1861 to '63; Julius Spaulding, 1865 to '66; Orin W. Orcutt, 1866 to the present time.

EAST ROXBURY.—Shubael Wales, 1830 to '42; Stillman Ruggles, 1841 to '43; Samuel Ruggles, 1843 to '52; Jacob Wardner, in 1852, and present incumbent.

Merchants:—Among others beside what I have previously named, I remember Woodward, Thresher, A. N. Tilden, Ed. Ferris, J. Riford, Mansfield, I. Brigham, E. P. Burnham, A. N. Tilden & Son, the two last firms at present doing good business. Asa Taylor was the first to keep store in town.

E. N. Spaulding's steam-mill burned down in November, since I wrote up the manufacturing business, and another one was well under way here when I came from Roxbury. Stephen Butterfield has been station agent and telegraph operator nearly the whole time since the railroad came to Roxbury. E. N. Spalding is a prominent business man, dealing heavily in lumber. Will Spalding, his son, is now "dispatcher" in an office in Boston.

THANKS are especially due O. W. Orcutt, Aaron Webster and Zed Stanton, Esq. I have received considerable information from three grand-daughters of Samuel Richardson—Mrs. York, Mrs. Woodard and Mrs. Youngs; also from O. Richardson, a former resident of this town. Many have no doubt felt interested who have devoted no time, therefore much will be left out, inevitably, which cannot fail of being a source of regret to their posterity; for, however this may seem to us of to-day, to whom much of this history is familiar, future generations will peruse it with the greatest interest, and every incident of the hardships, privations and heroism of the pioneers, related at many firesides by our children's children.   S. B. M.

ROXBURY CENTENNIAL CELEBRATION.

The day chosen for the Celebration fell on Tuesday, fair and fine as one could wish. The procession of citizens and visitors formed at the town-house, and led by Northfield Cornet Band, drum corps, militia, old folks' temperance organization, grange and civilians, marched to a charming little grove near the depot, where a stand had been erected for music and speakers, tables laid for an old-fashioned dinner in a little vale just below, tended by young ladies, picturesque in short waists, enormous puffed sleeves and narrow gored skirts, guiltless of trimmings. Among the visitors who were assigned seats of honor upon the stand were Philip Cram, the first child born in Roxbury, from Brookfield; Mrs. Orcutt, widow of Samuel Orcutt, and mother of those residing in Roxbury and Northfield of that name, the oldest person present, being 94 years of age. There were 39 persons over 70, 30 of them being over 80.

96

HISTORICAL ADDRESS,

(BY Z. S. STANTON, ESQ.)

Delivered at Roxbury, Aug. 22, 1876, Maj. Allen Spaulding, president of the occasion; a large concourse of citizens and visitors present; from which we extract the portions pertaining strictly to the history of the town not already covered by the papers of Mrs. Mansfield, given:

"Many of the early settlers of this township were veterans of the Revolution. Doubtless the tract of land now known as the town of Roxbury was never the permanent home of the Indians. Yet it may be inferred from the geographical position of this portion of our State, that the Indians, in their predatory excursions against the colonial settlements of New England, passed through here. The Iroquois, Cossuck and St. Francis tribes frequented this portion of our State at various times while on their hunting excursions, and doubtless the smoke of their camp-fires wended up from this little valley many times. In the fall of 1780, the town of Royalton was pillaged and burned by a band of Indians from Canada, who on their return passed through the west part of Brookfield, and probably the east part of this town. Arrow-heads and other relics have been found here at various times, which prove conclusively that the red man was here at a time previous to any white man's emigration to this township. Nov. 6, 1780, this township was granted, and it was chartered by the Governor, Council and General Assembly of the State, Aug. 5, 1781, to Benjamin Emmons and 64 others, nearly all of whom were residents of Windsor County. I think two of these persons afterwards resided in this town. Among the names of those to whom this township was chartered, I find those of Thomas Chittenden, Paul Spooner, and others prominent in the early history of Vermont. Besides the land chartered to those men, there was chartered one right for the use of a seminary or college, one for the use of a county grammar school, one for the purpose of the settlement of a minister of the gospel, one for the support of the social worship of God, and one for the support of an English school or schools in this town. The proprietors of this township held their first meeting at the house of Benjamin Burtch, an innholder in Hartford, County of Windsor, Nov. 20, 1783; Hon. Paul Spooner, moderator, and Briant Brown, clerk. A committee, consisting of Briant Brown, Esq., Capt. John Strong, Elisha Gallup, Abel Lyman and Asa Taylor were chosen to examine this township, and to lay out 100 acres to each proprietor as a first division, with the allowance of five per cent. for highways. They were also instructed to procure a surveyor, chainmen and provisions. They held an adjourned meeting Dec. 25 the same year, and voted to lay a tax of 10 s. lawful money, on each proprietor's right or share of land, for the purpose of paying the expenses of surveying. This tax was to be paid in money, wheat, beef or pork, at cash price. They chose Capt. John Strong collector, and Major Joel Mathews, treasurer. They also voted a tax of 2 s. lawful money, on each proprietor's right or share of land in this township, for the purpose of defraying charges that had arisen in procuring the charter. It is impossible to ascertain just how many meetings were held by the proprietors of this township, or when the survey was made. I think, however, that the survey was not made at this time, and possibly not until several years later. There was a proprietors' meeting held at the house of Asa Edgerton, in Randolph, Aug. 6, 1788; Major Elijah Paine, moderator, and Deacon David Bates, clerk. A vote similar to the one taken at Hartford, with the addition of another division, was passed. It is possible that the survey of the township was made previous to this time, but I have no authority for saying so. Each proprietor had one lot in each division. On the 21st day of May, 1789, the first settlement was made in this township.

Mr. Huntington, the first settler, was an elderly man, and was accompanied by several children, some of whom had arrived at maturity at that time. Three of his sons, Jedediah, Thomas and Jonathan were quite prominent in town affairs when the town was organized. I am not able to say who the next settlers of this township were, but soon after Huntington and Richardson came here, Mr. Isaac Lewis settled in this town-hip, and Messrs. David, Robert and Jonathan Cram located on the farms now owned and occupied by Messrs. Chatterton, Bowman and Clough. [See previous account of.]

Jacob Wardner came to this town in 1801, and built a log house on the farm now owned by H. A. Thayer. The next year he moved his family to this place. He was a German, and was born on board a vessel while his parents were emigrating to this country, and he used to boast that he 'never was born on the face of God's earth.'

. . . .

Samuel Robinson and Samuel M. Orcutt were at one time associated in mercantile business, and occupied the room now used by J. F. Pearson as a harness shop. This was the second store kept in town. They did a good business, and to use my informant's own words, 'There was not so many Bostons then as now; then the Granger did not trouble the merchant, and the potato bug did not bother the Granger; then the merchants drew their molasses without the help of patent gates, and sold new rum without a license.'

Elijah Ellis lived where Mrs. Brackett now does. He built the house at this place, and it was the first house built in town that was arranged for the use of stoves, I am informed. He had no fire-place or 'stack of chimneys,' as they were called, and people thought it a great departure from the old ways. Ellis also built the first clover-mill in town. [See Mrs. Mansfield's record.]

About this time Moses Woodard lived where Peter Gilbert now does, whose son was the noted manufacturer of the frames of saddles. There was a tavern kept here for some time, and the place was known as the center of the town. Below Woodward's, on the road leading to where the village now is, lived James Bancroft, who was for many years town clerk, and has left upon the town records some splendid specimens of penmanship, that might well serve for copies for many at this day. There were in 1810 but three houses where the village now is—the house of Mr. Burroughs, near where Mrs. Martell lives, and two others, near where Charles Leonard now resides. At this time, 1810, there was a considerable portion of the town settled.

After the return of our volunteers from Plattsburgh, with the exception of town meetings and trainings, the town was comparatively quiet. These trainings were held at various places, sometimes at Billa Woodard's and Capt. Orcutt's, on the east hill, and often near the tavern of John M. Spaulding. Mr. Spaulding kept this tavern, and was also proprietor of a saw-mill and grist-mill at this place. Then one day in each week was set apart for the grinding of salt. Coarse salt was the only kind of that commodity that could be obtained, and as the thrifty housewives then, as now, took great pride in making good butter, they had of necessity to grind their salt at the grist-mill. Mr. Spaulding built the hotel in the village in 1830. He was an energetic business man, and accumulated a handsome property for those honest days. For many years the town meetings were held at dwellings in various parts of the town. I find by consulting the town records that these meetings were held at the houses of the following-named gentlemen,

in the order that they occur: Jedediah Huntington, Samuel Richardson, Christopher Huntington, Lemuel Smith, Ichabod Munsel, Billa Woodard, Samuel M. Orcutt and Luther Ainsworth. After this they were held at the village, in the meeting-house and hotel hall, until the town-house was built, in 1854.

The verd antique marble was discovered in Roxbury, 1833, by a gentlemen named McCain.

No State in the Union has a better record in connection with the war of the rebellion than Vermont—and no town in the State has a better one than Roxbury. With a population of 1060, Roxbury gave the Union army 95 brave soldiers, 8 of whom re-enlisted. Co. H, 6th Vt. Regt,, under command of Capt. D. B. Davenport, was recruited in this town in the fall of 1861. Besides this company there were residents of this town in many other regiments. Twenty-six of these died in the service of their country. . . . . . .
. . Besides these, there were of those who enlisted from other places, but who were residents of this town, two that died—Homer Pearson in a rebel prison, at Salisbury, N. C., and Samuel Shepherd, who was a member of a Massachusetts regiment, in the service. In all, 29 men of this town fell in the defense of human liberty. I wish that this town might imitate the action of other towns, and erect a monument to the memory of these martyrs.

So far as manufacturing is concerned, Roxbury has done but little, and doubtless the wealth that is obtained here must come through the hard hand of the farmer. Mr. Shubal Wales, who kept tavern at East Roxbury many years ago, was also proprietor of clothing works at that place, but it was not a very extensive concern.

The people here have to a considerable extent, been dependent upon itinerant preachers. After Mr. Huntington removed to Canada, the settlers at East Roxbury secured the services of Elder Seaver, of Williamstown, and meetings were held in the school house. Elder Hovey also held meetings there, and soon after a Calvinist Baptist church was formed. There has been, I think, a church organization there ever since. Their present church, the First Christian, was organized in Feb., 1863. Rev. Henry Howard is now their pastor. The union house of worship was built in this village in 1839. Previous to this, the meetings were held in school houses, and sometimes in barns. Considerable excitement was occasioned at the time the first minister in town was ordained. In those days, there were many lay preachers, and one of these, a man named Culver, was privately ordained and laid claim to this lot, together with all the improvements that had been made upon it. The selectmen of the town objected to this, but Culver would not yield, and then they endeavored to have a preacher named Smith, better known as "Happy John," ordained. He declined, and Ophir Shipman was next appealed to. He consented, and was the first regularly ordained minister in Roxbury. He held the value of the land without improvements. The result of this strife was the destroying of the Baptist church at this place.

My fellow townsmen, in conclusion, let me say that I would that this task of chronicling a history of our town might have been performed by abler hands than mine. With the short time alloted me I could, of course, give nothing but a rough sketch of those incidents brought most vividly to my notice. I trust they are in the main correct. My thanks are due those who have so kindly furnished me with material, and I hope the day is not far distant when a fuller and more complete history may be written. If you derive half the pleasure in listening to this that I have in learning of those pioneers in our town, I shall be satisfied. I think we are too apt in this fast age not to look back to the lives and deeds of those who have gone before. Said Edmund Burke, "A people who do not look back to their ancestors will not look forward to their posterity," and still there are many to-day if called upon to give the maiden name of their grandmother would be unable to do so. To know more of those whose places we now fill, to learn of their virtues, to know wherein they erred, is our right and duty. In our little mountain town, away up among the Green Mountains, we have no great history to write of, no mighty deeds of valiant men to chronicle, no biography of some brilliant person who has gone from here and startled the world with his genius, for no native of Roxbury has been, to my knowledge, a member of Congress or of the State Prison either, but simply a story of hardy men and brave women seeking and making their homes among these hills. There are times when, perhaps, we may wish for a more genial clime and a more fertile soil, but none of us after living here a series of years will fail to love these hills, for it is our home. When we consider the changes that have been wrought in our State and nation during the past century, we know that our little town has kept pace with the rest. How different the scene of to-day and the one Samuel Richardson gazed on when

first he came here. At our feet still murmurs that little mountain stream that sparkled in the autumn sunlight of 86 years ago, but how changed is the rest. Then it was an unbroken forest, with naught but wild beasts for inmates; now it is teeming with the marks of improvement. The iron horse is going at lightning speed through our valley; step to yonder telegraph office and in a moment's time a thought of yours may be flashed to the Golden Gates of the Pacific, or, sent beneath the ocean's bed, may be heard on another continent; on our hillsides are evidences of great improvements, machinery supplants labor, and the products of other climes may be ours at prices almost nominal. Forth from these hillsides come a thousand sparkling streams with water pure and clear as our lives should be; across these hills the strong, invigorating air is ever waving, giving health and happiness, and here in our peaceful homes ought to be found hearts grateful to the Giver of all these blessings. But the tottering forms of these aged ones who have assembled here to-day, tell us plainly that it is but a brief happiness we have to enjoy here, and that with each return of this golden harvest time, new mounds will have been made in our valleys and on our hillsides, marking the spot where some one is resting from his labors, and may God grant that when the last summons shall come, and the places we now occupy shall know us no more, that our lives shall have been such as to bear well the scrutiny of the Great Hereafter.

—

A CENTURY OLD STORY.

BY MRS. SARAH BRIGHAM MANSFIELD.
(Read at the Roxbury Centennial.)

Ah! what more inspiring theme
For poet's pen or poet's dream
Than to go back an hundred years—
To dream of all the hopes and fears,
The heart-throbs and the pain
Of those who lived, and loved, and died—
Who felled the forests, dark and wide—
Who, with unswerving, constant toil,
Cleared these broad acres, tilled the soil,
Themselves a home to gain.

A hundred years, or less, ago
Deep waters had their ebb and flow;
The willow bowed its graceful head
Above the water-lily's bed,
Where stands this village now.
The bear and wolf roamed without fear,
With now and then a moose or deer,
And the primeval forests rang
With shrieks of panther—the birds sang
Their loftiest, sweetest strains, I trow.

The red man oft-times wandered through
These olden woods; ah! brave and true
Were they who mid th' green hills of Vermont
Sought and found homes; my word upon't,
A nobler, truer race

Than those old yeomen ne'er were seen;
Though brown of cheek, nor graceful mien
Had they, their record shows
A list of deeds that brighter glows
As years come on apace.

In a sweet glade, beside a wood,
A century gone, a cabin stood;
A purling brook trilled joyously along,
And bird-notes echoed back the song,
While little children fair
Joined in the chorus at their play:
What wonder that their hearts were gay—
From the dread war papa had come,
To spend his days in peace at home;
How light seemed every care!

'Twas springtime; adder-tongues were up;
'Neath the dry leaves the arbutus' cup;
Rude troughs still caught the flowing sweet
From the rock maple; tiny feet
Made fairy footprints all around.
One little lad, with crisp brown curls,
And full white brow, fair as a girl's,
With dusk-bright eyes, brim full of glee,
Pet of that humble home was he—
Humble, yet with love crowned.

"O, let me mind the fire," he cried, "to-day,
And watch the sap, to see it boil away;
You go to dinner, one and all—
Please let me stay; I'm not so very small,
I'll have you all to know;
I'm a big boy, 'most eight years old,
And not a bit afraid; now do not scold,
For won't I make the kettle sing!—
And don't forget my lunch to bring—
I'm starved almost!—now go."

And so they left him, bright-eyed Ned;
"He'll keep all right, we know," they said,
"And feel as proud as any king—
The little, pompous, silly thing,
To think such work is play."
And while they dined, the mother brought
A dainty lunch of trout they'd caught,
And good sweet bread, both brown and white:
"Now haste thee, husband, from my sight,
Nor linger by the way;
"My heart is sad—oh! strangely sad—
For fear of harm to the dear lad;
I know he's brave—as brave as good—
But wild beasts lurk in the deep wood—
Oh! haste thee to our child."
"Fie! fie! upon thy woman's fears;
The boy is safe—dry up thy tears;
And when he comes with me to-night,
Thou'lt smile upon this foolish fright—
He loves the deep woods wild."

Yet, as his hurried steps drew near,
Why blanched his cheek with sudden fear?
Ah! what was there his keen eye scanned?
Prints of moccasined feet on every hand,
With the bare ones of little Ned;
An arrow and a wooden spoon—
But where the boy they left at noon?
The frantic father called in vain;
Sad echo answered back the strain—
Forever lost! it said.

On through the forest, dark and wild,
The frenzied father sought his child;
Through mountain gorge, o'er hill and dale,
Till steps grew slow, cheeks wan and pale,
He sought, but never found.

Spring, summer, waned, and autumn came,
Rich with ripe fruits and golden grain;
But from that pleasant cabin home
The light and joy for aye had flown—
No little narrow mound,

Rose-strewn, where they could go and weep,
And know their darling was asleep
Beneath the flowers; no such relief
Had those poor hearts; in silent grief
They passed each weary day.
White grew the mother's raven hair,
Deep care lines on the brow once fair,
Watching and waiting all in vain;
The dear one came not back again—
He was lost to them for aye.

——The stolen child was a grand-uncle of the writer.

OUR ROXBURY VISIT.

When in print so far as with Middlesex,
we had no certain historian for Roxbury
engaged, but learning by chance correspondence that Mrs. Sarah Brigham Mansfield was residing at Roxbury, made her a
visit with much confidence, we had found
the best person in the town to write out
the historic record of Roxbury. While
visiting Mrs. Mansfield, we also made a
little trip into the Mad River Valley, that
we had never dreamed of as so pretty;
heard Rev. P. B. Fisk in his address at the
Fair at Waitsfield, and visited the birthtown of the Brigham family and Mrs.
Laura Brigham Boyce. Mr. and Mrs.
Mansfield pointed out many an old site
named in our Fayston history, fresh from
the press; now Mr. M., the old home site
of his father, which strangely the writer
had somehow overlooked.

RILEY MANSFIELD, born in Winchendon, Mass., came from there when 19
years old, with an ox-team, by marked
trees, through the heart of the Vermont
wilderness, and located in the valley of
Fayston, clearing himself a farm and
rolling up the logs for his first log-house.
He lived in this town till his death, and
raised a large family, and was one of the
principal landholders of his day, as the
Fayston records attest. His farms and
mortgages on farms covered much of the
territory of the town; but he was no oppressor. A neighbor under embarrassment came to him one day, and said, "I
want you to buy that 50-acre lot of mine.
If I can turn it into money, I can save my
farm and myself from ruin." "I will take

it," said Mr. M., and paid him his price for the land. The man afterwards said to him, "You saved me and my family from utter failure." A little later, hard times again came, and the neighbor was again in deep gloom. How he could meet his taxes he did not know. He had some fine sheep, but sheep were down in the market; no one wanted to buy for half their worth. The melancholy man came down one afternoon to see if Mr. M. would not buy his sheep. Mr. M. was absent. He told his story to Mrs. M., and said he knew of no one else who would give him the worth of his sheep, but he thought that Mr. M. might, and let him have the money. Mrs. M., sorry for the man, and knowing the neighborly spirit of her husband, told him that she thought Mr. M. might buy the sheep, and she would tell him when he came home, and she thought he would be up there that night. The man left a little encouraged. Mr. M. did not return till late. Mrs. M. told him, but it was 10 o'clock before he had his chores done, and he put off going up till the next morning. He went up then, but the man had hung himself in the night. His wife said to Mr. M., "Had you come up last night, it would have saved his life." Mr. M., although no ways obligated, always regretted that he had not gone up that night, late as it was.

He brought apple-seeds from New Hampshire, and planted orchards around his old homestead 63 years ago; trees yet remain there that sprang from the seed he planted then. Mr. M. removed from where he first settled to a farm on Mill brook, where he made his home the last 25 years of his life. His first home was adjoining the old Brigham farm on Fayston hill. His house was within 20 rods of where George Boyce now lives. He sold to Mr. Brigham and Mr. Griggs a part of their farms (old Stephen R. Griggs was the one who committed suicide).

From Obituary.—"Riley Mansfield, of Fayston, died Jan. 14, ——, aged nearly 77 years; another of our oldest and most respected citizens is gone, almost the last of the pioneer men who came to our town in its early settlement, or before it had become largely settled or improved. He came 56 years ago, and helped by his lifelong industry to make the wilderness to blossom as a garden. At 23, he was converted at a camp-meeting, and united with the Methodist church, of which he was a member at time of his death. In 1822 he married Betsey Chase, who died Mar. 11, '73. Of a large family, but one son, Martin Mansfield, is now living. He was respected for his sterling worth; there lives no man who will say, 'Uncle Riley,' as he was called by all his neighbors, ever knowingly cheated him one cent. Of his sudden death he seemed to have a premonition. He began to feel unwell Wednesday afternoon, and died on Friday near midnight. About an hour before he died, he dressed himself and laid down again on his bed, apparently comfortable, and died as an infant hushed to sleep in its mother's arms."

After his death it was found he had written in his diary the Sabbath evening before, the following:

"JAN. 9, SABBATH EVENING.

Now we know not what is before us; we frequently hear of people being found dead, and as you all, my dear children, are away from me, the thought came to me that I might never see any of you again. Oh, what a feeling came over me! I felt that I could not go to bed without writing a few words of entreaty that you would not let the busy scenes and cares of this life hinder you from preparing for the life to come. Oh, do think of the life that never, never ends! Think what folly it is to make overmuch provision for the flesh only to be enjoyed a few days! It is the height of folly for people to live as most do, and for professors of religion to live as all the world do, laying up treasures on earth. What I wrote on the other page (of this diary), was after I was ready to go to bed, but after these thoughts came to me, I made another fire and sat down and wrote this, hoping you might find it, and hoping it might have some influence on your lives. It may be your loving father's last request."

It was his last request to his children, for he never beheld their faces again, his death on the next Friday night being so unexpected, they were not sent for until all was over.

BETSEY CHASE,

who lived on Waitsfield Mountain, mother of Mrs. Riley Mansfield, of Fayston (see previous, page —), used to tell many tales of almost incredible hardships and privations. Her husband, Thomas Chase, served in the Revolutionary War, and she cared for her little family as best she could, as they were very poor, in the springtime subsisting upon milk and leeks (wild onions), and such small game as she could get, being an adept in the use of a rifle or shot-gun. At one time, when the army was in desperate need of recruits, and they were pressed into the service with but very little ceremony. When it was known officers were in town for that purpose, many poor fellows, who much preferred to remain by their own firesides to enduring the perils of war, would hide until the enlisting officers had left town. They, learning this, devised a plan to catch them by letting loose their cattle in the night, and concealing themselves to watch for the men to come out and care for them. Several times one night Mrs. Chase heard the tinkling of her old cow-bell in her corn-field, and each time marched resolutely out and drove old "Crumpie" into the yard, making all fast, and returned to the house, to have the same repeated, until the recruiting officer and men with him wearied out (at last,) made themselves and their errand known, and when told her husband was already in the service, was somewhat chop-fallen, but declared she was a brave woman, fit to be a soldier's wife. She was a strong, robust woman, and never seemed to know the meaning of the word fear. She often said she would as soon meet the devil in the dark as a man. Whether this was a bit of sarcasm on the "sterner sex" she never explained. Some of her superstitious neighbors called her a "witch," for her prophecies often came true, and they feared nothing so much as her displeasure, "lest some evil should come upon them." This rather pleased her than otherwise, as in this way she kept some disorderly neighbors very submissive. She died in Waitsfield, April, 1852, aged over 90 years.

The account of Riley Mansfield and Thomas and Betsey Chase belong to the towns of Fayston and Waitsfield, but having been overlooked at home, we include them with this near neighboring town, and the more easily, as Mrs. Mansfield has most cordially and permanently connected herself here as the historian of the town, though the family have now all removed from Roxbury and reside at Fairhaven.

MR. BURNHAM'S REMINISCENCES.

Deer.—Mr. E. P. Burnham, merchant at the village, told us he can remember some 50 years ago, when the deer used to herd together in spruce thickets on these mountains in the winter, and when the snow melted in the March days, and froze at night, making a crust, the hunters would be out the next morning for the deer. He says he has been on these mountains many times when the deer were so thick you could not count their tracks—the tracks were like a thousand sheep in the snow. The hunters frequently shot and brought in several deer at a time. He distinctly remembers when they brought in five at one time.

He was graphic in his remembrances of Crandall, of whom Mrs. Mansfield has some anecdotes on the foregoing pages.

"Some 50 years ago," says Mr. B., "there lived in this town a man by the name of John B. Crandall, but who was named and called by all his townsmen Judge Crandall, a drinking, miserable being, but a man with natural talent. He would get into debt and get sued, and defend himself in the courts. He managed his own case and plead his own cause before the jury, and usually with success. Judge Weston brought a suit for debt against him one time, however, in Randolph, when Crandall thought he would have some help, and engaged one of Judge Weston's students to help defend him. When the cause came on, the student arose to argue Crandall's case, but, awed by the presence of his master, began to hesitate. Crandall stood it for a moment. He had an inveterate habit of spitting when excited. For a moment he sat spitting, when, arising, drawing his ragged, slightly liquorfied form up to its full height, he spit once, twice, thrice. Said he, 'Sit down! sit down! You are afraid of the d——d cuss; let me try him!' He did try him, and won his case out and out with the jury, to the great amusement of all who heard the defense. He had a family. His own boys took after him in drinking, but had none of his power of wit and argument. I think they were more like their mother, who was a famous talker, but not well balanced. Some neighbors in of an evening, the old lady would sit and tell over her wise things; the old man, under the influence of liquor, in his chair sit and doze, and when she had chatted away and told her long yarns till late, arouse himself up and say, 'A dumb fool always knows the most.'"

The poor old man, of marked ability, but a wreck from his bad habit, died at last, and his curious old wife and his uneducated sons following in his steps, that never were any benefit to the community; but in the third generation, under the influence of a better education, the ability of the grandfather again cropped markedly out. His grandsons have the strong natural ability without the dissipation of their grandfather or fathers, and make fine men.

— •

THE 90TH BIRTHDAY PARTY
of Mrs. Betsey C. Spalding, of which Mrs. Mansfield has briefly spoken, was, indeed, a very unique and pleasant gathering, and as the oldest birthday party ever celebrated in Roxbury, should perhaps have a little more notice. Her five children, all living, were present: Erastus N., Billings, Mrs. Brackett, Mrs. P. Wiley, Mrs. A. N. Thompson, her daughter-in-law and her sons-in-law, and the grandchildren in part: Mrs. L. P. Thompson, from Clarence, Ia.; Mrs. Arthur Bradley, of Malden, Mass.; William Wiley, of White River Junction; Charles, of St. Albans; Edwin and Delia Wiley, Clinton Brackett, George Tilden, with their husbands and wives and four great-grandchildren, "uncles, cousins and aunts." Over the front door was "Welcome!" in cedar; within, the mammoth cake on the table, "a pyr-

amid of snowy whiteness, crowned with an exquisite white rose with silver leaves," a rose-pyramid rising beside, the gift of the great-grandchildren, of ninety rosebuds, rare specimens, just bursting into beauty, that filled the room with their delicious perfume; over the wall above, "1791 and 1881;" another table—an elegant bouquet of hot-house flowers from St. Albans friends, a mound of asters, artistically arranged, very handsome, from Mrs. E. P. Burnham, with letters of regret from friends who could not come, on the table. The photographer was there, and views taken of the family gathered about the aged mother in front of her house. Then there was the bountiful supper in the town-hall, five long tables, the central one laid with the mother's old-fashioned mulberry ware and silver of " ye olden" solidity and style; and after, the birthday address by Rev. Eli Ballou, of Bethel, who referred to Mrs. Spalding's coming to Roxbury when the town was but a wilderness, being one of the first settlers. He spoke feelingly of the kind, loving mother she had been, how deserving of all their love and respect; this occasion would remain a bright spot in their memories. Mrs. S. was born in Strafford, Ct., married John Spalding at 20, and came to Roxbury.

—

NORA, BLOSSOM OF THE MAY.

BY A. WEBSTER.

Where departed kindred sleep,
And the living come and weep,
Laid we, on a vernal day,
Nora, blossom of the May.

Seven summers' suns and flowers,
Seven autumns' russet bowers,
Eight sweet springtimes, fair and gay,
Saw our blossom of the May.

Mild was she, and sweetly fair,
Azure eyes and nut-brown hair;
Voice that rivaled warblers' lay,
Had our blossom of the May.

Earth is sad now she is gone,
Heaven another charm has won;
Where to meet, we hope and pray,
Nora, blossom of the May.

Rest, sweet blossom, rest in peace,
Where all pains and sorrows cease;
In our hearts shall ne'er decay,
Nora, blossom of the May.

Nora, blossom of the May,
Pride of her parental spray,
Sweetly bloomed and passed away,
Nora, blossom of the May.

dwellings, stores and shops (log-houses excepted) should be assessed at two per cent. of their value, if in the judgment of the listers their value did not exceed $1000. And if valued at more than $1000, at three per cent. The law also specified how personal property should be set in the list, as above. Wooden clocks were not taxed. Attorneys, physicians, merchants, mechanics, etc., were assessed in proportion to their gains.

1820: 86 polls at $20, $1720; 1990 acres of improved land at .08 of appraised value, $1366.42; 103 houses and lots at .04 appraised value, $247.06; 9 mills, stores, etc., at .06 appraised value, $48.60; 140 oxen at $10, $1400; 429 cows and three-year olds at $6, $2574; 169 cattle, two-year olds at $5, $845; 132 horses, three years old and upwards, at $14, $1848; 26 two-years old at $7, $182; 22 one-year old at $4, $88; 1 stallion at $50, $50; 5 brass clocks at $10, $50; 1 gold watch at $10, $10; 20 common do. at $5, $100; $1100 money at .06, $66; total, $11295.08; 34 militia polls and 9 cavalry horses were exempt from State taxes.

1830: 252 polls at $10, $2520; 3690 acres of land at .06, $1558.60; 541 houses and lots at .04, $1401.40; 14 mills, stores, etc., at .06, $62.40; 281 oxen at $2, $562; 712 cows and other cattle of three years old, at $1.25, $890; 254 cattle of two years old at .75 each, $190.50; 25 horses and mules, three years old, appraised at less than $25, at $1, $25; 180 over $25 and less than $75, at $3, $540; 6 at $75, at .06, $36; 43 two years, at $2, $86; 33 one year, at $1.25, $41.25; 2797 sheep at .10 each, $279.70; 7 carriages at .06 of appraised value, $6.30; 8 brass clocks at $3, $24; 20 watches at $1, $20; $3350 money on hand, etc., at .06, $201; $90 bank stock at .03, $2.70; 2 practitioners of medicine assessed, $35; 1 merchant and trader, do., $30; total, $8511.85; 148 militia polls and 6 cavalry horses, exempt.

In 1840, the list amounted to $10373.54. Later lists were assessed nearly as at present, and are as follows:

	Polls.	Real.	Personal.	Gd. List.
1850	266	$281,774	$32,023	$3,675
1860	312	304,473	46,547	4,134
1870	340	374,573	71,936	4,848
1878	326	296,652	67,807	4,260

FAYSTON.

BY MRS. LAURA BRIGHAM BOYCE.

This township is in the S. W. corner of the County, 20 miles from Montpelier; b. N. by Duxbury, E. by Waitsfield, S. by Warren and Lincoln, W. by Huntington and Buell's Gore; 6 miles square; land elevated, lying in large swells, except along Mill brook and Shephard's brook, where there is some intervale. Shephard's brook runs through the North part of the town, and empties into Mad river in Waitsfield. It affords ample water power, and several flourishing mills are in operation on its banks.

There was an extensive beaver meadow on this stream, and many of the trees on its banks were partly cut down by these animals. The brook received its name from one Shephard, who used to hunt beavers here.

Mill brook runs through the South part of the town, in an Easterly direction, and empties into Mad river in Waitsfield; this stream has good water-power, and several mills and one tannery are located on it. There is considerable good lumber in town, especially in the more mountainous parts, the most valuable of which is spruce. As many as 7,000 or 8,000 clapboard logs are annually cut in Fayston, besides the common lumber, ash, basswood, etc. There is also a good deal of hemlock, the bark of which is used extensively in tanneries. The spruce and hemlock lumber is a source of profit to the inhabitants. The maple is abundant, and there are many valuable sugar orchards; some have a thousand handsome second growth trees in one body. This adds an item to the income of the farmer, at the prices that have prevailed for maple sugar and syrup of late years.

The soil is strong and fertile, though not as easily tilled as a more sandy loam. These fertile upland farms are well adapted to dairying, as the sweetest grass is found here, and water as pure and soft as ever drank, two indispensable requisites for the dairy. Dairying is the chief source of income of a greater part of the inhabitants, though wheat and oats are raised here in

23

abundance, but potatoes more especially. Corn is often a remunerative crop; but not so sure as on the intervales.

Fayston was granted Feb. 25, and chartered Feb. 27, 1782, to Ebenezer Walbridge and his associates. It was first settled by Lynde Wait in 1798. In 1800, there were 18 persons in town.

Lucia Wait, daughter of Lynde Wait, better known as Squire Wait, was born in 1801, the first child born in town; subsequently, Wait Farr, a son of William Farr, was born, and received a lot of land from Griswold Wait, as being the first male child born in town. From which we see in those primitive days the weaker were oppressed by the stronger, as they are still. There was no orthodox reason why Lucia Wait should not have had that lot of land as her birthright—except that *she wasn't a boy.*

The town was organized Aug. 6, 1805. James Wait was the first town clerk; Thomas Green the first constable; and Lynde Wait, Rufus Barrett and William Williams the first selectmen. Aug. 27, 1805, there was a town meeting called to petition the General Assembly to be set off with other towns from Chittenden County, which was not granted until some time in 1810 or 1811, when Fayston became a part of Jefferson County.

The first highways were surveyed in 1807, by Edmund Rice, surveyor. The first school district was organized in 1809, and consisted of the whole town, but subsequently, in 1810, we believe, it was divided into two districts. The first tax levied on the grand list was in 1807, which was 5 cents on a dollar, to be worked out on the highway. The first tax levied on the grand list to be paid in money was in 1810. It was 1 cent on a dollar, and we have no doubt was as hard for these people as were the excessive taxes during the war for their descendants. The taxes levied on the grand list in Fayston during the war in one year were $10.79 on a dollar of the grand list, making a poll tax of $21.58, and school and highway taxes besides, which must have made another dollar. This was in 1864. There were several other bounty

taxes raised during the war, but this was the heaviest. Fayston paid her war debt as she went along, and can show a clean record. In 1812, the town voted to raise 1 cent on a dollar for the support of schools, which was to be paid to the town treasurer *in grain.* At this time there were 25 children in district No. 1, between the ages of 4 and 18.

In March, 1809, William Newcomb, William Rogers and Marjena Gardener were elected "hog howards," an office now obsolete, and exactly what its duties were, even then, we are unable to learn. But it was an old-time custom to elect newly-married men to that *notable* office, which might have been no sinecure after all, as the swine in those days all ran where they listed, and unless they were much less vicious than their modern descendants, it must have needed three "hog constables" to a town to have kept them in order.

In April, 1808, William and Paul Boyce, two Quakers, emigrated from Richmond, N. H., and settled near beaver meadow, on Shephard's brook. This was the first opening in what is now called North Fayston. There is a little romance connected with this same William Boyce. It seems that William's susceptible heart had been touched by one Irene Ballou, a Quaker maiden of his native place, and when he had made a beginning on his new home in the woods he began to be lonely, and feel the need of a helpmate to wash his wooden plates and pewter porringer, and also to assist him in picking up brush, planting potatoes, and several other things wherein the good wives made themselves useful in "the olden time," being then truly *helpmates* for men, instead of help spends, as many of the more modern wives are. So William journeyed to Richmond to claim his bride. He tarried long, and when he returned it was not the gentle Irene who accompanied him. Whether he met with a fairer Quakeress than she, and lost his heart with her against his will, or whether Irene was averse to going into the new country, among the bears and wolves, tradition saith not, but that it was not the latter reason we may infer from her farewell to him: "William, I wish thee well, I hope the Lord will bless thee, but I know He wont." Says one of his descendants: "I think He didn't, for he was always in some sort of trouble or other." Let the fate of William be a warning to all young Quakers, as well as those who quake not at all, to always keep their promises.

BOYCE FAMILY OF FAYSTON.

PAUL BOYCE married Rhoda Palmer, of Waitsfield, and here on the farm they first rescued from the wilderness, they lived to a ripe old age, and were finally buried in the cemetery not far away.

Their son, ZIBA WENTWORTH BOYCE, always resided in town until his death, 1877, age, 63. He received but a common school education, but by his own efforts, ultimately became a thorough scholar, and taught school many terms. Later he served the town in various capacities, and up to the time of his death was noted for his fine mental endowments. He was often jocosely called the "wisdom of North Fayston," and not altogether without reason. He was a writer of considerable ability, both in prose and verse. His two daughters inherited his talent for writing, more especially his younger daughter, Mrs. Emongene Smith, now a resident of Dubuque, Iowa. The eldest daughter, Mrs. S. Minerva Boyce, has always remained at the homestead.

When Ziba W. was quite a young lad, his father sent him one night with his brother after the sheep, but they having strayed from their usual pasture, they failed to find them. In the morning they found what there was left of them, eleven having been devoured by the wolves during the night.

On one occasion Paul Boyce was going off into the woods with his oxen, when he met a bear with two cubs face to face. The meeting was not a remarkably pleasant one to him; he being a Quaker and averse to fighting, was pleased when the bear turned and trotted off.

About the year 1809, Stephen Griggs emigrated from Pomfret, Conn., and settled about one-half mile from Esquire Wait's

farm. He resided there as long as he lived, and his companion, who survived him many years, died there. The place has never passed out of the family, a granddaughter at present residing there. This farm and the Brigham farm are the only ones in South Fayston which have never passed out of the families of the first settlers.

Deer-yards were frequently found on the eastern slopes of the hills. The early settlers used to hunt them in winter when the snow was deep, so that they could not escape. Buck's horns were often found in the woods. Sable were quite abundant. Ezra Meach, of Shelburne, passed through the town in 1809, setting his line of traps for sable, and blazed trees along his route. He found it quite profitable business, as these animals were exceedingly good in the western part of the town. The panther, the great dread of the juvenile community, was often seen, or supposed to be seen, but never captured in this town.

UNCLE JOHN'S INDIAN RAID.

Some time about 1803, there were then five or six families settled in what is now known as South Fayston. There were Uncle John and Uncle Rufus Barrett—I call them Uncle John and Uncle Rufus, as these were the names by which I knew them in my early childhood, albeit they were both young men at the date of my story. There were Squire Wait and Thos. Green, and if there were others I do not know their names.

Now at that time the raising of a new house or barn was a job that required plenty of muscle and new rum, for they were built of logs, and very heavy.

On a certain day, somebody in Warren was to raise a barn, and as the country was sparsely settled, everybody was invited far and near, and all the men of Fayston went except Uncle John. Whether he stayed at home to guard the women and children from the bears and wolves, tradition saith not. I only know he "tarried by the stuff," and all went well till near sundown, when suddenly there burst upon his ears a long, wild cry, between a howl and a whoop. Uncle John was on the alert; he listened with bated breath a few moments; louder and nearer than before came that terrible howl, this time in a different direction.

"'Tis the Indian war whoop," said Uncle John ; "no doubt we are surrounded, and the men all away." He stood not upon the order of going, but went at once. Uncle John was no coward, and if the redskins got his scalp, they should buy it dearly, he resolved, and seizing his gun, bidding his wife to follow, he ran to alarm the neighbors, and get them all together, that he might defend them as long as possible. In a short time every woman and child in the settlement was ensconced in Uncle Rufus' domicile, with all the firearms the settlement contained, the door barricaded, and all the preparations made to receive the red-skins that one man could do, aided by a few courageous women. They listened, with hearing made acute by fear, for the repetition of the war whoop. Now they heard it evidently nearing them —Uncle John loaded all the guns—now they heard it further away. With pale faces and palpitating hearts, they awaited the onset. The twilight shades deepened, the night closed in, but still the Indians did not attack them.

Now there was an additional anxiety among the inmates of the little cabin, for it was time for the men to be returning from the raising, and as they were unarmed, they would fall an easy prey to the Indians.

Meanwhile the men, having finished their labors, were returning home, all unconscious of the danger menacing them. They reached home, but were surprised to find those homes deserted. "Come on to my house," said Uncle Rufus, "perhaps the women were lonesome, and have gone to make my wife a visit." So, not knowing what else to do, they went on. Yes, there was a light at Uncle Rufus', sure enough, and a glance sufficed to show that there was some unusual commotion within. What could it be?

"Hark, I hear voices," cried one of the women, "it is the Indians this time, sure."

The children began to cry, and I suppose it would have been very delicate if the women had fainted, but they did no such thing.

"What are you all about here? why don't you let us in?" cried Uncle Rufus, shaking the door. The door was opened speedily, and instead of being scalped by the Indians, they fell into the arms of their astonished husbands.

"What is all this pow-wow about, anyway?" said one. Then Uncle John explained how he had heard the Indian war-whoop off in the woods, and had gathered the women and children there together for protection. The men burst into a loud laugh. "It was the wolves," said Squire Wait, "we heard them howling on the mountain as we came home. I'll be bound there isn't a red-skin within 50 miles."

Uncle John was somewhat crestfallen, but he was rather glad after all that it wasn't Indians, for he preferred to have his scalp in its proper place, rather than dangling from the red-skins' belts.

Some time in 1814, there was a rumor current of great treasure buried by the Spanish Legions at the forks of Shepherd's brook, and William Boyce, having a desire for "the root of all evil," resolved to find it. He engaged one Arad Sherman, a man of such magical powers that in his hands a witch-hazel rod performed as many antics as the rod of Aaron, and they went about the search. Arad took the enchanted rod, and lo! it pointed out the exact location of the buried treasure, but it remained for them to dig and get it. It had been revealed to Arad that they must dig in the night time, and no word must be spoken by any one of the number during the whole time of the digging, else the treasure would be lost to them. So one night they started on their secret expedition. Nothing was heard but the dull thud of the bars in the earth, and grating of the spade. The earth was obstinate, but they were determined no powers of earth should cheat them of their treasure. The hours wore on, when suddenly William's bar struck against the iron chest containing the treasure, with a sharp "clink." Overjoyed at their success, William forgot the caution and cried out "I've found it!" At that instant the box shook with an ominous rattle, and sank down, down, far below the sight of their longing eyes, taking the bar and all with it, says the tradition. Frightened nearly out of their wits, they "skedaddled" for home, sadder if not better men, and the treasure remains buried there to this day.

In the winter of 1826, a beautiful doe was run down Shepherd's brook to Mad river, near Jason Carpenter's and brought up in an open eddy out of the reach of the dogs. Judge Carpenter caught it in his arms, and, seven or eight hunters coming up just then, he told them that they could not have the doe, but each one of them might go and select a sheep from his flock, if they would go home about their business. Nothing but the beautiful doe would satisfy these blood-thirsty hunters, and, seizing the deer by main force, they killed it on the spot.

Pigeons were abundant. One device for keeping them off the grain patches was a boy threshing a log chain around a stump. They used also to construct bough houses on the edge of the field, and draw a huge net over the baiting place, thus securing dozens at a haul. Partridges were caught on their drumming logs in snares, or, if not there, the gunner was sure to find them in some thicket. So it came to be a proverb, "hunted like a partridge."

In early days Uncle Moses Eaton used to bring corn from Richmond on the backs of two horses, the roads not being passable for any vehicle.

On his journey Uncle Moses met Uncle Joe Clark, of Duxbury, at Pride's tavern in Waterbury. "Now," said Uncle Joe, "you will want some pork to go with that corn, and you just call at my house, and tell Aunt Betsey to put you up a good clear piece of pork." The next time they met Uncle Moses said, "I called on Aunt Betsey, as you told me, and she raised her hands and blessed herself, saying, "What on airth does that man mean, sending any one here for pork, when he knows that we haint had any kind of meat in the house

for six months?" But Uncle Joe enjoyed the joke hugely.

In Fayston there was considerable snow on the 8th and 9th of June, 1816, and everything was frozen down to the ground. The trees put out new leaves three times during that season, having been cut off twice by frost; hardly anything ripened, and the settlers saw dreary times.

WILLIAM NEWCOMB

came to the township quite early in its settlement, and finished his days here. He built one of the first framed houses in town, Esquire Wait's being the first; Mr. Newcomb and Merrill Tyler each built theirs the same year, but I am unable to learn in what year. Mr. Newcomb's farm was occupied by his son Hosea many years, but has passed into the hands of strangers. The old house was burned during a high wind, in Oct. 1878.

Dr. Dan Newcomb, son of Hosea Newcomb, was born and reared here, but has been for several years a practicing physician in Steele County, Ill. He is also the author of a medical work entitled, "When and How," a work of considerable merit. Don Carlos, another son, is a prominent wholesale merchant of Atchison, Kansas.

NATHAN AND JACOB BOYCE

In 1808, Nathan Boyce and his wife, Zeviah, came to Fayston, and settled on Shephard's brook, near Paul Boyce, of whom he was a relative, and also of the Quaker faith. Nathan Boyce died many years ago; his wife in 1856, aged about 90, I think. She resided with her son Jacob, who died in 186-. His wife still survives him, at the age of 81 (1878. She is still living, Aug. 1881.) She lives on the old farm with her son, Seth Boyce. The farm has always remained in the family.

Jacob Boyce had 4 sons and 4 daughters, all of whom, save one, are settled in Fayston or the immediately adjacent towns.

BRIGHAM FAMILY.

In 1809, Gershom Brigham and family emigrated from Winchester, N. H., and settled in South Fayston, near Lynde Wait's. Elisha, their third child, was then 17 years old, and eventually settled on the same land, his other brothers and sisters finding other homes. His parents resided with him while they lived, and their bones rest in the little green grave-yard on the old Wait farm. Elisha lived here to ripe old age, raising a family of 11 children, all of whom are now living except one daughter, who died at the age of 42. The two eldest sons and the two youngest daughters of this family have some literary talent, having all contributed to the press acceptably, in prose and verse. The eldest son, [See separate notice of Dr. G. N. Brigham].

Elisha Brigham died in 1863, aged 70 years ; his widow in 1876, aged 77. The old home that she had resided in for more than 40 years, took fire in some mysterious manner, and was burned in the early morning hours, when her demise was hourly expected. She was borne from the flaming house to the home of a neighbor, and breathed her last in the very house whence she went on her wedding day to be married 59 years before.

Mrs. Brigham was a woman of remarkable powers, mental and physical. Left an orphan by the death of her mother at the age of 12, she came from Randolph, Vt., her native place, to reside in the family of Esquire Wait, so she became early identified with the history of the town. Her remarkably vigorous constitution and ambition to excel, fitted her for the position of a pioneer's wife, and she endured the hardships and deprivations consequent on the building up of a new place, with great fortitude. With a large family of her own and many cares, yet she acted as nurse for half the town, and such was her skill in the management of the sick, that the old physician, now dead, used always, if he had a critical case, to send for Mrs. Brigham, and said, with her to nurse them, he felt pretty sure of bringing his patients through. Her very presence and touch seemed to bring healing with them.

When Mrs. Brigham was a fair, young wife of 19, she was small, lithe and supple, with nerves of steel, and she never shrank from any of the hardships of her life. They then made sugar nearly a mile from the house. It was growing late in the

spring, and Mr. Brigham was anxious to be about his spring's work, and his wife, being equally anxious for a good supply of sugar, offered to go with her sister, a girl of 17, and boil in the sap. Taking the baby with them, they started for the sugar-camp. It was late in spring and quite warm, and babies were not killed by a breath of fresh air in those days. They boiled sap all day, Mrs. B. gathering in some sap near the boiling place. In the afternoon they heard a good deal of barking off in the woods, but supposed it was some hounds after foxes. Mr. Brigham did not get up to the sugar-camp to bring down the syrup till nine o'clock, they staying there alone until that time: A neighbor passing through the camp early the next morning, found a sheep dead at the foot of a tree where Mrs. Brigham had gathered sap at sundown. The sheep was still warm when Mr. Brigham arrived on the spot. On looking around, they found 20 sheep had been killed by the wolves. Mrs. Brigham and her fair sister did not care to boil till nine o'clock the next night.

On one occasion Mrs. Brigham, desiring to get some weaving done, mounted an unbroken, 3-years-old colt, that had never had a woman on his back before, and started on a ride of 4 miles through the woods, to Wm. Farr's, with a bag of yarn fastened to the saddle-bow. There was only a bridle-path part of the way, and the colt was shy, but he found his match in the little woman of scarce 100 pounds' weight, and carried her safely to her destination. Her business dispatched at Mr. Farr's, she started homeward by another route, having occasion to call at one William Marsten's, who lived far up on the road leading over the mountain into Huntington, and from thence homeward by a route so indistinctly marked, blazed trees being the guide, she mistook a path worn by the cattle for the traveled road, and did not discover her mistake till she came up to the pasture fence. Nothing daunted, she took down the fence, passed over, then replaced it, and went over, being then so near home that she felt pretty sure of her whereabouts. After the colt became better broken, she used often to take one child in her arms and another behind her, and go to the store, 3 or 4 miles distant, or visit a distant neighbor, or to go to meeting.

JOTHAM CARPENTER

was the first settled minister, and received the minister lot of land in this town. How many years he remained here I know not, but he has one son now living in Brookfield.

Preaching has generally been of a desultory character, owing to the fact that North and South Fayston are divided by a natural barrier of hills, that makes it far more convenient for the North section to go to Moretown, and the South part is more accessible to Waitsfield, so that it seems probable that the different sections will never unite in worship. The people in N. Fayston have an organized Baptist society, and have quite frequent preaching, and some years hire a minister, and many years ago, the Methodists had quite a large society in So. Fayston, but it has been dismembered a long time, and most of its former members are dead, and those remaining have united with the Methodist church in Waitsfield.

John and Rufus Barrett were among the early settlers, and one Thomas Green, but as they have no descendants remaining in town, I cannot tell when they settled here, but they were here as early as 1803, it is believed.

Elizabeth, widow of John Barrett, died in Waitsfield a few years since (1878) aged 93 years. She survived her husband many years.

One Jonathan Lamson died in town several years ago, at the age of 84. His wife lived to the age of 107 years. Timothy Chase died at the age of 91; his wife, Ruth, some years earlier, over 80. Lynde Wait, the first settler, moved from town many years ago, and eventually went West, and I have learned, died at an advanced age, over 80. Nearly all the early settlers whom I have known, lived to ripe old age, but they have passed away, and with them much of the material for a full history of the town. I have gathered as much as I could that is reliable, but even the last two, from whom I have elicited most of the facts recorded here, have now gone to their long homes, and much that I have gathered here would now be forever sealed in silence, had I began my work a little later.

CAPT. ELLIOT PORTER,

the first captain of the militia in the town, was born in Hartford, Vt., 1785, married Sidney Ward in 1811, and soon after removed to Fayston, where they began to clear them a home in the North part of the town, where they resided till their death. He died at the age of 89; his wife at 86. They had 8 children. William E. Porter, their son, died at 57; 4 sons are now living.

WILLARD H. PORTER,

son of Elliot, has always resided in town, near where he was born, and has served the town in almost every official capacity. He has been town clerk 31 years, school district clerk 25 years, treasurer 14 years, justice of the peace 30 years, and in that capacity married 86 couple. He has represented the town 6 sessions, including 1 extra session, and has attended 2 constitutional conventions. Mr. Porter says the first school he attended was in his father's log-house chamber; the scholars, his eldest brother, himself and one Jane Laws; the teacher's name, Elizabeth Sherman. Mr. Willard Porter has done more business for the town than any other person now living.

WARREN C. PORTER

served as a soldier during nearly the whole war of the Rebellion, and has taught school 24 terms. Dr. Wilfred W. Porter, see separate notice. Walter, the youngest son, remains on the old homestead, and it was his care to soothe the declining years of his parents as they went slowly down the dark valley.

There was no death occurred in the family of Elliot Porter for 50 years.

WILLIAM SHERMAN

was among the early settlers of Fayston, though I am not informed in what year he settled here. He represented the town in the general assembly, and held other town offices. His daughter, widow of Eli Bruce, still lives on the old homestead that he redeemed from the wilderness.

ELI BRUCE

was a long-time resident of Fayston, and did a large amount of business for the town, several times being the representative, and justice of peace for many years. He died at the age of 69. His daughter was the first person buried in the cemetery in N. Fayston.

SILAS W. FISHER

resides in N. Fayston, on the farm where he has lived for 50 years. His wife has been dead some years. He has two surviving sons; one in the West, and the other, C. M. Fisher, is constable of Fayston at the present time—1878. He died in 1879.

BENJAMIN B. FISHER

was the first postmaster in town, and held the office till his death, and his wife held the office 4 years afterwards. Truman Murray is the present incumbent.

RILEY MANSFIELD

came to the town when he was quite a young man, and passed his days here, dying in 1876, aged 75; his wife in 1874; out of a large family, there is only one surviving child of theirs.

JOSEPH MARBLE

came to Fayston in September, 1809, and with his wife Susan passed the remnant of his days here, dying at the age of 84; his wife at 81. They had 11 children, two only are living (1878.) One daughter in Wisconsin, and Benjamin on the farm where his father began 70 years ago. He is I think now over 80 years of age—is still living, aged 86. Cynthia, daughter of Joseph Marble, and widow of Peter Quimby, died Aug., 1878, aged 74.

One fall, Joseph Marble, Jr., had a log-rolling, to build a new house, the old one giving signs of failing up. In the evening the rosy cheeked lasses from far and near joined with the athletic youths in a dance. It wasn't the "German," nor waltz, nor polka, but a genuine jig. It was a merry company who beat time to the music of a corn-stalk fiddle in farmer Marble's kitchen, the jocund laugh and jest followed the "O be joyful," as it went its unfailing round, which it always did on such occasions. They grew exceedingly merry, and one fellow, feeling chock full and running over with hilarity, declared "When they felt like *that* they ought to *kick it out.*" So they put in "the double shuffle, toe and heel," with such zest that the decayed sleepers gave way. Down went floor, dancers, corn-stalk fiddle, and all, into the cellar. Whether the hilarious fellow "kicked it out" to his satisfaction, we are not informed, but if his fiddle was injured in its journey it could be easily replaced.

In 1830, a little daughter of William Marston, 4 years old, strayed from home, and wandered on and on in the obscure bridle path. She came out at one Carpenter's, in Huntington, having crossed the mountain, and spent a day and a night in the woods; and beasts of prey, at that time were numerous upon the mountains.

Jonathan Nelson had a son and daughter lost in the woods about 1842. The boy was 12 years of age, the girl younger. After a toilsome search, they were found on the second day, unharmed, near Camel's Hump.

In 1847, the alarm was given that a little son of Ira Wheeler, 4 years old, had not returned from school. The neighbors turned out, and searching all day returned at night without any trace of the lost one. The mother was almost distracted. The search was continued the second day with no better results. I remember hearing my brother say, as he took a quantity of provisions with him on the third day, that they were "resolved not to return home again until the boy was found either dead or alive," though many thought that he must have perished already, either from hunger and fatigue, or from the bears infesting the woods. He was soon found in the town of Duxbury, several miles from home, having been nearly 3 days and nights in the woods. He had carried his dinner-pail when he started from school at night, and providentially some of the scholars had given him some dinner that day, so that his own remained untouched.

This being the second time the men had been called out to hunt for lost children in 5 years, some of them were getting rather tired of the thing, whereupon Ziba Boyce drew up a set of resolutions and read them on the occasion, after the child was found, and all were feeling as jolly as such weary mortals could. I have not a copy of them all, but it was resolved " that mothers be instructed to take care of their children, and not let them wander off into woods to be food for the bears, or for the neighbors to hunt up."

There have been no more lost children to search for in Fayston since that, so we may suppose it to have been effective.

Fayston, along with other towns, has suffered from freshets at various times. In the year 1830, occurred what was known as the "great freshet." Buildings were swept away, one person was drowned, and others barely escaped. The famous "Green Mountain slide," which began within a few feet of the summit, where the town is divided from Buel's Gore, in sight of the homestead where I was born, occurred in the summer of 1827. It had rained quite hard some days, and the soil, becoming loosened, gave way, carrying with it trees, rocks, and the debris of ages, on its downward course. Gathering impetus as it advanced, for the mountain is very steep here, it went thundering down the mountain side a distance of a mile or more, with a crash and rumble that shook the earth for miles around, like an earthquake. One branch of Mill brook comes down from here, and, being dammed up by the debris of this grand avalanche, its waters accumulated till it became a miniature lake, then overleaping its barriers it rushed down to its work of destruction below. In July, 1858, a destructive freshet visited Fayston, and the towns adjacent. It had been exceedingly dry, and water was very low. At 7 o'clock in the afternoon, on Saturday, July, 3, the workmen in the mill of Campbell & Grandy were desiring rain,

that they might run the mill. They got what they desired, only got too much; for instead of running the mill they ran for their lives, and let the mill run itself, as it did very rapidly down stream, in less than 2 hours after the rain commenced. The old saying "it never rains but it pours" was verified; it came in sheets. I remember watching the brooks surging through our door-yard; we felt no alarm, thinking a thunder shower not likely to do much damage. We retired to rest, and slept undisturbed, not being in the vicinity of the large streams. We learned in the morning every bridge between Fayston and Middlesex, but one, was swept away. Campbell & Grandy's mill went off before 10 o'clock, and the house pertaining to the mill was so much undermined by the water, the inmates left, taking what valuables they could with them. Mr. Green's family also deserted their house. The water was several feet deep in the road, but, the storm soon subsiding, the houses did not go off.

A clapboard mill owned by Brigham brother, on Shepherd's brook, was ruined. Not a mill in town escaped a good deal of injury. Many people left their houses, expecting them to be carried down the seething flood, and but one bridge of any account was left in town, and the roads were completely demoralized!

This storm seemed a local one, not doing much damage except in the towns in the Mad river basin and on tributary streams. I have heard it speculated that two rain clouds met on the mountain ridges. Be that as it may, I think two hours' rain seldom did such damage in any locality.

In the freshet of 1869, Fayston suffered less than many other towns, but several bridges were carried off, the roads cut up badly, mill dams swept away, etc.

The mill rebuilt on the site of the one swept away in 1858, this time owned by Richardson & Rich, was again carried off, but as considerable of the machinery was afterward found, Mr. Richardson determined to rebuild, putting it a few rods lower down the stream. He has built a fine, large mill there, and feels secure this mill shall stand.

Fayston is a very healthy town. There are several living in town over 80 years of age.

[This was written in 1867.]

ELISHA BRIGHAM

was born in old Marlboro, Mass., 1792. In the common school he obtained all the education he ever had beyond the poor chance of gleaning a little, here and there, from a limited supply of books, amid a multitude of cares at home; but at the age of 12, he had mastered most of Pike's Arithmetic; performing more examples by the feeble light of an old-fashioned chimney fire-place, than at school. So engaged was he that he often went to bed on a difficult problem, to dream it out on his pillow. From Old Marlboro, the family removed to Winchester, N. H., and there hearing of the emigration to the Winooski, and Mad River Valleys, they cast lots with the pioneers to this then wilderness country, and removed on to the tract of land owned in the present homestead. Elisha, now 16, began to take the lead in business, his father being very infirm. About half a dozen families were settled in the south part of the town, having made little openings in the forest, with no well worked road into the town. He and two other members of the family, came the first year to roll up the log-house. The next year all came on, and a family of 8 persons, several children younger than himself, seemed to be dependent on him, even so young, as a foster-father and a guardian. He commenced levelling the old forest trees, and bringing into tillage, meadow and pasturage. Early and late he toiled, and year by year the meadow widened, and the line of woods receded.

In the earliest business transactions of the town, we find the name of Elisha Brigham. There was hardly a year from that time till his death, but what he held some town office. But what most distinguished him was his exact honesty. No man could ever say that he defrauded him of the least in this world's goods. He would rather suffer wrong than to do wrong. He never could oppress the weak, as, instinctively, his whole nature prompted him to espouse their cause. And his religious example was the crowning glory of the man. He was the real pioneer of Methodism in the town; for many years leader in all their social meetings, and around him grew up a thriving class. In this earlier history of the community it might well have been christened the home of the good. Class-leader and chorister, he guided them encouragingly on, and yet his manner was never exciting, hardly, even, could it be said to be fervid or warm; but solid goodness, tenderness, and genuine interest in all that pertained to the soul's welfare, were manifest. The wavering came to him, for he never faltered; the weak, because he was a pillar of strength. He was a man of no doubts in his religious belief, and a man living not by emotion, but principle, and his home was one of hospitality; particularly was the preacher his guest.

In 1816, collector, often juror and selectman, many years lister, nearly always highway-surveyor, district clerk or committee man. In all his more active life, however, he was nearly alone in his politics, he being a thorough whig, while the town was intensely democratic. For which reason probably he was never sent to the Legislature of the State, as this seems to be the only office of importance which he at some time has not held.

At the age of 24, he married Sophronia Ryder. They had 12 children, but one of whom died in infancy; the rest were all living in 1863. One daughter died in July, 1866; the rest are all living, 1881. And in the fullness of affection and tenderness all will say he was a good father. Daily he gathered them around his family altar, while they lived with him, and sought for them the reconciliation of God. He walked before them soberly, patiently, peaceably. His soul seemed like an unruffled river, gliding ever tranquil and even in its banks almost alike in sunshine and in storm. He had no enemies; but was Grandfather, and "Uncle Elisha," to all the neighborhood. Even the old and young far out of his own immediate neighborhood, called him by the sobriquet of Uncle Elisha, and seemed to mourn for him as for a good old uncle. His family physician remarked of him after his decease, that he was "the one man of whom he could say, he did not know that he had an enemy in the world. He was a peacemaker."

ONLY A LITTLE WHILE.
BY MRS. LAURA BRIGHAM BOYCE.

Only a little while
Lingers the springtime with its sun and dew
And song of birds, and gently falling rain,
And springing flowers, on hillside and on plain,
Clothing the earth in garments fresh and new.

Only a little while
The summer tarries with its sultry heat;
Showering its smiles upon the fruitful land,
Ripening the harvest for the reaper's hand,
Ere autumn shall the fruitful work complete.

Only a little while
The autumn paints with gorgeousness the leaves,
Ere wintry winds shall pluck them from the bough
To drape the earth's dark, corrugated brow,—
Then hasten, loiterer, gather in thy sheaves.

Only a little while
The winter winds shall moan and wildly rave,
While the fierce storm-king walks abroad in might,
Clothing the earth in garments pure and white,
Ere the grim monarch, too, shall find a grave.

Only a little while,
Life's spring-time lingers, and our youthful feet
Through flowery paths of innocence are led,
And joyous visions fill our careless head ;
Too bright, alas ! as beautiful as fleet.

Only a little while
Life's summer waits with storm and genial sun,
With days of toil and nights of calm repose;
We find without its thorn we pluck no rose,
And spring-time visions vanish one by one.

Only a little while
Ere autumn comes and life is on the wane !
Happy for us if well our work be done,
For if we loitered in the summer's sun,
How shall we labor in the autumn rain?

Only a little while,
And winter comes apace; the hoary head,
And palsied limbs, tell of the labors past,
And victories won—ah ! soon shall be the last,—
And they shall whisper softly " he is dead."

W. W. PORTER

was born in Fayston, July 24, 1826. He was the 4th son of Elliot Porter and Sidney Ward, the former a native of Hartford, the latter a native of Poultney, Vt., and a daughter of Judge William Ward, judge in Rutland Co. 22 years.

Wilfred spent his time until he was 17 on the farm, and attending school winters ; at which time he commenced studying falls and springs, and teaching winters, attending the academies at Montpelier and Bakersfield, and working on the farm during the summer months until he was 22 years of age.

As early as fifteen he had set his mind upon the medical profession for life, and bent all his energies in that direction. Having studied medicine some time previously, he, at 22, entered the office of Dr. G. N. Brigham, and began the study of medicine, which he continued summers, teaching school falls and winters for 1½ year, when he entered the medical college at Woodstock, where he remained one term, and afterwards at Castleton, Vt., for two terms, graduating from that college in the fall of '51, when he came to Syracuse, and entered the office of Dr. Hiram Hoyt for a short time ; May, 1852, entered the school at Geddes as principal teacher for one year, and May 16, 1853, opened an office in that place to practice his profession, which he has continued until the present. At the close of his first year, the resident doctor of Geddes died, leaving him in full possession of the field. Dr. Porter rose rapidly, and by integrity of purpose and dealing, grew into a very large and lucrative practice, which he carried on for 15 years, as it were, alone, after which he had partners in the practice of medicine.

His practice gradually extended to the city of Syracuse, when, in 1875, the demand upon him for medical treatment from that city became so great that he opened an office there, which he alternately attends upon, with his home office in Geddes. He has been for 25 years a member of the Onondaga County Medical Society, and for one term its president, and a permanent member of the New York State Medical Society; also a member of the American Medical Association, and upon organization of the College of Medicine of Syracuse University, in 1872, he was appointed clinical professor of obstetrics and gynæcology the first year, and at the end of the year, professor in full, which position he still retains.

His skill in the treatment of diseases has

won for him a position in the esteem of the people to be envied by young practitioners, and his indomitable perseverance and endurance of body have enabled him to gratify, in a great measure, the laudable ambition of his earlier years—to be among the first in his profession. He was one of the first movers in the organization and establishment of a university at Syracuse, and since its beginning has been a trustee and closely identified with all its interests, and has been largely identified with the public schools of his town since his first residence there, being supt. of the schools of the town for some 2 years, and trustee of the village school for some 25 years; also being president of the board of education.

He and his wife are warmly attached to the Methodist Episcopal church, and are not only liberal supporters of the same, but of any enterprise they regard as looking to the building up of good society.

In the year 1853, Nov. 13, he married Miss Jane, daughter of Simeon Draper and Clarissa Stone, of Geddes; children, Clara A., George D. (deceased), Wilfred W. Jr., Jane and Louie.

LONGEVITY RECORD IN 1881.

Ruth Chase died in 1865, aged 84; Timothy Chase in 1875, 93; Benj. Corliss, in 1865, nearly 91; Henry Morgan, 1868, 84. The wife of Henry Morgan (in Northfield), over 80 years. Her home was in Fayston. James Baird died in 1870, aged 81; Geo. Somerville, 1870, 80; Margarett Strong, 1870, 98; Elizabeth Lamson, in 1872. Her friends differed as to her age; some claimed she was 104; others that she was but 102. Her husband, Jonathan Lamson, died some 20 years since, aged between 80 and 90; Jane McAughin died in 1872, aged 82; Capt. Elliot Porter, 1874, nearly 90; Sidney Porter, his wife, 1875, 86; Joseph and Susan Marble, over 80; Zeviah Boyce, 1856, aged about 90; Mehitable Tyler, 1855, between 80 and 90. Elizabeth Barrett died in Waitsfield in 1873, aged 93. She was for many years a resident of Fayston, but moved to W. a short time before her death.

TOWN OFFICERS 1871–1881.

Town Clerks, Willard B. Porter, 1871 to '80; D. S. Stoddard, 1880; S. J. Dana, 1881. *Representatives,* 1871, none; S. J. Dana, 1872; M. S. Strong, 1874; D. S. Stoddard, 1876; Seth Boyce, 1878; Nathan Boyce, 1880. *Treasurers,* D. S. Stoddard, 1871, '72; A. D. Bragg, 1875, '79; Seth Boyce, 1880, '81. *First Selectmen,* C. D. Billings, 1871; Dan Boyce, 1872; C. S. Dana, 1874; Seth Boyce, 1875; J. Patterson, 1876; M. S. Strong, 1879; John Maxwell, 1878, '79; J. P. Boyce, 1880, '81. *Constables,* Cornelius McMullen, 1871, 72; H. G. Campbell, 1873, '74: C. M. Fisher, 1875, '76, '79; S. J. Dana, 1877, '78; Allen S. Howe, 1880; M. S. Strong, 1881. *Grand Jury,* G. O. Boyce, 1871, '72, '73, '75; W. B. Porter, 1874, '76; C. S. Dana, 1877, '78; Seth Boyce, 1879, '80; R. Maxwell and Wm. Chipman, 1881. *School Supt.,* Grey H. Porter, 1871, '72, '73; Rev. J. F. Buzzel, 1874 to 1881. *Trustees of the Town,* Seth Boyce, 1873, '79; Geo. Boyce, 1877, '78, '80, '81. *Justices of the Peace,* Willard B. Porter, 1872, '74, '76, '78; G. O. Boyce, 1872, '74; D. S. Stoddard, 1872, '76, '78, '80; Z. W. Boyce, 1872, '74; H. H. Morgan, 1872; C. D. Billings, 1874; E. Ainsworth, 1874; S. J. Dana, 1876, '78, '80; O. S. Bruce, J. Z. Marble, 1878; Nathan Boyce, Stephen Johnson, Dan Boyce, 1880.

GERSHOM NELSON BRIGHAM, M. D.,

for 20 years a practicing physician at Montpelier, was born in Fayston, Mar. 3, 1820, was son of Elisha Brigham, who made his pitch in F. with the first settlers. His mother, Sophronia Ryder, whose mother was Lucy Chase, a relative of the Hon. Dudley Chase [See Randolph History, vol. II], was a woman of vigorous constitution and an active, original mind. Several ancestors in the Brigham line have been physicians, one of whom was Gershom Brigham, of Marlboro, Mass., the old ancestral town of the Brighams of this country, the stock tracing back to the parish of Brigham in Northumberland Co., England. Dr. G. N. Brigham received his education in our common schools, with a year in Wash. Co. Gram. Sch. and a half year at Poultney Academy, and studied medicine with Dr. David C. Joslyn, of Waitsfield, Dr. S. W. Thayer, now of Burlington, Prof. Benj. R. Palmer, now of Woodstock, graduating at Woodstock Medical College in 1845, attending three courses of lectures. He has practiced 3 years at Warren, then 3 years at Waitsfield; removed to Montpelier, 1849; attended lectures at the college of Physicians and Surgeons, N. Y., spending much time in the hospitals of the city, about which time he became a convert to homœopathy, and was the second person in middle Vermont to espouse the cause at this time so unpopular, and one of six who founded the State Homœopathic Society. He has educated quite a number of students in his office, among whom, his own son, Dr. Homer C. Brigham, of Montpelier, and Prof. Wilfred W. Porter, of the Medical Department in the Syracuse University. While at Montpelier he served a while as postmaster; was town superintendent of common schools; lectured on education, temperance and sundry scientific subjects, and has been a contributor to medical journals, and known to the secular press in essays and poetical contributions for over 25 years. He delivered the class poem before the Norwich University in 1870; published in that year a 12 mo. vol., pp. 180, "The Harvest Moon and other Poems" at the *Riverside Press*, which with additions came out in a second edition.

The Doctor has since issued a "Work on Catarrhal Diseases," 126 pp., and reports a work on "Pulmonary Consumption," nearly ready for press; that he has written this year, 1881, a play in tragedy, "Benedict Arnold," that he expects to publish. He is regular contributor to three medical journals, and has written for as many as thirty of the leading newspapers, East and West. He married, 1st, Laura Elvira Tyler, dau. of Merrill Tyler, Esq., of Fayston; children, Homer C., Willard Irving, Julia Lena, Ida Lenore. His first wife died Mar. 12, 1873. He married, 2d, Miss Agnes Ruth Walker, dau. of Ephraim Walker, Esq., of Springfield. They have one child. Dr. Brigham has resided since 1878, at Grand Rapids, Mich. His son, Dr. Homer C., is in practice at Montpelier. In his poetical writings—not a few— the Doctor has always inclined to the patriotic.

Aug. 16th, 100th anniversary of Bennington battle. At the meeting of the Vermonter's Society in Michigan, at Grand Rapids, Hon. W. A. Howard delivered the oration, and Dr. G. N. Brigham, the poem. We give an extract. In our crowded pages we have scarce room for poetic extracts, even, and this appears to be the musical town of the County. Such a flock of native poets, all expecting by right of manor, to sing in the history of their birth town, with the one who has written the most in this prolific field, we must begin to be brief. Haply, he has published too widely to be in need of our illustration:

FROM "THE BATTLE OF BENNINGTON."

When Freedom's cause in doubtful scale
Hung trembling o'er Columbia's land,
And men with sinking hearts turned pale
That 'gainst the foe there stood no braud,
    Vermont, thy banner rose.
Green waved thy lofty mountain pine,
Which thou didst make thy battle sign,
Then from the mountain fastness thou
Didst sally with a knitted brow,
    And tyrants felt thy blows.

The bugle blew no frightful blast
Where th' sulphrous smoke its mantle cast,
For oft thy sons in forest field
The heavy broadsword learned to wield
    In their old border frays.
Bred to reclaim the native soil
With sinewed limb and patient toil,
The forest path to stoutly fend,
Where foes did lurk, or wild beasts wend,
    No danger did amaze.

Free as the mountain air they breathe,
The vassal's place they dare disown;
The blade from scabbard to unsheath
And see the slaughters harvest sown,
    Ere wrong shall rule the day.
So when the midnight cry, "To arms!"
Did reach them at their northern farms,
They snatched the musket and the powder-horn,
And shook their brand with patriots' scorn,
    And gathered to the fray.

Vermont, thy soul's young life was there,
There from thy rocks up leapt the fire
That made thy hills the altar-stair
To holy freedom's star-crowned spire,
    While all the world did doubt.
In native hearts and native blades
The freeman's hope forever lives;
The soul that first in sorrow wades,
The most to human nature gives
    In sorest times of drought.

The hosts of Albion sleep secure,
The mountain path to them is sure,
And in their dreams they wait the day
To feast and drive the mob away,
　　And forage on the town,
That dream to England sealed her doom;
They roused to hear the cannon boom,
And see the mountaineers they scorned
In serried line of battle formed,
　　And on them coming down.

And who here making pilgrimage,
When told how, with their muskets clubbed,
Our sires from breastworks drove the foe,
How here were English veterans drubbed
　　By plowmen gloved in steel,
Shall say, the race keeps not to-day
The Spartan fire—
　·　·　·　·　·　·　·　·　·

Shall say, if with this trenchant warp
There runs not through a thread of gold;
Or if the Attic salt still flows
Through pulsing veins of later mold,
　　And pledges colored wine.
　·　·　·　·　·　·　·　·　·

From hence the field of Bennington
With Concord and with Lexington,
Upon the patriot's scroll shall blaze,
And virtue's hearts proclaim her praise,
　Till chivalry's page shall end—
Shall tell how Mars did glut his rage,
How screamed the eagle round her nest,
When death or freedom was the gage,
While war unloosed her battle vest,
　　And carnage rode a fiend.
　·　·　·　·　·　·　·　·　·

And where the nations strive and hope,
And in the breaking darkness grope,
Here may expiring faith still burn,
And see the patriot's emblem turn
　　Above this crimson sea.

From another poem on the same subject:

How grand thy towering cliffs, where twines
　The hemlock's green to wreath thy crown;
How bright thy peaks when day declines,
　As there thy glory settles down.

When stirred the border feud, how rang
　The note of war;
　·　·　·　·　·　·　·　·　·

And where the wolf ran down her prey
By grange girt in with woodland dun,
The ranger hurried to the fray,
There flashed the border-guardsman's gun.

And when a mightier cause called for
Thy sons to draw the sword　·　·
　·　·　·　·　·　·　·　·　·
The bugle gave the hills its blast.

And men in buckskin breeches came,
　Their waists slung with the powder-horn,
Their hearts with freedom's spark aflame,
　And battled till the STATE was born.

·　·　·　·　·　thy border cry
Rang to the Northern cliffs for help,
When Allen mustered for old Ti.,
And drove from there the lion's whelp.

From there to Hoosiek's bloody flume
Marched forth our sires with hearts aflame,
And snatched the British lion's plume,
And wrote for us a storied name.

From a remembrance to Vermont:

O, bring the spring that plumes the glen,
　And hearty be the greeting;
We'll think in kindness of the men
　Whose hearts to ours gave beating;
Nor shall their armor rust
Taken by us in trust.

　·　·　·　·　·　·　·　·　·

Bathed in the noon of peace, green, green
　Forever, be those hills;
Green where the hoar-frost builds her screen,
　And winter's goblet fills,
The frost and cedar green!

Queen Virgin of the Ancient North,
　Throned spirit of the crags,
Who called the sturdy Aliens forth
　To weave thy battle-flags.
We take the sprig of pine,
Proud of our lineal line.
Vermont! Vermont! Our childhood's home,
　Still home where'er we roam.

MISS SUSAN GRIGGS.

BY ANNA B. BRAGG.

Many efficient teachers of our district
schools have been reared and educated in
this town, though the greater part have
followed teaching but a few terms before
commencing "life work," but Miss Griggs
has made teaching the business of her life,
and in years of service, number of pupils,
and different branches thoroughly learned
and imparted to others, has no equal here,
and perhaps but few in our whole country.
She was born in this town, Feb. 1814.
From her earliest schooldays, her book
was her favorite companion, often upon
her wheel-bench, that sentence after sentence of some coveted lesson might be
committed to memory, while her hands
spun thread after thread of wool or flax,
working willingly for herself and her
brothers and sisters, as was the custom in
those days.

When 12 years of age, her father, an
earnest Christian man, died, leaving his
wife and little ones to struggle along the
path of life alone in God's care. But as in
his life he had often said, "Susan is our
student," so in all her young days after
she seemed to hear his voice encouraging
her to give her time, talents and life to the
work of Christian education. She began
teaching in the Sabbath-school at 13, and
at 16 in a district-school, where for many
years her time was spent, and in attending
school, as she completed the course of

study at Newbury Seminary. In 1850, she was one of the teachers sent out to the South and West by Gov. Slade. She taught one year at Wilmington, N. C., and then went to Wolcottville, Ind., under the direction of Gov. Slade, a small village in a new town, first teaching in the family of George Wolcott, with the addition of a few neighbors' children; then in a small school-house. The school so increased, Mr. Wolcott, the founder of the village, built a convenient seminary at his own expense, furnished with musical instruments, library, apparatus, etc. Here she taught for 17 years, principal of the school, having sometimes one or two assistant teachers, and often a hundred pupils. Beside the common and higher English branches, there were often classes in German, Latin, French and painting, and always in music, vocal and instrumental, and always a literary society, and always a Sabbath-school, in which she taught a class, and was sometimes superintendent. She says "these years were full of toil, but bright with hope that minds were there awakened to the beauties of the inviting realms of purity and truth."

After a short rest with a brother in Missouri and another in Wisconsin, she resumed teaching in Fort Wayne College, Ind.; afterward in Iowa about 2 years, and is now in Kendallville, Ind., one of a corps of 12 teachers; 60 pupils under her charge. "Many will rise up and call her blessed."

Mrs. Celia (Baxter) Brigham, of Evart, Michigan, contributes the following for the Baxter family:

EBER H. BAXTER AND FAMILY

came to Fayston in April, 1831, and lived there 20 years. They had 14 children; one died in infancy. They removed to Michigan with 10 children—two remained in Fayston—in 1851. Albert Baxter, eldest son, had then lived in Mich. about 6 years. He has been for the last 20 years connected with the *Grand Rapids Eagle*; is now editor of *Grand Rapids Daily Eagle*. Albert, Celia—Mrs. C. B. Brigham; Rosina—Mrs. R. B. Cadwell, now in California; Edwin, lawyer in Grand Haven, Mich.; Uri J., lawyer in Washington, D. C.; Sabrina—

Mrs. S. B. Cooper, Evart, Mich.; and Vienna I.—Mrs. V. I. B. Corman, Lowell, Mich., of the Baxter family, are more or less known as occasional authors in prose and poetry. Twelve children, the father now in his 80th year (1879) still survive. Ira C., sixth son, left his body on the field of Chickamauga, Sept. 20, 1863. E. H. Baxter was town clerk and justice of peace in Fayston for several years.

MRS. CELIA B. BRIGHAM

has written many years for press, and for many newspapers and journals short poems. She has sent us for her representation in the dear old birthtown, a rather pretty collection, for which we can make room only for the following:

TO MY SLEEPING BABE.

Gently, little cherub, gently
  Droop those weary eyelids now;
Slumber's hand is pressing lightly,
  Softly on thy cloudless brow.

Meekly, little sleeper, meekly
  Folded on thy guileless breast
Dimpled hands of pearly whiteness—
  Lovely is thy "rosy rest."

Calmly, little dreamer, calmly
  Beats that tiny heart of thine—
As the pulses of the leaflet,
  Rocked to rest at eventime.

Softly, little darling, softly
  Dies away thy mother's song;
And the angels come to guard thee,
  Through the night hours, lone and long.

Sweetly, blessed infant, sweetly
  Fall their whispers on thine ear;
Smiles are on thy lips of coral—
  Snowy pinions hover near.

TO AN UNSEEN MINSTREL.

The lark may sing to the chickadee,
From his lofty azure throne,
Nor feel the thrill in the maple tree,
Where his listener sits alone;
Even thus, thy spirit sings to me—
Hearest thou the answering tone?
From their sunward flight, can thy tireless wings
Ever fold where the forest warbler sings?

Thou callest the voices of long ago
From level-trodden graves,
As the wind may call an echoing note
From out the dark sea caves—
As the burning stars of heaven may call
To the restless, heaving waves—
That, ever-changing beneath their gaze,
Can answer only in broken rays!

THE NEGLECTED BIBLE.

Precious, but neglected Bible!
Let me ope thy lids once more,
And, with reverential feelings,
Turn the sacred pages o'er.

Source of joy and consolation,
　　Vainly does thy fount supply
Me with life's pure crystal waters—
　　Lo! I languisit, faint and die!

Not because is sealed the fountain
　　That could soothe the keenest woe;
Not because the stream unfailing
　　Hath one moment ceased to flow;
But because my thirsty spirit,
　　Seeking bitter draught, passed by,
Heedlessly, the living waters—
　　Lo! I languish, faint and die!

Descriptive of how many a Vermonter
felt in 1851, is a little "sonnet" below, by
ELISHA ALDIS BRIGHAM, sent me by Mrs.
Brigham, that her husband may, as well as
herself, have a little niche in the history of
their native town:

SONNET.

O, tell me not of Liberty's bright land!
　Where man by brother man is bought and sold:
　To toil in sweat and tears, for others gold,
　Obedient to a tyrant's stern command;
　Where children part upon the auction stand
　To meet no more, and weeping parents torn
　Asunder—slave-bound captives long to mourn,
　Are scattered far and wide, a broken band.
　Where Justice on proud Freedom's altar sleeps,
　Where mercy's voice is never heard to sigh;
　Where pity's hand ne'er wipes the tearful eye
　Of Afric's exiles, who in misery weep—
　The millions three who wear oppression's brand;
　Oh! call it not sweet Freedom's happy land!
Fayston, Feb. 1851.

A whole budget from natives in the
West: We will not give any one's long
piece entire; but not having the heart to
leave any son or daughter who knocks at
the old Green Mountain door, out entirely,
even if they are unfortunately a "poet,"
we shall give some one short extract, or
sonnet for all who have sent home their
pieces for Fayston, and let the dry old,
only statisticians, growl as they may. Here
comes the Fayston men and women of the
pen for a page or two: First, a long poem,
almost a news-column, fine print, "written
in my chamber at Washington, on the anniversary eve of the assassination of President Lincoln." We will have six or seven
verses from

THE ANNIVERSARY OF THE ASSASSINATION.

BY U. J. BAXTER.

Why sound the bells
So mournfully upon the air of night?
Why volley forth the guns upon the night,
　With sudden peal that tells
Of darkling horror and of dire affright?

The morn shall ope
With a dread tale that tells of dark eclipse—
Of a dark deed that throws its black eclipse
　On all a nation's hope,
And smites the joy that filled a nation's lips?

Stricken and low!
Aye, let us weep—weep for the guilt and crime—
The ingrate sense—the coward guilt and crime!
　Dissolve in tears and woe
The darkling horror of this monstrous time!

His name breathe not,
His thrice-accursed name, whose brutal hand—
Whose foul, polluted heart and brutal hand
　A demon's purpose wrought,
And whelmed in grief our glad, rejoicing land.

. . . .

A nation's heart bowed with him in the dust
　　We turn our hope in vain
To seek a chieftain worthy of his trust.

No marvel here!
Two kingliest come not haply born and twinned—
Each age its one great soul, nor matched, nor twinned,
　　Owning no mortal peer—
So is his glory in our age unkinned.

His mantle fell--
On whom is not yet shown—yet sure its folds
Are buried not—its rich and loving folds
　　Shall lay some blessed spell
On him who most his noble spirit holds.

Great chieftain! rest!
Our hearts shall go as pilgrims to thy tomb;
Our spirits mourn and bless thy martyr tomb;
　　We deem thy lot is blest;
Our love shall rob our sorrow of its gloom.

All coming time
Shall ne'er despoil thy glory of its crown—
Each year shall set its jewels in thy crown--
　　Each day bell's passing chime
Shall add a tongue to speak thy just renown.

LITTLE BEN.

BY SARAH BRIGHAM MANSFIELD.

In a lonely spot in a dismal street
Little Ben sat chafing his bare, cold feet,
And so hungry, too, for nothing to eat,
　　All the long day had poor Ben.
His mother, alas, had long been dead—
So long, he could just remember, her and
The sweet pale face as she knelt by his bed
　　And prayed God to bless little Ben.

The twilight deepened, how dark it grew,
And how heavily fell the chill night dew,
And the moaning winds pierced through and through
　　The form of poor little Ben.
"Oh! why am I left here alone," he cried,
"Dear mamma told me before she died
She was going to Heaven; Oh, mamma," he sighed,
　　"Why don't you come for poor Ben?"

"Can you be happy, tho' in Heaven a saint,
While I am so cold, so weary, so faint?
Dear mother, dost hear your poor darling's plaint?
　　Oh, come for your own little Ben!"
The morning came with its rosy light,
And kissed the wan cheeks and lids so white.
They were closed for aye! in the lone night
　　An angel had come for poor Ben.

THE FIRST FLOWER OF SPRING.

BY ZIBA W. BOYCE, (deceased.)

The first April violet beside the bare tree,
Looking gayly up seemed to be saying to me,
" I come with yon robin, sweet spring to recall,
There caroling above me the glad news to all—
How pleased all your feelings--your eye and your ear;
With gay exultation you welcome us here;
But in the soon future, surrounded by flowers,
And Summer bird's plumage, far gayer than ours,
Forgotten the perils we willingly bore—
First messengers telling of winter no more."
I thought of the bird, and the flower, and then
Confessed it is thus with all pioneer men.
Let them labor and suffer new truths to disclose,
Their wants or their woes there's nobody knows.
The world owns the work when the labor is done—
They, the bird and the flower, forgotten and gone.

THE RAIN.

BY MRS. D. T. SMITH.

When from winter's icy spell
Burst the brooklets in the dell,
    With a song;
When the early robins call
From the sunny garden wall,
    All day long;
When the crocus shows its face,
And the fern its dainty grace,
    And the daffodil;
And the dandelion bright
Decks the field with golden light
    On the hill;
When the Spring has waked a world again,
And the apple-blossoms whiten,
And the grasses gleam and brighten,
Then we listen to the rythmic patter of the rain.

When the lilies, snowy white,
Gleam upon the lakelet bright,
    'Mid their leaves;
And the twittering swallows fly,
Building nests for by and by,
    'Neath the eaves;
Roses blush i' the dewy morn,
Bees their honey-quest have gone
    All the day;
And the daisies, starry, bright,
Glisten in the firefly's light
    As they may;
When Summer decks the mountain and the plain,
When she binds her golden sheaves,
Then she tilts her glossy leaves
In the splashing and the dashing of the rain.

When the maple forests redden,
And the sweet ferns brown and deaden
    On the lea,
Straightly furrowed lie the acres,
And we hear the roar of breakers
    Out at sea;
When the birds their columns muster,
And the golden pipins cluster
    On the bough,
And the autumn breeze is sighing,
Springtime past and Summer dying,
    Here and now;
And autumn winds are filled with sounds of pain
When the katydids are calling;
Then the crimson leaves are falling
Through the weeping and the moaning of th' rain.
Dubuque, Iowa.

THE MOSS-COVERED TROUGH.

BY S. MINERVA BOYCE.

That moss-covered trough, decaying there yonder,
    I remember it well when but a child;
Though years have flown by, I still love to wander
    Along the old road by the woodland wild.

Ah! yes, I remember when full and o'erflowing,
    With the clear, sparkling nectar, so cool;
The old farmer came with his bucket from mowing,
    And we drank from his cup, then trudged on to
        school.

And then 'neath the low-spreading maple close by it,
    Were gathered the wildlings of May;
There blossomed the hat of a lad who drew nigh it,
    And blue-bird and robin sang sweeter that day.

Though now thrown aside, to give room for another,
    All neglected, and moss-grown, and old,
I still find a charm to be found in none other,
    Were it carved e'er so lovely, or plated with gold.

Long ago the old farmer finished his mowing,
    Filled his last bucket, " reaped his last grain;"
Then went just beyond where seed-time and sowing
    Will never recall him to labor again.

And here we give, if we may nip at
will, the buds, for which we only have
room, a pretty extract from SABRINA BAX-
TER, born in Fayston:

BUDS AND BLOSSOMS.

We walked within my garden
    On a dewy, balmy morn—
. . . .
We paused beside a rose-bush,
    The swelling buds to note—
To drink the gushing fragrance
    Which round us seemed to float;
. . . .
One bud we'd viewed but yesternight,
    When very fair it grew—
We'd waited for the morrow's light
    To see it washed in dew,
A worm had found the curling leaf,
. . . .
Had marred the bursting budlet,
    Had withered stem and flower.

Alas! for earthly happiness,
    In bitterness I cried,
Naught beautiful, naught lovely,
    May on this earth abide!
A blight is on the floweret,
    A blight is on the grove,
A doubly blighting power upon
    Those objects that we love!

" Mortal! " the voice seemed near,
    And musical the tone,
Are there no buds, whose brightness
Outshines the garden rose?
What worm has nipped the blossom?
    Who answereth for those?

" Within the human garden
    How many a floweret lies,
Despoiled by reckless gardener—
. . . .
And in the whispered lays we heard,
    And from the flowers there smiled,
A plea for human rose-buds—

25

Taking a skipping extract from EMOGENE
M. BOYCE:

I paused once more, gave a few lingering looks
At the dear olden place, the remembered nooks:
The orchard, the garden, the dark, silent mill,
The little red cot at the foot of the hill,
Where the little trout brook, still murmured along;
The old lofty pines sang the same mournful song,
When with father and mother, we children four,
Had gathered at eve 'round the old cottage door.

SOLDIERS OF FAYSTON.

BY DORRIC S. STODDARD.

The notes of war that rang through the
land in the winter and spring of 61 were
not without their effect upon the town of
Fayston. Her hardy sons willingly re-
sponded to their country's call. The following is the record of services rendered
and lives given, who served for their own
town in the order of enlistment:

THOMAS MAXWELL, the first resident o
Fayston to respond to the call for volunteers. He enlisted May 7, 1861, at the
age of 20 years, in Co. F. 2d Vt. Reg.; was
discharged, by reason of sickness, Feb 21,
1863; re-enlisted Mar. 20, '64, in Co. F.
17th Vt. Reg.; severely wounded in the
Wilderness May 6, '64. The ball entered
the neck, passed through the roots of the
tongue, and lodged in the base of the
head, where it still remains; discharged
June 17, '65.

MARK AND LUTHER CHASE, brothers,
enlisted Aug. 14, '61, in Co. H. 6th Vt.;
aged 26 and 18 years. Mark was discharged May 29, '62; reenlisted Nov. 27,
'63; taken prisoner, and died at Andersonville, Ga., July 3, '64. Luther died in
hospital Jan. 31, '62.

GEO. SOMERVILLE, age 23, enlisted in
Co. G. 6th Vt., Aug. 29, '61; discharged
June 23, '62.

JOHN H. HUNTER, age 41; enlisted
Sept. 2, '61, Co. H. 6th Vt.; chosen corporal; discharged; reenlisted Dec. 15, '63;
lost an arm in the service; finally discharged Mar. 10, '65.

GEO. L. MARBLE, age 30, enlisted in
Co. G. 6th Vt., Sept. 10, '61; reenlisted
Feb. 8, '64; taken prisoner Oct. 19, '64;
supposed to have died in Libby Prison.

WM. M. STRONG, age 19, enlisted in Co.
G. 6th Vt., Sept. 23, '61; served 3 years;
mustered out Oct 28, '64.

ALLEN E. MEHUREN, enlisted in Co. G.
6th Vt., Sept. 27, '61, age 23; discharged
by reason of sickness, Feb. 4, '63.

CORNELIUS MCMULLEN, age 29, enlisted
in Co. B. 6th Vt., Oct. 3, '61, re-enlisted
Dec. 15, '63, transferred to Co. H. Oct.
16, '64, served till the close of the war,
mustered out June 26, '65.

HENRY C. BACKUS, age 24, enlisted in
Co. G. 6th Reg't., Oct. 7, '61, promoted
sergeant, mustered out Oct. 28, '64.

WARREN C. PORTER, age 37, enlisted
Oct. 15, '61, in Co. G. 6th Vt., served 3
years, mustered out Oct. 28, '64.

CHESTER S. DANA, age 33, enlisted in
Co. B. 10th Vt., July 18, '62, chosen 5th
sergeant, promoted to 1st ser'gt., sick in
general hospital much of the latter part of
his service, discharged May 22, '65.

LAFAYETTE MOORE, enlisted in Co. F.
2d Vt. as a recruit, July 30, '62, age 26,
died in the service Feb. 29, '64.

HEMAN A. MOORE, age 21, enlisted
in Co. F. 2d Vt., Aug. 2, '62, mustered
out June 19, '65.

ELI GIBSON, recruit in Co. G. 6th Vt.,
enlisted Aug. 13, '62, age 22, died in the
service April 7, '64.

LEWIS BETTIS, a resident of Warren,
enlisted for this town in Co. G. 6th Vt.,
Aug. 13, '62, age 37; transferred to the
Invalid Corps, Jan. 15, '64.

JOHN CHASE, age 23, enlisted in Co. G.
6th Vt., Aug. 13, '62; mustered out June
19, '65.

NATHAN THAYER, age 23; enlisted in
Co. H. 6th Vt., Aug. 13, '62; discharged
June 3, '63.

NELSON J. BOYCE, age 32; enlisted in
Co. G. 6th Vt., Aug. 16, '62; transferred
to the Invalid Corps July 1, '63.

LESTER H. HARRIS, age 25; enlisted
Aug. 18, '62, in Co. F. 2d Vt.; died May
18, '63.

The following 17 soldiers all members
of Co. B. 13th Vt., (9 months), enlisted
Aug. 25, '62; mustered in Oct. 10, '62, at
Brattleboro; mustered out at the same
place July 21, '63; the battle of Gettysburg being the only one in which they
participated:

GEORGE O. BOYCE, 2d serg't., age 28;

with others of his company taken prisoner by rebel guerrillas while going from Camp Carusi to Fairfax station with supply teams, May 14, '63. They were paroled the next day, and returned to the regiment.

Dorric S. Stoddard, 3d corporal, age 28; William E. Backus, age 22, detailed scout; John Baird, age 20, died of fever soon after returning home; Matthew Blair, age 27, afterwards re-enlisted in 56 Mass., killed in the Wilderness; Charles D. Billings, age 19, died at Camp Carusi May 19, '63; Chauncey Carpenter, age 39, re-enlisted Dec. 31, '63, in Co. C. 17th Vt., discharged May 13, '65; Samuel J. Dana, age 29, wounded at Gettysburg; Royal S. Haskins, age 21; Charles C. Ingalls, age 18, re-enlisted Sept. 1, '64, in Co. G. 6th Vt., mustered out June 19, '65; Stephen Johnson, age 21, re-enlisted Aug. 26, '64, in Co. G. 6th Vt., mustered out June 19, '65; Ziba H. McAllister, age 21, re-enlisted in Cavalry Co. C. Nov. 30, '63, transferred to Co. A. June 19, '65, mustered out June 26, '65; Levi Nelson, age 20; William Nelson, age 26, Daniel Posnett, age 47, Winfield S. Rich, age 24, Reuben Richardson, age 45, transferred to Co. H., re-enlisted Nov. 30, '63, in Co. H. 6th Regt., discharged May 12, '65.

William G. Wilkins, age 18, enlisted in Co. F. 2d Vt., June 16, '63, discharged Jan. 21, '64.

Robert Hoffman, age 21, enlisted in the 3d Battery, Oct. 19, '64, discharged June 15, '65.

John W. Palmer, enlisted in Cavalry, Co. C. Nov. 28, '63, age 23, transferred to Co. A. June 21, '65, mustered out Aug. 9, '65.

Judson W. Richardson, age 29, enlisted in Co. H. 6th Vt., promoted corporal June 19, '65, and mustered out June 26, '65.

Charles O. Dyke, age 18, enlisted Nov. 30, '63, in Co. H. 6th Vt.; mustered out June 26, '65.

Myron Mansfield, age 18, enlisted Dec. 2, '63, in Co. H. 2d U. S. Sharp-shooters; transferred to Co. H. 4th Vt., Feb. 25, '65; supposed to have died at Andersonville.

Benj. B. Johnson, age 20, enlisted Dec. 3, '63, in Co. G. 6th Vt.; transferred to

Vet. Res. Corps, Dec. 4, '64; mustered out July 15, '65.

Wm. H. Johnson, age 18, enlisted Dec. 3, '63, in Co. G. 6th Vt.; pro. corp. Sept. 23, '64; serg't. June 20, '65; mustered June 26, '65.

Charles B. Corliss, age 18, enlisted Dec. 3, '63, in Co. G. 6th Vt.; discharged June 28, '65.

Anson O. Brigham, age 21, enlisted Dec. 5, '63, in Co. H. 6th Vt.; trans. to invalid corps, and discharged June 28, '65.

Calvin B. Marble, age 18, enlisted Dec. 9, '63, in Co. G. 6th Vt.; mustered out June 26, '65.

Edwin E. Chaffee, age 18, enlisted Dec. 9, '63 in Co. H. 6th Vt.; pro. corp. June 19, '63; must. out June 26, '65.

Asa E. Corliss, age 20, enlisted Sept. 7, '64, in Co. G. 6th Vt.; must. out July 19, '65.

John W. Ingalls, age 28, enlisted Sept. 16, '64, but did not enter service.

This town also furnished 14 non-resident soldiers, of whom I can give but a meagre report, as follows:

Geo. Arnold, Francis E. Buck, Thomas Bradley, 1st army corps; Sidney Dolby, 54 Mass. (colored); Wm. W. Green, Philip Gross, 1st A. C.; Wm. J. Hopkins, cav.; John J. Hern, 1st A. C.; Randall Hibbard, 1st A. C.; Frederic Kleinke, 1st A. C.; Nelson Parry, Co. B. 7th Vt.; Nicholas Schmidt, 1st A. C.; John S. Templeton; James Williamstown, 1st A. C.

The following persons were furnished under draft, five of whom paid commutation: Hiram E. Boyce, Eli Bruce, Jr., Nehemiah Colby, Charles M. Fisher, Julius T. Palmer, and one, Nathan Boyce, procured a substitute.

This town probably furnished from her own residents as many, if not more, soldiers for other towns than were credited to her from non-residents, the record of some of which is given as follows:

Andrew J. Butler, Co. H. 6th Vt.; Hiland G. Campbell, 3d Vt. Battery; Alba B. Durkee, Co. I. 9th Vt.; Timothy Donivan, Co. H. 6th Vt.

In Co. G. 6th Vt.: Edward Dillon, G. W. Fisher, James N. Ingalls, Robert Maxwell and Samuel Maxwell. In 3d Vt.: Wm. W. McAllister. In Co. G. 6th Vt.: James H. Somerville, Ichabod Thomas. Dexter Marble lost a leg in the service, in a Wisconsin regiment.

Thus I have given as best I can from memory, and from data at command, an imperfect record of Fayston and Fayston men during the rebellion. Undoubtedly the foregoing record is not perfect, yet I think it is substantially correct.

Probably no town in the state suffered more financially than this. During the latter part of the war when large bounties were demanded by volunteers, and paid by wealthy towns, Fayston, to save herself from draft was obliged in one year (1864) to raise for bounties and town expenses the almost unheard of sum of $12.50 cents upon every dollar of her grand list, thus subjecting the owner of a simple poll list to the payment of a tax of $25. Yet this enormous sum was paid immediately, with scarce a murmur of complaint, and not a dollar left to be a drag-weight upon tax-payers in after years.

Fayston can look back upon her financial record as a town, and the military record of her soldiers with no feelings but those of honor, satisfaction and pride; knowing that the privations and valor of her sons in the field, and the liberality of her citizens at home all contributed their mite to keep the grand old flag still floating over a free and undivided nation.

GRAND ARMY REPUBLIC'S RESPONSE TO SUMNER'S BILL FOR ERASING OUR BATTLE RECORDS.

BY D. S. STODDARD.

Blot out our battle records, boys,
  Charles Sumner's bill doth say;
Forget that you were soldiers once,
  And turn your thoughts away.

Yes, turn your thoughts away, my boys,
  So noble, brave and true;
Forget you lugged a knapsack once,
  And wore the army blue.

Flaunt not that starry flag, my boys,
  With Lee's Mills, on its fold,
'Twill make some rebel's heart ache, boys,
  To see it there so bold.

And blot out Savage Station, too,
  And likewise Malvern Hill;
That was a noisy place, you know,
  But blot it out, you will.

Fort Henry, too, and Donelson,
  Where Grant "Surrender" spake,
In such decided tones it made
  The rebel Pillow shake.

And Shiloh, too, and Vicksburg, where
  One Fourth of July day,
Brave Pemberton his well-tried sword
  At the feet of Grant did lay.

And Cedar Creek, and Winchester,
  And Sheridan's famous ride:—
Forget it, boys, forget it all,
  It hurts the rebels' pride.

And Fredericksburg, and Antietam,
  Where cannon rang and roared;
And Gettysburg, where three long days
  Grape shot and shell were poured.

Where thousands freely gave their lives,
  And drenched with blood the sand,
To stay the flow of Treason's tide
  In Freedom's happy land.

And Richmond, too, and Petersburg,
  And the Wilderness, forget;
And comrades dear who fought so well,
  Whose sun of life there set.

Forget, my boys, you ever marched
  With Sherman to the sea!
Deny you ever fought against
  The rebels under Lee!

And Appomattox Court House, too,
  Where Lee dissolved his camp;
And gave his long and well-tried sword
  To General U. S. Grant.

Those names, we've loved them long, my boys,
  And oft a glow of pride
Has thrilled through every vein, to think
  We fought there side by side.

And oftentimes, my comrades dear,
  There comes a sadder thought—
The price, the price! by which our land
  These cherished records bought.

And now shall we erase those names,
  And make our battle-flags,
Which e'er have been the soldier's pride,
  Nothing but worthless rags?

No more shall read those glorious names
  While swinging in the breeze?   •
No more our hearts shall swell with pride
  To think of bygone deeds?

And must we suffer all this shame
  To please that rebel horde,
Who brought the war upon themselves
  By drawing first the sword?

Then we must ask their pardon, too,
  For what we've done and said;
Tramp down the graves of comrades dear,
  And honor rebel dead.

And I suppose the next kind thing
  That Sumner'll want is this,
That we get down upon our knees,
  And rebel coat-tails kiss!

Now, comrades, when all this appears,
  'Twill be when we are dead!
When every man who fought the rebs
  Sleeps in his narrow bed!

Rich, district clerk, to support the school on the grand list; Robert Waugh and Nathaniel Pitkin, school com.; Aaron Elmer, collector. Voted, that no one shall have a right to take any child into his family to attend school, unless he take one for a year, and that the selectmen shall act in conjunction with the committee in examining the school teacher, and to raise $34 to support schooling.

At town meeting, Mar. 25, 1801, Caleb Pitkin, mod., voted to divide the district; set up the old school-house at vendue, to be sold to the highest bidder; sold the house for 2½ bushels of wheat, on 6 months' credit, to Aaron Elmer; 12 squares of glass, to Solomon Gilman, for 1 bush. of wheat; 75 nails, to Nathaniel Dodge, for 1 peck of wheat; boards, to Robert Waugh, for 9s. 6d., to be paid in wheat; table, to Joshua Pitkin, for 2 bush. 2 qts. of wheat; chair, to Joshua Pitkin, for 3 pecks, 4 qts. of wheat. The selectmen organized the inhabitants on the river road into a school district, beginning at Hart Roberts' on the north, Capt. Skinner's at the south, Nathaniel Pitkin's on the west, and Samuel Wilson's and Joseph Wells' on the east. Stephen Rich, Samuel Paterson, Caleb Pitkin, were selectmen.

So the old school-house was sold, a little, square, log-building, covered with bark; a big stone chimney, with an opening above for the smoke to go out and the rain to come in, and the grand old forest for play-ground, and did it not ring with the merry shouts of childhood? They needed no gymnasium then. Were there not the trees to climb, the birds' nests and squirrels to hunt, and partridges and woodchucks to look after? The children did not sing in school in those days. They had to sit straight, keep their eyes on the book, and their toes on the crack. They hardly dared breathe in school-time, there was such an awe of ferule and rod. The children did not sing in school, but the bird's song they heard through the open window, and when the noon-time came, the children joined the chorus, and the old woods rang again.

It seems the inhabitants not included in the river district, were all in one other district. Afterwards districts were divided and arranged, as the inhabitants increased, according to their needs. But it was not until about 1812, that a school-house was built on the river near Joshua Pitkin's. Schools were kept in a portion of a dwelling-house, and sometimes in Caleb Pitkin's old house. In the mill district, now the village, the first school-house was built in 1821. The first school in this district was taught by Miss Comfort Gage, in the summer of 1820, in Capt. Martin Pitkin's barn, on the place where the writer resides. There was a school a number of years in the Dwinell district, before the convenience of a school-house was enjoyed. Four winters this school was kept in Simeon Dwinell's kitchen. This to some housekeepers might have seemed an inconvenience, as the house was small, and Mrs. Dwinell had 8 children of her own. But she doubtless got along nicely, washing days and all. The children must be educated; in those days troops of little ones were not so much in the way.

In 1805, a committee was appointed by the town to act in concert with the selectmen in purchasing a piece of ground for the burial of the dead, and the grave-yard near J. H. Eaton's was bought of Nathaniel Dodge.

Mar. 1797, Thomas McLoud, of Montpelier, and Sally Dodge, of Marshfield, were united in marriage by Joseph Wing, Esq., of Montpelier, the first marriage in town. Joshua Pitkin, Esq., was the first justice of peace, and Dec. 10, 1801, he married Ebenezer Wells to Susannah Spencer, the first marriage by a citizen of the town.

Feb. 1, 1803, a town meeting was called to see if the town would form themselves into a Congregational society, and also to see if they would agree to settle a minister. The vote stood 17 in favor and 70 against.

Bears, wolves and deer were very numerous in the early days of Marshfield. The wolves made night hideous by their howlings, and it was no uncommon thing to kill a bear or deer. Joshua Pitkin, in his

26

journal, speaks of killing 8 deer at different times, and one bear story belonging to our region has in it sufficient of the tragic to warrant insertion here.

One season early in September the bears began to make depredations in the corn, on the Skinner farm, now Wm. Martin's. Solomon Gilman, one of the early settlers, who was a great sportsman, promised to watch for the bear, and put an end to his suppers of green corn; he took his stand at night in the field, waiting the arrival of the depredator. The bear came on, and was soon helping himself, when with true aim, the hunter fired. The bear gave one great spring, and came directly on, or over him. He felt his time had come. The blood was flowing! He caught the lacerated intestines in his hands, replaced them as he could in that moment of desperation, wrapped the long skirt of his overcoat about his body, holding it firmly with both hands; had just strength enough left to shout for help, and to run a short distance. Help soon came. They assisted him to a place of safety, and folding back his overcoat, a double handful of bruin's entrails fell to the ground! Mr. G. lived long to be the terror of the denizens of the forest, but it was years before he heard the last of being killed by a bear.

At another time, Mr. Gilman was pursuing a bear through some woods where Mr. Ira Stone was chopping. Seeing the bear rapidly approaching, Mr. Stone sprang upon a large rock. The bear came up. Mr. Stone attempted to strike him with his axe, but one blow of the bear's paw sent the axe to the ground. They now clinched. Mr. Stone attempted to grasp the bear's tongue, but instead, the bear crushed two of his fingers. They rolled to the ground, the bear uppermost. Just now Mr. Gilman came near, and taking aim, shot the bear through the head. The crushed fingers was all the serious injury Mr. Stone received.

The settlers made quite a business of selling ashes, and afterwards, a larger one of making salts for sale. The beautiful elms, of which there were many on the river banks and in other places, were cut down, piled and burned for this purpose, and a great deal of other valuable timber. Salts sold well, so the day and the long night were often spent in boiling salts, and more than one woman has lent a hand at this work.

There are only two ponds which lie wholly in this town—Nigger Head, of circular form, and about half a mile in width, and Nob Hill ponds. Long pond lies partly in Marshfield and partly in Groton. Mud pond has within a few years dried up. Our county map shows other ponds in our eastern portion, but by actual survey it is found that neither of these are our side of the line. Our township is somewhat hilly, but in only one case are we entitled to the name of mountain.

NIGGER HEAD

mountain, in the north-easterly part of the town, is a steep precipice, 500 feet high, in one place 300 feet perpendicular. It is an imposing sight, so bold, precipitous and grand—nature enthroned in one of her wildest phases. On its dizzy heights we have a remarkably fine view of the surrounding regions, and of the bright waters of the beautiful pond below, and nowhere can one get a better view of the fearful precipice, than in a little boat on the waters at its base.

Winooski river passes through this town from north to south, more than half of the town lying on the east. It receives many tributaries in its course. Lye brook, the outlet of Pigeon pond in Harris' Gore, is a considerable stream, and falls into the river a little south of the center of the town.

A part of the south portion of Marshfield is more easily convened at Plainfield village, which really extends a little into our town than at our own village. As a consequence our people in that vicinity attend church at Plainfield, while a portion of the people in Eastern Cabot, on Molly's brook and vicinity, attend church at Marshfield.

On the east side of the river a large quantity of good timber remains uncut, and there are also on this side of the river very large quarries of granite, beautifully clear, and of superior quality, and should the time come when a railroad shall pass up through this portion of our town, the value of these forests and quarries will be estimated very differently from what they are now. As far as farms are cultivated on this side of the river, they are pretty good.

About the year 1825, quite a settlement was made on this side, some 2½ miles east of where the town-house now stands. So many families moved in, that a log school-house was built, and at one time there was a school of 30 scholars; but the land proving better for pasturage than tillage, after a few years the settlement was deserted. These large pastures are now owned by wealthy farmers.

The town is in every part well-watered. The east part is noted especially for its pure, soft, cold springs. There is also hardly a farm in town but what has one or more good sugar orchards, and the amount of sugar made here any year is large. Through the kindness of E. S. Pitkin, Esq., I have the following statistics of the manufacture of maple sugar here in the spring of 1868, which is above the average: Sugar orchards, 108; sugar made in 1868, 140,350 pounds, or more than 70 tons; 18 orchards made each 2,000 and upwards; 40 made less than 2,000 and more than 1,000 pounds.

WATER PRIVILEGES.

Molly's brook, from the easterly part of Cabot, unites with the Winooski soon after entering this town. On this brook, just above the junction, are Molly's Falls, which are worthy the notice of the traveler. They can be seen to advantage from the stage-road, a mile above the village. The water falls in the distance of 30 rods, 180 feet. Were we writing fiction, it would do, perhaps, to follow the figures of Thompson in his valuable "Gazeteer of Vermont," making these falls 500 feet; but we, who, in the clear mornings of summer can hear the roaring of the water, will have it just as it is, 180 feet. There is an amount of water-power here not often equalled. It would be difficult to estimate how much machinery might be kept in motion by the water which is precipitated over these falls. Then, on the river below, are a number of excellent mill-sites, and in addition to all these, Nigger Head brook, from where it leaves Nigger Head pond to its entrance into the Winooski, has a succession of falls, making good locations for mills; all the better, as the stream is never materially affected by drought.

Among our early settlers a good deal of attention was paid to orcharding. On the hill farms there are good orchards and fine fruit, both grafted and native. On the river, apple-trees have never done as well.

Aug. 22, 1811, there was a very great rise of water, and Joshua Pitkin lost grass sufficient for 15 tons of hay, by the over-flowing of his meadows, as his journal tells. In Sept. 1828, there was a great flood, and Stephen Pitkin, Jr's. clover mill, a mile above the village, was carried off; also many bridges. July 27, 1830, a great rise of water carried off nearly all the bridges on the river, and greatly injured the uncut grass on the meadows, and Aug. 1, 1809, there was a great hail-storm, injuring gardens and corn very much. The evening of July 5, 1841, there was a terrific hail-storm through a portion of the town. Vegetation was much injured, and very much glass broken. Aug. 20, 1869, there was a very sudden rise of water, buildings were injured, some small ones carried off, and bridges and other property destroyed.

A great gale was experienced here May 13, 1866. The wind was accompanied with rain, and 4 barns and some smaller buildings were blown down. Mr. Amos Dwinell was in his son's barn at the time, and was buried in its ruins, but extricated without much injury. A number of cows were in two of the demolished barns, but only a very few were seriously injured.

In the spring of 1807, snow was 4½ feet deep April 4, and when Joshua Pitkin began to tap his sugar-place, Apr. 15, it was 3 feet deep. May 15, 1834, there was a great snow-storm, more than 2 feet deep. In the winter of 1863 and '4, snow was very deep, fences covered for months.

We have also had our portion of fires. A barn was burned Oct. 1806, Jeremiah's

Carleton's blacksmith shop in 1827; after, an old house of Caleb Pitkin's, the dwelling house of Nathan Smith; the dwelling-house of Bemis Pike, Feb. 1835; new house of Hiram Goodwin, May, 1840; the starch-factory and clover-mill of Stephen Pitkin the night of Dec. 10, 1853, large shoe-shop of Henry Goodwin, May, 1860; house belonging to G. O. Davis, occupied by G. W. Nouns, who was severely burned, and the family just escaped with their lives. Mar. 1869, the saw-mill and shop, and all the tools of Calvin York.

CASUALTIES.

Betsey Swetland and another young lady were riding on horseback May 7, 1817, below the village, when she was killed by the fall of a tree. She lived only a few hours.

Mr. Jonathan Davis, an aged man, was burned to death by falling into the fire, probably in a fit, and Jonathan Davis, Jr., had a little son drowned in a water-holder at the door.

George Pitkin, 'while drawing wood alone, fell before the runner of the sled, and was crushed to death, Feb. 20, 1845.

Martin Bemis, son of Abijah Bemis, came to his death by slipping in the road, and a sled passing over him.

Mrs. Linton was accidentally shot, by a gun carelessly handled by a boy.

Mrs. Tubbs, an old lady, accidentally took some oil of cedar, and lived but a short time.

Mr. Graves had a little daughter scalded, so as to cause death. A child of Nathaniel Lamberton was scalded, so as to cause its death in a short time. Mrs. Benoni Haskins was burned, so as to cause death in a few hours. A little child of Francis Loveland was also burned to death some years since, and a child of Spencer Lawrence scalded, so as to cause its death.

A number of years ago, Mr. Asa Willis had a very remarkable escape from sudden death, while at work on a ledge of rocks, near where Daniel Loveland resides. There had been an unsuccessful attempt made to split open a granite rock 12 feet square, the lower edge of which lay on a large rock 15 feet high. The top of the lower rock was slanting like the roof of a house. While attempting to open the crevice already commenced in the upper rock, sufficient to insert a blast of powder, the rock split in two nearly in the middle, Mr. Willis falling between the parts, and he and they sliding from the large rock to the ground, 27 feet. The two pieces, when they reached the ground, stood in such a way that the upper edges leaned against each other, and the lower edges stood apart so as to leave a wedge-shaped cavity large enough to admit his body, and there he lay. No one was with him but Mr. Joshua Smith. On ascertaining that he was alive, Mr. Smith dug away the earth, and succeeded in extricating him from his perilous situation. Neither he, nor the physician, who was immediately called, thought him much injured, and, he lived to do a good deal of hard work, and yet it is thought he never entirely recovered from the effects of the shock.

IMPROVEMENTS.

The log houses of the pioneers soon gave way to better dwellings. At the present time nearly all the houses in town are of modern style and finish, but it is the barns that ought particularly to be mentioned. Many of them are large, beautifully finished and painted, and not surpassed by any in the vicinity.

THE TOWN CLERKS

have been, Stephen Rich 7 years, George Rich 7 years, Robert Cristy 9 years, Martin Bullock 16 years, Jacob Putnam 19 years, Jonathan Goodwin 2 years, Samuel D. Hollister 2 years, and Andrew English 24 years, from 1849 to his death in 1873; Geo. W. English 2 years, and Edgar L. Smith, elected in 1875, now in office.

REPRESENTATIVES.

The town was first represented in the Legislature in 1804, by Stephen Pitkin. He held this office in all 13 years, then by George Rich 3 years, Wm. Martin 12 years, Josiah Hollister 2 years, Alonzo Foster 2 years, Spencer Lawrence 2 years, Welcome Cole 2 years, Horace Hollister 3 years, Ira Smith 2 years, Stephen R. Hollister 2 years, E. D. Putnam 2 years, Hiram Potter 2 years, Asa Spencer 2 years, George A. Gilman 2 years, Ingals Carleton 2 years, Samuel D. Hollister 2 years, Andrew English 2 years, Bowman Martin 2 years, C. W. H. Dwinell 2 years, Wm. Martin, Jr., 2 years, and Preston Haskins 2 years. George Wooster, 1869–70; Moody Bemis, 1872; George Putnam, 1874; Levi W. Pitkin, 1876; Marshal D. Perkins, 1878; Mark Mears, 1880.

TOWN TREASURER.—George O. Davis, elected 1870.

SELECTMEN FROM 1876.

Eli G. Pitkin, 1876–77; H. P. Martin, 1876–78; J. H. Eaton, 1876; Willis Lane, 1876; Marcus R. Bliss, 1877–78–79; H. H. Hollister, 1879–80; Chester Sawyer, 1880; Levi W. Pitkin, Orin H. Smith, Daniel Holcomb, 1881.

TAVERNS.

Joshua Pitkin, Esq., raised the first tavern-sign Oct. 1805. He continued to keep a public house many years. The second tavern was opened by Charles Cate, where Erastus Eddy now lives. Joshua Smith moved into town from Ashford, Ct., in Dec. 1811, bought out Mr. Cate, and commenced keeping tavern, which he continued 17 years. He was a kind neighbor, accommodating to all, and travelers who called on him would never forget the exceeding drollery of his jokes. He died at the age of 84. His wife, one of our best women, still lives (1869) aged 87.

Capt. James English opened a tavern about the year 1811, where Obed Lamberton now resides, and kept a public house a number of years. He was a wheelwright and a highly respected citizen; removed to what is now the village; died in 1825, and was buried with Masonic honors.

Capt. Jacob Putnam bought out Capt. English in 1820, and kept a public house some years, and his son, A. F. Putnam, kept a number of years after at the old stand, and later at the village.

Dudley Pitkin commenced keeping a tavern at the old place occupied by his father, about the year 1824, and for a few years continued the business.

Daniel Wilson moved from Alstead, N.

H., in 1821, and settled in the village. He built and ran the first carding-machine in town. He also bought the place where the hotel now stands, and built there a one-story plank house. The place soon passed into other hands, and in 1826, was bought by Eli Wheelock, who put on another story, and made other additions to the house, and opened it as a hotel the same year. It has been used for a public house till the present time (1869), but so many additions and alterations have been made, that it would now be rather a difficult matter to find the original building. The property soon passed into other hands, was purchased by Horace Bliss, who remained in the tavern a number of years; then sold to Lyman Clark, who afterwards sold to Jabez L. Carpenter, and it has had a number of owners since. A. F. Putnam was proprietor 6 years, and sold to P. Stevens. The present occupant (1869) is P. Lee.

STORES.

The first store in town was opened as early as 1818, by Alfred Pitkin, son of Joshua Pitkin, Esq., in a one-story house just opposite his father's, and just where Wm. Haskins' house stands. After a few years Mr. Pitkin removed to Plainfield, and later to Montpelier. The first store in the village was kept by a Mr. Kimball. He stayed here only a short time.

Enoch D. Putnam opened a store here, Apr. 5, 1840, and continued to trade here till March, 1855, when he sold out and went to Cabot, and has recently removed to Montpelier. George Wooster went into partnership with Mr. Putnam in Sept. 1848. In May, 1858, G. & F. Wooster commenced trade in their starch-factory, but have since built a large store, and are doing a good business.

A. F. Putnam commenced trade In 1866, and is also doing a good business. Levi Bemis and some others have also been in the mercantile business in our village, and after a time have left for other places. Geo. A. Putnam is our present merchant (1881), and Mrs. Adams keeps a ladies store. A. F. Putnam, postmaster.

PHYSICIANS.

Dr. Bates came here in 1826. He located at Eli Wheelock's hotel; remained but a few months. In 1827, Dr. Hersey came here to practice. He boarded at Judge Pitkin's; remained about a year. About 1828, Dr. Daniel Corliss settled in our village, stayed a year and removed to Montpelier, (now East Montpelier, where he died.)

Dr. Asa Phelps removed from Berlin to this place in 1831, and still lives here. For many years he was the only resident physician. He has known as well as any other man, what it was to travel over our hills on a dark night, with the thermometer below zero, while the winds were all abroad—years ago. At that time, we had many more poor people in town, than now, On such nights after doing for the sick, if he could have lodging on the floor, with his feet towards the fire, he would put up till daylight. He was never known after such visits to complain of his fare, indeed sometimes, he had no fare to complain of. He has had a large practice—often without pay, never objecting to have counsel, and if superseded by others, " he kept the even tenor of his way," never speaking against the practice of other physicians; thus has secured universal respect.

Dr. Ezra Paine moved here in 1842, and remained here some 2 years.

Dr. George Town removed here from Montpelier in 1852, but after a few years, sold out and returned to Montpelier, but removed here again, and has a good practice.

Dr. J. Q. A. Packer, homœopathist, removed from Peacham here in 1865. He is doing a good business.

LONGEVITY.

A few persons here have attained to the age of 90 years. Dea. Spencer died at 90; Mrs. Capron over 90; Mrs. Cree, 94; Mrs. Austin, 94.

Mr. Joel Parker and wife resided in this place a year or two. Some few years since, Mrs. Parker had attained to the great age of 97, and on her birth-day sung two hymns to a neighbor who called upon her.

Mr. P. was 10 years younger. They have both recently died in Northfield, she in her 100th year.

Aged persons who have died in town within 3 or 4 years.—Daniel Young, 91, and his wife Lydia, 85; Sylvester Loveland, 88, and his wife. 84; Mary Bemis, 84; Samuel G. Bent, 81; Ira Smith, 80; Abijah Bemis, 86; Willard Benton, 83.

Aged persons now living (1881).—Dr. Asa Phelps, 85; Lucy Bemis, 86; Sally Dwinell, 86; Mary York.

MILLS.

The first saw-mill in town was built by Stephen Pitkin, afterwards Judge Pitkin, in 1802, on Lye brook. In 1812, he built the first saw-mill at what is now the village, and a grist-mill in 1818, which was used many years. The stone and brick grist-mill, now owned by Harrison F. Ketchum, was built in 1831, by Gen. Parley Davis and Truman Pitkin. About the year 1823, Simeon Gage built clothing-works at the south part of the village, but they were used only a few years.

LIBRARY.

There has been for 20 years, in this place, a circulating library, of historical works, travels, etc.

CONGREGATIONAL CHURCH.

BY MRS. DEA. A. BOYLES.

The first Congregational church in Marshfield was organized Dec. 24, 1800. By request of a number of persons in town, to be embodied into a visible church of Christ, Rev. Mr. Hobart and two brethren, Mr. Timothy Hatch and Peterson Gifford of Berlin, came and organized a church of 13 members. Selah Wells was the first deacon, and afterwards Gideon Spencer. For a number of years they had additions, both by professions and letters, and were supplied with preaching a portion of the time by ministers from the neighboring towns. Rev. Mr. Hobart of Berlin, Rev. Mr. Lyman of Brookfield, Rev. Mr. Wright of Montpelier, Rev. Mr. Worcester of Peacham, and also a Mr. Washburn and Mr. Bliss, were among those who occasionally ministered to them. About the year 1817, Rev. Levi Parsons, afterwards missionary to Palestine, was here, and preached a number of times. But they never enjoyed the blessing of a settled minister. Thus they continued till Dec. 8, 1825, when with the hope that they should enjoy better privileges, those members residing at the south part of the town, united with the church in Plainfield. The rest of the members, and a number of other persons who wished to unite with a Congregational church, thought best to form a church at the north part of the town, in the vicinity of the village, and by request, Rev. Mr. French of Barre, and Rev. Mr. Heard of Plainfield, came and organized a church, which still remains. Brothers Andrew Currier and Alexander Boyles, were chosen deacons. It has been supplied with preaching a part of the time. Among those who have labored here are Rev. Messrs. Kinney, Baxter, Herrick, Torrey, Waterman, Samuel Marsh, and Lane. Rev. Joseph Marsh labored here nearly 2 years. Through the summer of 1868, Rev. Mr. Winch, of Plainfield, preached at 5 o'clock every other Sabbath. There have been many removals and the present number of church members is small.

Record from 1869 to Aug. 3, 1871, by Rev. N. F. Cobleigh, pastor, then.—For several years there had been but little Congregational preaching in Marshfield, when in the spring of 1870, Rev. J. T. Graves preached half of the time for 6 weeks. Soon after, Rev. N. F. Cobleigh was engaged to preach half of the time for 1 year. The church had no church property, but in the spring of 1871, a new church was begun, a Sabbath school organized, and a library obtained. The church will be dedicated Aug. 16, 1871. The membership has more than doubled during the past year. Preaching services are now held every Sabbath. Rev. N. F. Cobleigh is to be settled as pastor Aug. 16th inst.

Record from Aug. 1877, to 1879, from Rev. Geo. E. Forbes.—From this time to the spring of 1877, Rev. Mr. Cobleigh was its pastor, and through his faithful efforts its membership was very largely in-

creased. Of the 57 who composed the church when Mr. Cobleigh resigned, only 9 were members in 1870. Aug. 16, the church was dedicated and the pastor installed. After Mr. Cobleigh's resignation in 1877, Rev. John Stone, of Berlin, supplied until early in 1878, when Rev. Paul Henry Pitkin, of Brooklyn, N. Y., was called to be its pastor. He was installed March 14; is its present pastor (1879.) Alexander Boyles, elected deacon in Aug. 1827, held office till his death, Nov. 27, 1876. The other deacons have been Andrew Currier, Silas Carleton, Benjamin Boyles and Mervin Roberts.

CHRISTIAN CHURCHES.

BY MISS A. BULLOCK.

About the year 1815, Elder John Capron commenced preaching in this town, and soon after removed his family here from Danville. There was a revival of religion, and a church was organized about this time. They believed the Scriptures, together with the spirit of God, a sufficient rule of faith and practice. They were blessed with more or less prosperity till 1825, when some of them considered some articles setting forth their faith and covenant, as necessary and proper for a Christian church. This caused a division, but finally there was a reorganization under the pastoral care of Elder Capron, Dec. 15, 1836, the two blending together again. Between this time and March 5, 1844, 44 persons united with this church, a part living in Calais, and a part in Marshfield. Among this number there were many of whom we believed "their record is on high." Elder Capron had but little educational advantages, was of warm and energetic temperament, and many remember him justly, as a friend and brother in adversity. He moved from this town some time after the death of his excellent wife, who was kind to all and ever had a word for the afflicted. She died June 14, 1848, and was buried in our soil, and her memory still clings to our hearts. Elder Capron being the first settled minister in town, was entitled to, and received the town's minister lot of land. He removed to

Stowe. [See history of Morristown. Ed.]
He was married a second time, and died
some years since.

About the year 1839, there was another
church of the Christian denomination organized in the North-west part of the town,
under the direction of Elder Jared L. Green.
This church was subjected to very hard
and severe trials. Many of its members
sleep in the dust, some are scattered to
other parts, while others are living and
striving for the better land.

ADVENT CHURCH.

Feb. 6, 1867, another church was organized here of 6 members, believing in the
advent of Christ near at hand, under the
pastoral care of Rev. J. A. Cleaveland.

BAPTIST CHURCH.

From the early settlement of the town
there have been residents here who have
maintained the views of the Baptist church.
More than 30 years ago a church of this
denomination was organized, consisting of
members in Barre, Plainfield and Marshfield. The larger number resided in Barre
and Plainfield, and this church will probably be mentioned in the history of one of
those towns. [Barre has left it, we think,
to Plainfield.—Ed.]

UNIVERSALIST SOCIETY.

BY REV. A. SCOTT.

Universalism was introduced into this
town by Daniel Bemis, a Revolutionary
soldier, who moved here from Conn. in
1809. Soon after Ebenezer Dodge, Jr.,
and Robert Spencer became associated
with Mr. B. in religious faith. The first
preacher of this faith here was Rev. Wm.
Farewell, in 1818. From this time there
was occasional Universalist preaching here
till 1854, by Revs. L. H. Tabor, Benjamin
Page, Lester Warren, and it may be some
others.

In 1854, Daniel Bemis, Junior, Edwin
Pitkin, Jonathan Goodwin, Abijah Hall
and others united and secured the services
of Rev. Wm. Sias for one-fourth of the
Sabbaths for this and the next year.
During 1855, the friends organized, under
the name of " The Universalist Society of
Liberal Christians in Marshfield." The

society for the year 1856 and '7, enjoyed
the labors of Rev. Eli Ballou for one-
fourth the Sabbaths.

In 1827, an association was formed
called "The Union meeting-house society," for building and keeping in repair a
church they erected in the village in the
north part of the town; the only church
edifice in town till 1859. [In 1831, when
the first list of shares prepared apportion-
ing the time to the several denominations,
the Universalists were represented by four
shares, owned by Sam'l. Ainsworth, Daniel
Bemis, Jr., and Cyrus Smith.] In 1857,
this association repaired and modernized
the church, making it neat and pleasant,
both external and internal. Some of the
other societies, desiring more room at this
time, relinquished their interest in the
church. The property being sold to pay
the assessment upon it, it fell into different
hands, and at the present writing, 1869,
three-fourths of the occupancy is given to
the Universalist society. This change in
the occupancy of the house gave a new impetus to the cause in the town. This society has since sustained public worship
one-half of the Sabbaths, excepting 1866
and '7, during which they sustained it every
Sabbath. These years were supplied as
follows : 1858 and '9, by Rev. Eli Ballou ;
1860, Rev. M. B. Newell ; 1861, '2 and '3,
by Rev. E. Ballou ; 1864, by Rev. Olympia
Brown ; 1865, by Rev. L. Warren ; 1866,
'7 and '8, by Rev. A. Scott. Revs. Newell, Brown and Scott lived in the town
during their ministrations. The society
was united, and at the present time, 1869,
is in as good, if not better, condition than ·
at any former period, having raised more
money for the support of worship one-half
of the Sabbaths, than it had ever before
done. Rev. L. Warren is to labor with it
from May 1, 1869. Connected with the
society and congregation are some 40 families, beside many single individuals of
other families. There is also a small Sabbath-school, for the use of which there is
a reading library of 150 vols. The church
property is worth from $3,000 to $3,500,
¾ of which is given to the occupancy of
the society.

From paper of Rev. Geo. E. Forbes in 1879—Universalist record continued.—In 1869, Rev. Lester Warren was engaged to preach one-half of the time till the spring of 1873. In July of this year, Rev. Geo. E. Forbes was settled over the society. For 2 years the Plainfield society united with this for his support. The remainder of the time he has preached for this society exclusively, and is its present pastor.

The Union Sabbath-school, composed of scholars from the different denominations occupying the church, was continued until 1871. Since that time the Sabbath-school here has been connected with this society; present number, about 90, officers and pupils. A. H. Davis was its superintendent in 1871 to '75, when he was succeeded by C. H. Newton. Under the ministry of Rev. L. Warren in 1871, a church was organized, which at present numbers 43 members. John E. Eddy and Abial H. Davis were elected deacons, and still hold the office. Ira H. Edson was the first church clerk, succeeded by D. R. Loveland and C. H. Newton, present clerk,

METHODIST CHURCH IN MARSHFIELD.

In May, 1826, Stephen Pitkin, Jr., married the writer, a daughter of Gen. Parley Davis, of Montpelier. A few months before she had been baptized by Rev. Wilbur Fisk, and united with the M. E. church on probation. Previous to their marriage Mr. Pitkin had also experienced religion. In Jan. 1827, there being no Methodists in Marshfield at that time, they both united with the Methodist church in Cabot; he as a probationer, being baptized by Rev. A. D. Sargeant, of the N. E. Conference, and she, by letter, in full connection. In 1827, the union meeting-house was built at Marshfield, and a committee appointed to divide the time for occupying the house between the different denominations owning it. A few Sabbaths were set to the Methodists, though Mr. Pitkin was the only Methodist pew-holder. Rev. N. W. Aspinwall, preacher in charge at Cabot, appointed and attended meetings here on these Sabbaths alternately with his col-

league, Rev. Elisha J. Scott. In Feb. 1828, the first quarterly meeting was held, weather stormy. The meeting commenced Saturday, P. M. Several ministers and one minister's wife were in attendance, and all were entertained at our own house—a small frame-house, never encumbered with clapboards.

The next year Sophronia and Sally Cate were baptized by Rev. Hershal Foster—the former now Mrs. Guernsey, of Montpelier. These two, with Mr. Pitkin and myself, and a Mrs. Whittle, constituted the first Methodist class in Marshfield, organized in the autumn of 1829, Mr. Pitkin class-leader and steward. What seasons of interest were the class-meetings and prayer-meetings of those days! The next to join were Samuel G. Bent and wife. Our numbers increased very gradually; at most, we occupied the church only ¼ the Sabbaths. Rev. Solomon Sias, Rev. Stephen H. Cutler, Rev. E. J. Scott, and others, spoke to us the words of life. About 1834, the first wife of Andrew English, Esq., proposed to the writer, we should get the children of the neighborhood together for a Sabbath-school. As we had preaching at the church so little, we met at our homes alternately, at 5 o'clock. This we did many months, till we had a good-sized school, when it was proposed to take our Sabbath-school to the church, where it was duly organized, Jeremiah Carleton, Esq., first superintendent. A library was procured, and the school prospered. It was strictly a union Sabbath-school. The desk was supplied by ministers of different denominations, and our Sabbath-school went on. For a number of years the Methodists were supplied with preaching ¼ the time, by preachers who lived in Cabot. After that, we were united with Woodbury and Calais, and supplied in that way. A few united with the little band from year to year, but deaths and removals kept our number small. Some of these death-bed scenes were, however, remarkably happy. Especially was this the case in the death of Loammi Sprague.

The first preacher sent here by Conference was Rev. David Packer, who died a few years since in Chelsea, Mass. He resided on East Hill, in Calais.

At this time preachers received but a very small salary, and the members were often scattering and poor. After being in Calais a few weeks, Mr. and Mrs. Packer one morning ate their last food. Almost an entire stranger, Mr. Packer did not feel that he could beg. After uniting in family prayer, he retired to an old barn on the place, while she sought her closet, and each alone committed their case to the father of the stranger and the poor.

A mile away from them lived a young farmer, not a professor of religion. As he started after breakfast for the hay-field with his hired help, something seemed to impel him to stop. He must go back to the house and carry some provisions to the new minister. It was of no use to say, "I'm not acquainted with them, I know nothing of their needs," he must take them some food. He told the men they might go to mowing, he must go back. He went back, told his wife his feelings, and they together put up meat, potatoes, flour, butter and sugar, and other things, a fair wagon load, and *he* took it over, and found how blessed it was to give, and *they*, how safe to trust in God.

Slowly did the little church increase, never having preaching more than one-fourth of the time for many years.

In 1851, the Congregationalists and Methodists agreed to unite and support preaching. First for 2 years they would have Congregational preaching, and then Methodist for the next 2. Rev. Mr. Marsh, Congregational, was our first minister, and at the close of the two years Rev. Lewis P. Cushman was appointed by Conference, and spent 2 years with us. In those years a number were added to the church. Mr. Cushman is now a missionary in Texas; his little daughter, Clara, so well remembered by us, started last October as a missionary to China.

Before the close of Mr. Cushman's first year Mr. Pitkin died, and as he had been very influential in procuring and sustaining preaching, and there was no one to then take his place, the effort was now aban-doned, and for a number of years we had no stated preaching. At length, in 1859, a few concluded to make one more effort, and Rev. Joshua Gill was stationed with us. The Union church had passed mostly into the hands of the Universalists, and we had no preaching place. We needed a church, and one was put up and covered in '59, and finished in 1860. The house was the right size, well furnished. Our next minister was Rev. Geo. H. Bickford, an excellent preacher, and one of the best of men. He died some years later at Barton. His last words, his hand upon his breast, closing his eyes, that grand old doxology, the *gloria*, "Glory be to the Father, the Son and the Holy Ghost." Rev. C. S. Buswell came next 2 years. Rev. James Robinson was stationed here in 1865, Rev. Joseph Hamilton in 1867; both years we had some additions. In 1869, Rev. James Spinney was appointed here. No. of vols. in S. S. library, 450.

In 1871, Rev. J. Hamilton was with us again, and stayed one year. In 1872, Conference made Rev. C. P. Flanders our pastor, succeeded in 1874, by Rev. C. A. Smith, who was with us 3 years, followed by Rev. G. H. Hastings in 1877, in 1879 by Rev. O. A. Farley, and in 1881 by Rev. C. H. Farnsworth, our present pastor. Our members have gradually increased; our present number is 73.

In the spring of 1870, we bought of Bemis Pike a good house and garden for a parsonage; cost, $1,800.

Feb. 3, 1878, our church was burned. The society had just put down a new carpet, and a new organ and new lamps had been purchased, which, together with our large Sabbath-school library, was all consumed, and no insurance. What a loss for us! But after mature deliberation we decided to rebuild. The Church Extension Society gave us $200, Rev. A. L. Cooper $50, and a few other friends smaller sums. January 16, 1879, our new church was dedicated, sermon by Rev. A. L. Cooper. The church is built in the Norman Gothic style of architecture, nicely finished and furnished throughout, warmed from the vestry beneath, and free from debt.

Since we have had a church of our own, our Sabbath-school has been prosperous, and never more so than at the present time. It is large, numbering over 80. The present superintendent is J. B. Pike.

STEPHEN PITKIN,

whose history is so interwoven with early Methodism in Marshfield, was very unassuming in his manners, and very strong in his temperance and anti-slavery principles. He belonged to the old Liberty party when in this town; their caucuses were opened with prayer. He had a great aversion to pretension. He once lent his sleigh and harness to a man calling himself John Cotton, to go to Barnet, to be gone three days. Cotton was quite a stranger, having been in our place but 6 weeks, during which he had boarded with my husband's brother, working for him a part of the time, and the rest of the time selling clocks he had purchased of a Mr. Bradford, in Barre. Four days went by. On inquiry, Mr. Pitkin found that the clocks had been purchased on trust, and all sold for watches or money; that he owed $60 toward his horse, and that he had borrowed of the brother with whom he boarded, horse-blanket, whip and mittens. It seemed sure he was a rogue. What could be done? Pursuit was useless after such a lapse of time. Mr. P. felt his loss severely; he had little property then, and what he had, was the product of hard labor; but he always made his business a subject of prayer. About 3 weeks passed away. One evening, having been out some time, he came in, and with his characteristic calmness, said, "H—, I shall not worry any more about my sleigh and harness; I think I shall get them again." "Why do you think so?" said I. His answer was, "I have been praying God to arrest Cotton's conscience, so that he will be obliged to leave them where I can get them, and I believe he will do it," and from this time, Wednesday evening, he seemed at rest on the subject. The next Tuesday morning, as he stepped into the post-office, a letter was handed him from Littleton, N. H., written by the keeper of a public house there:

Mr. Pitkin—Sir:—Mr. John Cotton has left your sleigh and harness here, and you can have them by calling for them.
    Yours, &c.,   JOHN NEWTON.

He started for Littleton the same day, some 40 miles, found the sleigh and harness safe, with no encumbrance. The landlord said the Wednesday night previous, at 12 o'clock, a man calling himself John Cotton came to his house, calling for horse-baiting and supper. He would not stay till morning, but wished to leave the sleigh and harness for Mr. Pitkin, of Marshfield, Vt. He also requested the landlord to write to Mr. Pitkin, and said he could not write, and that he took them for Mr. Pitkin on a poor debt, and started off at 2 o'clock at night, on horseback, with an old pair of saddle-bags and a horse-blanket on a saddle with one stirrup, and no crupper, on one of the coldest nights of that winter. None of the other men to whom he was indebted received anything from him, or ever heard from him after.

[This brief sketch of this so worthy man cannot be better completed than by the following lines we have in our possession, which were written by Mrs. Pitkin after his death:]

"I have loved thee on Earth,
    May I meet thee in Heaven!"

Thrice, since they laid him with the dead,
Have Autumn's golden sheaves been laded,
Thrice have the spring-birds come and flown,
    And thrice the flowrets bloomed and faded.

Yet, yet the far-off birds returning,
    The harvest sunset gilded o'er,
The flowrets springing, blooming, fading,
    But whisper, "he will come no more."

That hymn of praise, that voice in prayer,
    On memory's zephyrs back to me,
Thrilling my inmost soul, they come
    Like midnight music on the sea,

In these dear haunts, beside this hearth,
    There is for me no answering tone.
We knelt together by her grave,
    I weep and pray by theirs alone!

Oh, "pure in heart," in purpose firm,
    To me be thy meek mantle given;
One faith, one hope was ours on earth,
    God grant us one bless'd home in Heaven.

In the winter of 1866, a lodge of Good Templars was organized here. Good has been accomplished, and it is hoped much more may yet be done. The present number of members is 101.

DEA. GIDEON SPENCER

Came first to Marshfield from East Hartford, Conn., in company with Caleb and Martin Pitkin in the spring of 1792. That summer and the next they worked clearing land, and preparing for the coming of their families, returning for them in the fall. February, 1794, Mr. Spencer, Caleb Pitkin and Aaron Elmer removed their families to this wilderness, and commenced the settlement of Marshfield. From Montpelier they came with hand-sleds without roads over snow 4 feet deep. Daniel, oldest child of the Spencer family, was 4 years old. This family had the first daughter, born in town, and their son, Horace, was born the day the town was organized. Their location was a mile from either of the other settlers. So neighborly were the bears, Mr. Spencer found it necessary to take his gun when going after his cow, which had the whole forest for pasture.

He was chosen deacon of the Congregational church, soon after its organization; was active in sustaining meeting, and attained the great age of 90 years. His wife, a daughter of Capt. Isaac Marsh, a woman of energetic and social habits, died at the age of 86.

CALEB PITKIN

married Hannah, daughter of Capt. Isaac Marsh, and came first to Marshfield as a surveyor. He was rather retiring in his manners, but had a vein of pleasantry which made him agreeable company, and he had a good education for the times. He was a good reader, and often when no minister was present, read the Sunday sermon. His trade was a mason, and the original stone-chimneys of the first dwellings were laid by him. His wife was social, and a worker. He removed to Peacham a few years before his death, Apr. 1813, at the age of 40. His widow returned to Marshfield, and lived some years after the decease of her husband. The oldest son, James, still lives on the old place. One son, a physician, has deceased, and a daughter lives in Burlington.

JOSHUA PITKIN, ESQ.,

born in East Hartford, Conn., arrived with his wife and three children in Marshfield on the 1st of Mar., 1795, and located where Wm. Haskins now lives. Not a tree was felled on the lot, excepting what had been felled by hunters in trapping for furs; but he went to work and soon had a spot cleared, a log-house up and ready to occupy. He raised a large family, and resided on the same place till his death. He kept the first public house in town, and was the first justice of peace. He and his exemplary wife united with the Congregational church. She died about 1821, and he married again. He commenced a journal of his life and business Mar. 28, 1796. The last record is dated June 10, 1847. He died June 25, 1847. His last words were, "I know that my Redeemer liveth," etc. Dea. Pitkin of Montpelier, his second son, kept the first store in town. None of his descendants remain in Marshfield.

HON. STEPHEN PITKIN

came with his wife into this town March 1, 1795. He had a large farm, pleasantly located, where Bowman Martin now resides. He was very well educated for the times, and possessed of a strong mind, and great energy. His keen eye, and commanding look gave evidence he was one to lead others, rather than one to be led. His influence was great in the business transactions of the town. He was the first town representative; held the office in all, 13 years; was first militia captain, eventually became a major, and was assistant county judge 4 years.

He was considerate of the poor, and the writer is informed by his nephew, James Pitkin, Esq., that in the cold season of 1816 and '17, when almost no provisions were raised, he bought salmon at Montpelier by the barrel, when he had to be trusted for it himself, and sold it out to those in need, taking his pay when they could work for it. He continued to reside on the same farm till his death, which took place May 22, 1834, age 62. He raised a family of 13 children, 12 of his own, one dying in infancy, and one, the motherless babe of his brother, Levi, he and his excellent wife adopted and brought up as their own. His oldest son, Horace, settled in town, but after a few years, removed to Central Ohio, where he recently died. His second son, Edwin, an enterprising citizen, settled in town, raised a large and intelligent family, was considerably in town business,—and was for many years the principal surveyor in the vicinity. He died a few years since. His third son, Truman, settled in Marshfield first, subsequently in Montpelier, where he died, leaving 3 sons and one daughter. One of his sons, Gen. P. P. Pitkin, resides in Montpelier, and the other two at the West. His 4th son, Stephen Pitkin, Jr., will be particularly mentioned in another place in this history. The two youngest sons went West, where one died a number of years since. Three daughters still live, one in Iowa, and two in Massachusetts.

CAPT. STEPHEN RICH,

born in Sutton, Mass., at 15 became a soldier in the Revolutionary war, as a substitute for his father. He was at the taking of Burgoyne, and in a number of other battles. He came to Marshfield in Feb. 1798, and settled where his grandson Samuel D. Hollister now resides. He was the first selectman of Marshfield and first town clerk; held the office 7 years. His only son George, was also town clerk 7 years. He removed to Montpelier, where he died. Capt. Rich filled various town offices, and was an esteemed citizen. He accumulated a large property, and had, besides the son mentioned, a family of five daughters. He resided where he first settled till his death, at the age of 83. His wife, a woman of uncommon energy, survived some years after his decease.

CAPT. JOSIAH HOLLISTER.

Born in E. Hartford, Ct., came to Marshfield about the year 1806. He married Phebe, daughter of Capt. Stephen Rich, in 1809. He acquired a large property, was respected by his townsmen, and had a fair share of town offices. He represented the town in the legislature of the State 2 years, and was chosen captain of a company of cavalry. He died at the age of 52.

HON. HORACE HOLLISTER.

Born in E. Hartford, Ct., in 1791; when a young man came to Marshfield, and resided one year with his brother Josiah, and then returned to Ct.; was married to Ruth P., daughter of Capt. Stephen Rich, and moved to Colebrook, N. H., first in 1817, and to Marshfield in 1821. Like his brother, he was very successful, shared largely in the confidence of the people, and was very much in public business. He was a man who had an opinion of his own, and dared express it. He was elected to most of the town offices; was overseer of the poor many years; also, assistant judge 2 years, and senator 2 years. He died recently, aged 76.

HON. WILLIAM MARTIN.

BY MRS. SOLOMON WELLS, OF PLAINFIELD.

Among the early settlers of Marshfield, was Wm. Martin, born in Francistown, N. H., July 28, 1786. In 1800, his father and family moved to the frontiers of Vermont. William worked out mostly till 21, to help support his father's family. He worked at South Boston a part of the time, and on the first canal that was built at Cambridge, and went to Canada, owing to the scarcity of money in Vermont, and worked. He had no education except what he picked up, without attending school. At 18, he enlisted in a company of cavalry; was chosen at once an officer, and rose from one grade of office to another to colonel. At the time of President Monroe's visit to Vermont, he commanded the company that escorted him into Montpelier, and took dinner with the President. He continued in the militia, was in the war of 1812, and at the battle of Plattsburgh.

In 1809, he married Sabra Axtell, of Marshfield, and moved that summer to Plainfield, where he lived 4 years, and then bought a farm in Marshfield, about a mile above Plainfield village, where he resided till 1840. His farm was one of the finest upon the head waters of the Winooski. He had 5 boys and 2 girls, two

of whom are now dead. He held many of
the town offices; was constable and collector 25 years; 12 years representative,
and a number of times was one of the assistant judges of the County Court. Up
to 1840, much of his time was spent in
public business. He then moved to Montpelier (now E. Montpelier,) afterwards
returned to Marshfield, but finally removed
to Rockton, Ill., where he now resides.
His wife is still living (1869,) but has been
blind for 16 years. He is a man of fine
social qualities, and was always hospitable
and kind to the poor. He acquired a
handsome property, and an accuracy in
doing business which but few men possess.
He was many years a member of the Congregational church in Plainfield.

JACOB PUTNAM, ESQ.

BY HON. E. D. PUTNAM, OF MONTPELIER.

My father, Jacob Putnam, moved from
Alstead, N. H., to Marshfield, with his
family, himself and wife, 3 boys and 3
girls, in the spring of 1820. He also
brought with him his father and mother,
Joseph and Miriam Putnam. They were
among the first settlers of Hancock, N. H.,
where my father was born in 1784. He
bought the farm of James English, Esq.,
on the river road, 2 miles south of the village, 220 acres, for which he paid $1,400.
He afterwards sold 50 acres, and the remainder was sold in 1868 for $6,200. This is
about a fair sample of the rise of real estate
in the town in the last 50 years. Mr. English moved to the village, and built a house
and wheelwright shop. There were at
that time a saw and grist-mill, and only
two houses within what are now the limits
of the village. The land where the village now stands was then but partially
cleared, and there were no settlements
east of the river, except in the extreme
N. E. and S. E. corners of the town, and
there was but little money in the country.
Most of the business transactions were in
neat stock and grain. When anything of
any considerable value was bought on
credit (as was usually the case,) notes
were generally given, payable in neat stock
in Oct., or grain in Jan. following. When

the prices of the stock could not be agreed
upon by the parties, three men were selected as appraisers, their appraisal to be
binding upon the parties. A pair of good
oxen were worth about $50 to $60; cows,
$12 to $15; corn and rye were worth 50 cts.
per bushel; oats, 20 cents; potatoes, 12 to
20 cents. Good crops of wheat were generally raised in town, and I can recollect
of wheat being carried as late as 1824, to
Troy, N. Y., for a market. There was no
manufacturing to any considerable extent
done in this country as early as 1820.
Nearly all the clothing was made at home
by hand. The spinning-wheel and loom
might be found in almost every house, and
among my earliest recollections is the buzz
of the wheel and the thumping of the old
loom, and whenever there came a pleasant,
sunny day in March, the flax-break might
be heard at almost every farmer's barn,
and very well do I recollect the "big
bunches" of woolen and linen yarn which
"ornamented" the kitchen of the old
homestead, spun by my mother and sisters. The words of Proverbs, "She seek-
eth wool and flax, and worketh diligently
with her hands," were peculiarly applicable
to my mother. In addition to making all
the cloth for clothing the family, she made
hundreds of yards of woolen and linen
cloth, and exchanged it at the store for
family necessaries. These days have
passed. A spinning-wheel is rarely seen
now; if found at all, it is stowed away in
some old garret, a relic, and the sewing-
machine is annihilating the needle. Are
people happier now than they were then?

My father enjoyed the confidence of the
public; was town clerk 19 years, and occasionally held other town offices. He
lived on the same place where he first
bought 36 years, to the time of his death,
in 1856, aged 72 years. My mother died
in 1864, aged 81. They lived together 52
years. Their children are all living, except
the eldest son, Thomas B., who died Apr.
30, 1830. The youngest son, A. F. Putnam, is the present postmaster of Marshfield. My grandfather died in 1826, aged
83 years; my grandmother in 1835, aged
91.

JONATHAN GOODWIN, ESQ.

BY MRS. H. L. GOODWIN.

Jonathan Goodwin was born at Concord, N. H., May 27, 1784, where he passed his youth and early manhood. He was one of a large family. Were it not for the experience of the late war, it would be difficult for a person in these days to realize the bitterness of party-spirit and controversy, even among kindred, which existed before and during the war of 1812. At a family gathering where politics were discussed, Jonathan being a Democrat, and the other members of the family Federalists, a brother remarked, "as there was a prospect of war, it would be a good time for him to show his patriotism and courage, if he had any." He replied, "it was a pity those who had so much sympathy for the enemies of their country, were not in a position to afford them the aid and assistance they would naturally wish to give." These remarks were never forgotten. Jonathan enlisted as recruiting sergeant, was afterwards lieutenant and captain; was stationed at Saco, Me., Boston and Plattsburgh. At the latter he received an injury from which he never recovered, and was a pensioner the remainder of his life. It is worthy of remark that during the 7 years he was in the United States' service, although at that time the custom of using ardent spirits was almost universal, he never indulged in it, not even after being assured by his physician that probably he would not survive the campaign without it. In 1814, his family moved from Concord, N. H., to Randolph, Vt. After his discharge he removed to Chelsea, and in 1839, to this town to reside with his eldest son. The following summer they built a house, and occupied it one winter. In April it was burned.

It was burned on Saturday. The next day, Elder Capron announced from his pulpit that on Monday the inhabitants would meet to assist Messrs. Goodwin in getting out timber for another house-frame. On Monday, men enough came to cut the timber, hew it, frame it, draw it over a mile, and raise a house, 28 by 34 feet, in a day.

He passed the remainder of his life in Marshfield; was justice of peace, town clerk 2 years, postmaster 2 years, and often administered on the estates of the deceased, and gave general satisfaction. Although in early life his opportunities for education were limited, he was a person of more than ordinary information, especially in history and the Bible, of which he was a daily student.

In early life he united with the Baptist church in Concord, but during a season of religious interest in Chelsea, was drawn to a more thorough examination of the Scriptures than ever before, which led to his embracing the doctrine of the final redemption of all, in which belief he afterwards continued till his death, Jan. 1867, aged 82, generally respected as a man and a Christian.

REV. MARCUS M. CARLETON,

son of Jeremiah Carleton, Esq., was born in Marshfield, 1826. When about 15, he made a profession of religion, uniting with the Congregational church in Barre, where he resided with his uncle. He soon after decided to be a foreign missionary, and from hence devoted all his energies to procuring a suitable education. He first entered Middlebury College, but removed to Amherst College, Massachusetts, where he graduated, and on account of a chronic cough went south to study theology at Columbia, S. C. After finishing his course, he offered himself to the Congregational Board for foreign missions, but was not accepted, they fearing his health would fail; but determined in his resolutions he offered himself immediately to the Presbyterian Board by whom he was accepted, and sailed for India in 1865, where he has labored most of the time since. He was stationed first in Ambalia city, but the mission seeing him eminently fitted for an itinerant, set him apart for that work after a few years, since which he has lived most of the time in a tent, travelling from village to village in Ambalia district, instructing and preaching to the people, and having studied medicine, finding it very advantageous to him in his ministeral labors among the inhabitants, he also administers to them as a physician—sometimes his family accompany him in the tent; but during the hot season they generally remain among the mountains, where he sometimes rests with them during the hottest period. [An account of his family we will not repeat here, as we have already given the same in a notice of Rev. Mr. Carleton with his family in Barre—See No. 1, of this vol. p. 40. A member of the Carleton family tells me he is a man of herculean frame—physically and mentally a very strong man. In a letter to his father in 1879, an extract of which lies before me, he speaks of his good health as a source of great joy—seems to luxuriate body and soul in his nomadic preaching life.]

MARSHFIELD MILITARY RECORD.

SOLDIERS OF 1812.

This place furnished 8: Abijah Bemis, Phineas Bemis, Obadiah Bemis, David Cutting, John Waugh, Abijah Hall, Isaac Austin, and Philip Delan.

Lewis Bemis, a brother of three of these soldiers, was also from this town, though he enlisted from Barnet. His father and friends all resided here, and he should have a notice here. He belonged to the old 4th regiment, which was sent out under Col. Miller to the then territory of Ohio, to look after the Indians who were making depredations on the frontier settlements. At one time they came to the dwelling of a Mr. Harriman, (whose wife was the daughter of Alexander Parker of Montpelier, and sister of Mrs. James Pitkin of this town,) just about an hour after the savages had murdered and left him and his family. They pressed on, but failed to overtake the Indians, and soon after joined the main body under the infamous Gen. Hull on its way to Fort Detroit. Before arriving at Detroit, Col. Miller saw Hull's treachery, and accused him of it, and challenged him to fight a duel, both before and after their arrival, quite in vain; he surrendered the fort and army without firing a gun. In that fort, among our men, were a number of British who had deserted and joined our army. The next morning, and two or three succeeding mornings, our army was paraded and the British officers walked along and inspected it, and when they saw a British soldier, he was tapped on the shoulder, and commanded to step out. Where they had suspicions, and yet were not certain as to their being British subjects, they would question them. A number of times Mr. Bemis, though he never saw Ireland, was asked, " In what town in Ireland were you born"? Each time his answer was, " I was born in Paxham, in Massachusetts." One poor fellow, the first time they came round, succeeded in squinting his eyes so as fairly to deceive them, and after that succeeded in slipping down an embankment just in the right time to save his life. About 40 of these poor deserters were taken out and shot. The army, surrendered by Hull, was then taken to Quebec, and confined in a prison-ship on the St. Lawrence, where they were allowed but one half pint of water per day, though their prison was floating on the river, and if any one attempted to let down a cup for water, he was shot down. Three-fourths of the prisoners eventually died from the cruelties there received. The rest were eventually exchanged.

JESSE WEBSTER died in Marshfield, Oct. 20, 1878, aged 83 years. He was one of the Plattsburgh volunteers, and had an application for pension pending at the time of his death.

It is not known that any one enlisted from this town, in the war with Mexico.

But when the great rebellion broke out, that intensity of feeling which thrilled from the prairies of the West to the shores of the Atlantic, found an answering tone among our hills, and by our firesides. And as call after call for reinforcements came, the father left his family, the son his parents, in many cases, alas! to return no more.

> They came in serried ranks, the boys in blue,
> Who at their country's call no danger knew;
> Room! room! for Marshfield boys, our
>   soldiers true.

LIST OF SOLDIERS FURNISHED FOR WAR OF
THE REBELLION.

BY GEN. P. P. PITKIN, OF MONTPELIER.

Alphonso Lessor, Co. D, 2d Reg. Pro. Lt., wd.
Patrick Mahar, F, 2. Wd. & dis. Oct. 31, 62.
Alvah H. Miles, F, 2.
Chauncey Smith, D, 2. Died of disease in
army.
David P. Bent, G, 4. Died ; buried at Wash-
ington.
Byron Bullock, G, 4. Died of disease in army.
Hiram Hall, H, 3. Died.
John E. Aiken, G, 4.
Robert A. Spencer, G, 4.
Edward W. Bradley, F, 6. Wounded.
Homer Hollister, F, 6. Wounded in hand.
Asa H. Winch, 1st Bat. Died at New Orleans.
Joshua D. Dunham, 2d Bat. Died at New
Orleans.
George W. Nownes, C, First Cav.
Ira Batchelder, C, First Cav. Wounded.
Josiah O. Livingston, I, 9. Pro. Capt. Co. G,
Oct. 19, '64.
George N. Carpenter, I, 9. Pro. 1st. Lieut.
Benjamin F. Huntington, I, 9.
Vilas Smith, I, 9. Lost overboard Steamer
U. S. near Fortress Monroe.
John Q. Amidon, I, 11.
Jackson Blodgett, I, 11. Died.
George H. Wheeler, I, 11.
Harvey L. Wood, I, 11. Deserted.
Benj. F. Shephard, Jr., I, 11. Died in Hosp.
at Montpelier.
Robert H. Tibbetts, I, 11. Killed in battle.
Alvah A. Cole, I, 11.
Elbridge G. Wilson, I, 11. Killed in battle.
Francis H. Felix, I, 11. Injured in shoulder.
John W. Huntington, I, 11.
Lorenzo D. Mallory, C, 1st Cav. Pris'nr at
Andersonville ; exch'd, died on way home.
William R. Gove, C, 1st Cav.
Charles Nownes, C, 1st Cav.
Thaddeus S. Bullock, G, 4. Died in hospital.
Nathaniel Robinson, G, 4. Ball in hand,
cannot be extracted.
Calvin R. Hills, G, 4. Wounded.
William A. Webster, A, 4. Died at Ander-
sonville.
Wesley P. Martin, G, 4.
David B. Merrill, A, 4.
Smith Ormsbee, G, 4. Shot on picket, died
from wound.
Samuel Wheeler, A, 4.
John Bancroft, C, Cav. Died.
Parker S. Dow, C, 8 Regt.
Frederick H. Turner, H, 11.
David K. Lucas, 3d Bat.
Edmund H. Packer, 3d Bat.
Allen Phelps, Frontier Cav.
Moses Lamberton, do. do.
Edward L. Wheeler, do. do.
Leonard H. Fulsome, do. do.
Frank L. Batchelder, E, 4 Regt.
Ira Ainsworth, E, 4.
Patrick Moore, D, 8.
Lysander E. Walbridge, E, 8.
Theron T. Lamphere, E, 8.
Hiram Graves, K, 2.
Thomas Witham, K, 2. Died, prisoner.

George H. Nelson, D, 2. Badly wounded.
David Powers, D, 2.
Henry A. Rickard, D, 2.
Joseph S. M. Benjamin, B, Cav.
Francis H. Ketchum, C, " Badly wound-
ed with shell.
Eri McCrillis, C, Cav. Died at Andersonville.
Geo. W. Nownes, C, Cav. Died Andersonv'e.
Cyrus Farnsworth, H, 4 Regt.
Horace Burnham, C, Cav.
Charles M. Wing, B, Cav. Leg broken.
Norman W. Johnson, F, 2 Regt. Ball thro.
body and wrist, lived.
John O. Morse, I, 9. Died.
James H. Carpenter, H, 11.
John Graves, Jr. H, 11. Died at Andersonville.
Solon H. Preston, H, 11.
William W. Willey, H, 11.
Walter H. Morris, G. 3. Wounded.
Charles H. Newton, G, 4. Wn'ded with shell.
James Aylward, E, 17. Died.
John H. Amidon, I, 11.
Charles T. Clark, E, 17. Died.
James Clark, C, 17. Died.
William G. French, E, 17. Died.
Clark J. Foster, E, 17. Badly wn'ded in leg.
Benj. F. Huntington, E, 17.
Daniel Hogan, E, 17.
Wm. E. Martin, E, 17. 1st Lieut.; killed be-
fore Petersburg.
Harvey L. Batchelder, C, 13.
Martin L. Chandler, " "
Eli S. Pitkin, C, 13.
Charles A. Davis, C, 13.
Hudson J. Kibbee, " "
Sereno W. Gould, " "
Charles E. Shephard, C, 13.
Albert Sargeant, C, 13.
Willard M. Austin, C, 13.
Orson Woodcock, " "
Rufus H. Farr, C, 13.
Benjamin B. Buzzell, C, 13.
David Huntington, " "
Joseph Simmons, C, 13.
Lucius D. Nute, " "

In 1863 a draft was ordered; 34 men
were drafted, but only one, Cottrill Clifford, went into the service; 22 paid their
commutation money. Clifford served his
time, was discharged, and accidentally
killed on his way home. I do not find his
name in our list of soldiers ; probably he
was put in to fill up some regiment sep-
arately from our other men.

There went out 98 from us, 28 of whom
never returned. A few were brought back
to be buried, but most of our dead sleep on
Southern soil. In the vigor of young
manhood they went, one and another,
who were household treasures.

"The loved of all, yet none
O'er their low bed may weep."

Perhaps the last news of them was, "seen
on the battle-field," or "taken prisoner,"

and then long months elapsed ere one word could be heard to stay the anguish of suspense. At last came the fearful, "Died at Andersonville."

MONTPELIER & WELLS RIVER RAILROAD.

When the history of Marshfield was written eleven years ago, we had no railroad. About this time a charter was granted for the Montpelier & Wells River road, which passes through our town about a mile from the village. The town bonded itself in the sum of $17,500, and private subscriptions made up the sum of $30,000. All is paid but about half the bonds.

The first train of cars went through here Nov. 29, 1873. Of course the rejoicing was great.

A year or two later we were connected with the rest of the world by telegraph. The advantage to the public is not easily estimated. The railroad is doing good business. L. D. Nute is station agent and telegraph operator. A private telegraph is owned and run by George A. Putnam and L. D. Nute, from the depot to Putnam's store, where the post-office is located. Mr. and Mrs. Putnam are telegraph operators.

THE THANKS OF THE WRITER

are due to James Pitkin, Andrew English and E. S. Pitkin, Esqs., and others, for the assistance rendered her in this work; also to Miss Anna Pitkin, of Montpelier, for the loan of her father's journal.

—

[We have known our excellent historianess of Marshfield more than 20 years. Mrs. Pitkin was a favorite contributor in our "Poets and Poetry of Vermont," (1858,) in which see from her pen, "The Young Emigrant," "The Fugitive Slave," pages 333, 334. So well has Mrs. Pitkin written for us, and for the Montpelier papers in the past, *Zion's Herald* and other papers, we cannot forbear, not solicited by her, but of our own good will, to place a little group selected from her poems at the foot of her history here—Ed.]

A THOUGHT.

BY MRS. HANNAH C. PITKIN.

For thee, busy man, in a forest lone
A shoot hath started, a tree hath grown.
The axe-man, perchance, may have laid it low
For thy narrow house—it is ready now,
All ready—but mortal, art thou, art thou?

Maiden, thy dream of affection so warm,
Trust not. The shroud to envelop thy form
Is woven, is coming, by wind or wave;
'Tis thine, by a stamp which no mortal gave,
Thou canst not turn from the path to the grave.

Art thou toiling for wealth, the weary day,
Or thirsting for fame—there's a pillow of clay
On a lowly bed, 'tis waiting thee there,
The mould and the worm thy pillow will share;
Spirit, Oh, where is thy refuge—Oh, where?

TO THE ITINERANT'S WIFE.

BY MRS. H. C. PITKIN.

Out on the ocean, dark and wild
  A little bark was driven.
One kindly star looked out and smiled
  A precious boon from heaven;
It warned of threatening near,
Just, just in time the rocks to clear.

I stood upon a point of land
  Where ocean billows came,
A beauteous wave just kissed the strand,
  Then seaweed swept again.
'Twas gone, to come again no more,
But left a gem upon the shore.

A wanderer lone mid desert's waste,
  Beneath a burning sky,
Sank down at last despairingly,
  He felt that he must die,
My Island Home, so dear to me,
I never, never more may see!

Oh God! he cried. A tiny flower
  Just caught his closing eye,
And in its winsome loveliness,
  It seemed to whisper "try."
God lives, take heart, so o'er the main
He found his Island Home again.

So sister, like the star be thine
  To bless the tempest driven,
And point to poor despairing ones
  The narrow way to Heaven,
And in the wanderer's darkest hour,
Sweetly to win him like the flower.

In blessing be thou ever blest,
  Cheer age, and counsel youth,
And ever where thy pathway lies,
  Scatter the gems of truth.
And hear, when Death is lost in Life
Blessings on the Itinerant's Wife.

FROM AN HISTORICAL ACCOUNT OF MARSHFIELD.

CONTRIBUTED BY REV. GEO. E. FORBES IN 1879.

[After the Legislature of Vermont had approbated and passed the General Resolutions of 1878, to assist in finishing this work, the MS. history of Mrs. Pitkin, furnished to us for the work in 1869, having been sent to the Claremont Manufacuring Company of New Hampshire, and by them withheld four years, with the other Washington County papers sent, under their proposition to immediately print. We wrote to Mrs. Pitkin for a duplicate of her history. Unable, from the infirmities of her age and feebleness, from fully undertaking to so do, she engaged the assistance of Rev. Mr. Forbes, who gave us a very reliable and pleasant paper of about half the length of Mrs. Pitkin's paper, with which we were pleased and should have published, had we not fortunately meantime recovered Mrs. Pitkin's papers, which as they are the fullest record, as she was first invited to write, and is so eminently a Washington County woman, daughter of old Gen. Parley Davis, of Montpelier, and a long-time honored and beloved resident of Marshfield, we are assured no other writer could be so acceptable to Marshfield, and none other to the County, and so have given the papers of Mrs. Pitkin in full, nearly; and will here but append a few extracts from the paper by Mr. Forbes, containing information or points in it not in Mrs. Pitkin's paper; while we feel to express under the circumstances more thanks to Mr. Forbes than if able to give his paper more fully—Ed.]

Marshfield is situated in the eastern part of the County, and lies on both sides of the Winooski river, which flows through it from north to south. The soil is a mixture of clay and loam; the surface broken and hilly, is divided into productive farms. The river valley, and that part of the town lying west of it, contains the best tillage land, which has very largely been brought under cultivation. The eastern part, more rocky, is used principally for pasturage; although in the eastern part in some sections there are some good farms.

The original forests were heavy timbered with maple, beech, birch, spruce and hemlock, and some elm, fir, cedar and pine. In the eastern part there yet remains a considerable growth of spruce and hemlock, but it is rapidly being cut off for lumber. Sugar-maples are to be found in all parts of the town, producing quite as abundantly of sugar as in any other part of New England.

Besides the Winooski river privileges there are two or three streams which furnish good water-power the larger part of the year. It has not been utilized to any large extent, however, hence the town is not noted for its manufacturing interests. Molly's Falls, on Molly's brook, about a mile from the village, in a distance of 30 rods the water falls between 200 and 300 feet in a series of beautiful cascades. During high water the roar of these falls can be heard for several miles. A good view of these falls can be obtained from the road leading to Cabot. There is also a very pretty cascade on Nigger-head brook, about a third of a mile south of the village, where it is crossed by the road leading to the depot. The town has only one village, which is situated on the Winooski river, about a mile from the Cabot line. The Montpelier & Wells River R. R. crosses the town, running nearly parallel with the river from Plainfield until within a mile of the village, when it makes almost a right angle to the east, passing Nigger-head pond, and threading its way through a notch in the mountains to the Connecticut river. The Marshfield station on this road is one mile from the village, and 15 miles from Montpelier.

It is not known what white men first visited the town's location. This township was purchased of the Stockbridge Indians, (see Mrs. Pitkin's paper,) but it is not certain whether these Indians ever occupied this territory. At the time of the purchase by Mr. Marsh, they were residents of New Stockbridge, Montgomery Co., N. Y.

When the first settlers picked their dwelling-places, Mr. Pitkin settled upon the river near the place where Bowman P. Martin now resides; Messrs. Dodge and Spencer settled further south and west on the higher land. Here was the birth-place of the first child born in town, a son to Mr. and Mrs. Ebenezer Dodge, Sept. 17, 1794, the place of his birth about a mile north of Plainfield village; the place is still owned by descendants of the Dodge family.

The first "burying-ground" was purchased by, and for the use of the town. The first interment therein that has a stone to mark the spot was the infant twin sons of Joshua and Ruth Pitkin, died January 9, 1800. Stephen Pitkin, Jr., donated the land for the village cemetery, and the first interment in it was his adopted daughter, Eunice Sweeny.

There have been five church organizations in town. At present there are but three, as the Christian, and Calvinistic Baptist have become extinct. There have been 11 school districts in town. The present number is 10, each of which has a school of from 20 to 30 weeks per year. The school in village district has two departments, but employs two teachers only during the winter term, as a rule. The town has no academy, but competent teachers hold select schools at frequent intervals, affording educational facilities for those wishing to remain in town. And the seminaries at Montpelier and Barre, as well as academies in the vicinity, have drawn a considerable number of students from this town. There are but two persons, however, from this town who have received a full collegiate education. Rev. Marcus M. Carleton, missionary in India, and Prof. Curtis C. Gove, Principal of High School at Westport, N. Y.

The principal business of the town has been, and still is, farming. At present there is but little manufacturing being done. There is 1 boot-shop for making men's thick boots and overshoes, 2 harness-shops, 1 tin-shop, 1 photograph saloon, 2 cooper-shops, where are manufactured butter and sugar-tubs, and sap-buckets. Six saw-mills, one clap-board and three shingle mills. Two of the saw-mills are run by steam; the rest by water-power; one cheese-factory, and 1 starch factory. There is 1 blacksmith shop, 2 wheelwright shops, and 3 carpenter-shops, There is a hotel, and a patent medicine laboratory. There are 3 stores, and 3 churches. The town cannot boast of a lawyer. It has 3 doctors, Asa Phelps and George M. Town, allopathic; J. Q. A. Packer, homœopathic.

The town representatives from 1870 to 1879 have been: Moody Bemis, George A. Putnam, L. W. Pitkin, D. M. Perkins.

The population in 1840, was 1,156; in 1850, 1,102; in 1860, 1,160; in 1870,

1,072. The decrease which the census of 1870 shows, is doubtless owing to the abandonment of some of the smaller and most unproductive farms, and the Western emigration of many of the younger men.

LEWIS BEMIS.

There are a few pensioners of the war of 1812 yet living. One of the soldiers of this war, Lewis Bemis, enlisted at Barnet in 1808. His son, Daniel H. Bemis, of Lancaster, Mass., writes of him: "He enlisted at Barnet in 1808, and served 5 years in the 4th Reg't. of Regular U. S. Infantry. He was with Harrison in his march through the wilds of Ohio in pursuit of the Indians, and was in the battle of Tippecanoe, when over half of the men in his company were killed or wounded. The man on either side was killed, and he was slightly wounded in the face by a rifle ball. He was in 11 battles and 13 skirmishes with the Indians. He used to relate to his children the story of the soldiers' sufferings while on their march to join Hull, and through Ohio; how their thirst was so intense, that when they reached Lake Erie, in spite of their officers, large numbers threw themselves on the beach, and drank until they died from the effects of it. He was under Hull when he surrendered at Malden, near Detroit, and was a prisoner 26 weeks, during which time he suffered greatly, both for want of water and decent food. Their bread, he used to say, bore the mark on the package in which it was enclosed, 1804. He was paroled, and went from Halifax to Boston, where he arrived a few days before the term of his enlistment expired. He soon after enlisted again in a Company of Light Artillery, with which he went up and joined Gen. Macomb's army the day before the battle of Plattsburg. A part of the battery was stationed at the bridge-head at Plattsburg, and the remainder sent to Burlington, to prevent the British from landing and destroying that place. He was with that portion of the battery sent to Burlington, and so did not have any active part in the battle; but assisted in burying the dead. He was one of the party who

buried the British dead after the engagement. He was discharged after peace
was ratified, having served in all about 6
years and 6 months; 5 years under the
first enlistment in the 4th Infantry, and 18
months in the Light Battery. He died in
1855, at Clinton, Mass., where he is buried,
aged 73."

IRA SMITH.
BY REV. GEORGE E. FORBES.

He was the son of Joshua and Keturah
Smith; was born in Woodstock, Conn.,
Jan. 22, 1800. At 11 years, he came with
his parents to Marshfield. They moved
on to the farm now owned and occupied
by J. E. Eddy. During his minority, Ira
worked on the farm summers and attended
school winters until he was 18. The school-
house then stood near the present residence of Webster Haskins. Soon after
there was a school-house erected where
the village now stands, in which he taught
the first school. He was paid in grain, to
the value of $12 per month, boarding him-
self. In 1821, he purchased 300 acres of
wild land lying around the present site of
the Marshfield depot, which he cleared,
and cultivated 15 acres, spending a part of
his time there, and the balance in working
out, until he was 29, when, Jan. 4, 1829,
he was married to Hannah Jacobs, and
they settled at first on his cleared land,
but a short time after, as he purchased, and
they removed to, the home of his parents,
where they lived 11 years. For about 4
years after selling the home farm, he
rented different places, but in 1844, purchased a farm on which the remainder of
his life was spent. He died Sept. 18, 1880,
leaving a widow, one son, Orrin, who lives
on the homestead, and two daughters, now
Mrs. Levi Benton, of Marshfield, and Mrs.
C. H. Newton, of Montpelier. One son
died in the army, and a daughter married
E. B. Dwinell, but died a few years after,
and 4 children died quite young. Mr.
Smith held many of the town offices, being
regarded by the citizens as a man of worth
and integrity. He represented the town
in the Legislature during 1844-5. In politics he was a Democrat, and never failed
by his vote to express his faith in the doc-
trines of his party. His last public act
was to rise from the sick bed to which he
had been confined for several days, and go
to the polls to deposit his ballot for the
several State officers. He believed in the
vital principles of religion, but in accord-
ance with the general character of the
man, his faith found expression in deeds
rather than in word. In religious sympathy he was a Universalist, and gave his
influence and means to promote the interests of that society in town. His morals
were always above reproach. He was
temperate in deed and in word; drank no
intoxicating liquors, no tea or coffee, and
never used tobacco in any form; was fru-
gal and industrious, and consequently was
enabled to acquire a good property, while
generously responding to many calls for
the promotion of educational and benevolent enterprises.

He possessed an indomitable will and
wonderful endurance from the time that he
hired out as a laborer, at 9 years of age,
until he abandoned active toil, a short
time before his death. He met all duties
with a manly spirit, and evinced his willing-
ness to obey the primal law of life—labor.
He had a remarkably strong constitution,
and when his "golden wedding" was celebrated in 1879, he seemed nearly as hale
and hearty as a man of 60 years, though
even then there were premonitory symp-
toms of the disease which caused his death.
For nearly 2 years he suffered from a
cancer on the lower lip, and during the
latter half of this time, especially, did he
endure extreme pain and inconvenience in
taking food. But under all these trials he
exhibited great fortitude, and died resigned to his Maker's will. His funeral
was attended by a large concourse of citizens besides the numerous relatives, thus
testifying of the esteem in which he was
held by the entire community. The funeral services were brief; no formal eulogy
was pronounced; his life had preached its
sermon, and with a few words of comfort
to the bereaved ones, the last sad rites
were ended, and the body of this worthy
man was borne to its final resting-place.
His age was 81 years. "Though dead, he

yet speaketh," in his good, solid, practical life.

UNIVERSALIST CHURCH.
CONTINUED.

The Rev. Geo. E. Forbes continued as pastor until May, 1880. For 1 year succeeding this date the church had only occasional preaching services, and during this time its numbers were diminished by the death of two members. In May, 1881, the Rev. Eli Ballou, D. D., was engaged as pastor for one-half the time. This engagement continues at present, (Aug. 18, 1881.)

MARSHFIELD VOTED FOR THE GAZETTEER at the town-meeting held March 4, 1879, to send a subscription to Miss Hemenway for the whole work, attested by E. L. Smith, town clerk.

MIDDLESEX.

BY STEPHEN HERRICK, ESQ.

The town of Middlesex was chartered June 8, 1763, by Benning Wentworth, Esq., then Governor of the Province of New Hampshire, to the following grantees: Jacob Rescaw, Benjamin Crane, 3d, Seth Trow, Richard Johnson, Lawrence Egbert, Jr., James Campbell, David Ogden, Matthias Ross, Jonathan Skinner, Jehial Ross, Ebenezer Canfield, Daniel Ogden, Jonathan Dayton, Jr., Lawrence Egbert, Samuel Crowell, William Bruce, Robert Earl, Patridge Thacher, Joshua Horton, Job Wood, George Ross, Cornelius Ludlow, Nathaniel Barrett, Esq., Jeremiah Mulbard, John Roll, Jr., Joseph Newmarch, Nathaniel Little, Henry Earl, Richard Jennee, Esq., Gilbert Ogden, John Little, George Frost, Daniel Ball, Samuel Little, 3d, David Morehouse, Jr., Thomas Woodruff, John Force, Joseph Raggs, Jr., Capt. Isaac Woodruff. Daniel P. Eunice, Jacob Brookfield, Jonathan Dayton, 3d, Isaac Winors, Samuel Meeker, Jr., David Loomeris, John Cory. Jr., Alexander Carmica, David Bonnel, James Seward, Stephen Potter, Nathaniel Potter, Stephen Wilcocks, Thomas Dean, Jonas Ball, Amos Day, John David Lamb, William Lamb, William Brand, James Colic, Jr., William Hand, Robert French, Samuel Crowell, Jonathan Woodruff, Ezekiel Ball, Aaron Barnett.

THOMAS MEAD AND THE FIRST SETTLERS.

The first settler in this town 20 years subsequent to the above date made his first settlement here. Having succeeded in finding one of the best lots of land in Washington County, on the Onion River, 5 miles from Montpelier village, here Mr. Thomas Mead made his excellent location. The second settler, JONAH HARRINGTON, chose his location about 2½ miles from Montpelier on a superior lot of land. SETH PUTNAM came soon after with three brothers, Ebenezer, Jacob and Isaac, who were soon followed by Ephraim Willey, Ebenezer Woodbury, Ira Hawks, Solomon Lewis, Samuel Mann, Isaac Bidwell, Henry Perkins, Daniel Harrington, Samuel Montague, Nathaniel Carpenter, Daniel Smith, Hubbard Willey, Asa Harrington, Joseph Chapin, William Holden, Lovewell Warren, Jesse Johnson, Joseph Hubbard, David Harrington, Jonathan Fisher, Isaac Bidwell, Oliver Atherton, Robert McElroy, Nathan Huntley.

ORGANIZATION OF THE TOWN.

Copy of a record in the town clerk's office in Middlesex:

To Seth Putnam, Esq.:—

Sir—We, the Inhabitants of the town of Middlesex, petition your honor to grant a Warrant for the purpose of calling a town-meeting in said town of Middlesex on Monday, the 29 of March instant, at ten of the clock in the morning, for the purpose of Organization of said Town.

EDMOND HOLDEN,
LEVI PUTNAM,
SAMUEL HARRIS,
ISAAC PUTNAM.

Chittenden, March 15th, 1790.

In pursuance of the foregoing Petition, By the authority of the state of Vermont, you are hereby directed to warn all the freeHolders and other inhabitants of the town of Middlesex to meet at the dwelling-house of Seth Putnam, Esq., in said Middlesex, on Monday, the 29th day of March Instant, at ten of the clock in the morning. Firstly to choose a moderator to govern said meeting.

2dly, to choose a town Clerk, Selectmen, Town treasurer, and all other Town officers according to Law, and of your doings herein make due return according to Law.

Given under my hand at said Middlesex, this 15th day of March, A. D., 1790.

To Levi Putnam, freeholder of the Town of Middlesex. SETH PUTNAM,
Justice of the Peace.

Served the within Warrant by notifying the inhabitants by setting up a true copy at my dwelling house in Middlesex.

March 16th, 1790.

LEVI PUTNAM, *Freeholder*.

Mar. 29, 1790, According to within warrant being met, made choice of Levi Putnam, Modera'r ; Seth Putnam, Town Clerk ; Thomas Mead, Levi Putnam and Seth Putnam, selectmen ; Edmond Holden, constable and collector of taxes ; Lovewell Warren, Town Treasurer ; Jonas Harrington, Surveyor.   Attest,

SETH PUTNAM, T. C.

Recorded May 7th, 1790.

I find by the records in the town clerk's office that the honorable Seth Putnam was chosen to represent the town of Middlesex on the first day of September, 1807, and that the number of votes cast for representative was 30. The general reader will at first think it strange, to say the least, that the town had no representative till 17 years after its organization ; but may remember Vermont was not admitted into the Union until Feb. 1791.

SAMUEL MANN, one of the first settlers of the town, bought two lots of land 3 miles N. E. of Middlesex village. I bought the same lots Oct. 19, 1820, at which time I commenced an acquaintance with the inhabitants of Middlesex. I came into the town with my family Mar. 16, 1821. The venerable Thomas Mead was then very far advanced in years, and had a great number of children and grand-children. His son Thomas, and grand-son Thomas, lived in his house, and also Jacob Morris, who married his daughter, making in all four families. Mr. Thomas Mead was a church-going man and was much respected. There was no meeting-house in town until several years after I came, except a small house of one story, which was built by a very upright and benevolent man,

SAMUEL HASKINS,

who built it at his own expense to present to the Methodist church, which was then in a prosperous state here. He owned a saw-mill and grist-mill, and an oil-mill. While he was grinding large cakes of oil-meal, one of the stones, 6 feet or more in diameter, broke away from the axle-tree or shaft, and threw him backward against the oil-trough, and broke both of his legs. The stone which remained attached to the axle-tree rolled around swiftly against the other, crushing them nearly off, until the sufferer was released by a neighbor, who took away the stone and conveyed him to his house. Two physicians were soon in attendance ; both limbs were taken off, but the good man's sufferings soon ceased, and he passed away calmly. I was standing by to behold the solemn sight, and could truly say :

" How still and peaceful is the grave
  When life's valu tumult all is passed ;
  The appointed house by Heaven's decree
  Receives us all at last."

After the death of this generous man, the house was changed from a meeting-house to a dwelling-house, and thus remains. It stands near the S. E. corner of the town cemetery, owned and occupied by a grand-daughter of the deceased and her husband.

LOVEWELL WARREN,

one of the first settlers, was town treasurer in 1790. He was much esteemed by his neighbors. Leander Warren, a son of Lovewell, represented the town several times, and was much esteemed by his townsmen. Rufus Warren, a son of Leander, has also represented the town.

HON. SETH PUTNAM

had 3 sons. Holden, the oldest, represented the town several times. Roswell, the second, was an estimable citizen, much esteemed, and the reverend George Putnam was a minister of the Gospel, much esteemed. Hon. Seth Putnam made the town a present by deeding to the town a small lot of land for a cemetery, where his remains and the remains of a part of his family are buried. Their graves are enclosed by an iron fence. Almost all the first settlers of Middlesex were living here when I came. I think the number of men was about 210 who were heads of families, and they have all passed away from earth.

WILLIAM HOLDEN,

one of the first settlers, bought a lot of land about 1¼ miles from the village, the

VERMONT HISTORICAL MAGAZINE.

farm now owned by William B. McElroy. Mr. Holden had 5 sons, Horace, William, Xerxes, Moses and Philander. Horace Holden, chosen town clerk in March, 1820, held the office 32 years. At the end of 32 years, his son, William H. Holden, was chosen, and held the office 19 years. C. B. Holden, a son of Horace, held the office from March, 1873, to the time of his death, July 25, 1878, and James H. Holden appointed July 27, 1878, by the selectmen; held the office until September 3, 1878. Horace, William, Xerxes, Moses and C. B. Holden represented the town several times each, and have all passed away, and William H. Holden has also passed away.

JOSEPH CHAPIN

was born Oct. 28, 1758. His son, Joseph Chapin, Jr., was born June 25, in Weathersfield, Vt., in 1792. Joseph Chapin, Sr., settled in Middlesex when the town was quite new; his son, Joseph Chapin, Jr., was a farmer, and by industry and good economy, acquired a very handsome property for his children, and left a good name. His wife passed away many years before his departure. She was sister to Horace Holden. Joseph Chapin, Sr., lived to the age of 96 years, and was esteemed by all who knew him.

Joseph Chapin, Jr., had 2 sons. Hinkley, the oldest, was killed instantly. He was a brakeman on the cars, and received the fatal blow when passing through or under a bridge. William Chapin, his son, still survives and has held many important offices in town.

The Chapin family own lots in our beautiful cemetery, and the remains of their loved ones are deposited there. One of Joseph Chapin, Jr's., daughters, with her husband, Otis Leland, are living in sight of our beautiful cemetery, where they often visit the graves of their departed friends— their son, their parents and grand-parents, and brother who was killed on the cars.

JEREMIAH LELAND,

one of the first settlers, removed from Charlestown, N. H. He died soon after, I came to Middlesex, respected by all who knew him; left 3 sons, Rufus, James and

Jeremiah, all of whom have long since passed away, esteemed by all, and their remains are deposited in our cemetery, with the remains of all their partners in life. James, son of Jeremiah, was never married. Jeremiah, Jr., has left 4 sons, all now living, two of whom have represented the town, and Rufus has left two sons, who are now living, worthy men, much esteemed.

EBENEZER PUTNAM,

a brother of Col. Seth Putnam, was a man about 50 years of age when I came to live in Middlesex, in 1821. He was a very pleasant, social man, and worked with me to score timber for a barn. His son, Russel, hewed the timber. Soon after, Russel was taken sick. I visited him several times. His sufferings were very great before he passed away. He left several daughters and one son, whose name was Holden, who was a sheriff of good repute, and enlisted in the last war, and lost his life in the defence of his country.

JACOB PUTNAM,

another brother of Col. Seth Putnam, settled on a branch of Onion river in Middlesex, about 5 miles above Montpelier village. I became acquainted with him soon after I came to the town. He was a man of good understanding. I was associated with him and Nathaniel Carpenter in making an appraisal of all the real estate in Middlesex soon after I came. He died many years since. His son, C. C. Putnam, and C. C. Putnam, Jr., are persevering men and good citizens.

ISAAC PUTNAM, another brother of Seth Putnam, lived in Montpelier, and passed away to the spirit life, leaving a good name and a respectable posterity.

NATHANIEL CARPENTER

was one of the first settlers; voted for town representative in September, 1807; was town clerk in all 9 years, and a justice of the peace, I think, 30 years, or more. He died in the winter of 1837. In 1821, when I came to live here, he lived one mile from our village and 5 miles from Montpelier village. He had 4 sons by a second marriage; two or more by a previous marriage; his four last sons were, N. M. Carpenter, Don P. Carpenter, and Heman and Albert. Don P. Carpenter has been one of the side judges of Washington County Court, and Heman, judge of Washington County Probate Court, and N. M. Carpenter is a respectable and successful farmer. I know less of Albert, as he settled in a distant state.

CAPT. ROBERT MCELROY,

one of the first settlers, lived 2 miles from Middlesex village. His family were an aged mother, who emigrated from Scotland, his wife, 4 sons and 3 daughters. Ira, the oldest son, died single; Harry, the second son, had 3 sons, Clesson R. and H. L. McElroy, and Wm. B. McElroy. Lewis had 2 sons and Jeremiah 2 sons, in all, 7 grandsons. Capt. Robert McElroy and wife, mother and 4 sons, have passed away. Harry McElroy's third son, Wm. B. McElroy, was chosen town clerk, Sept. 3, 1878.

It will be observed by this that Capt. Robert McElroy has left a good record. In addition to the above I think it is my duty to state that Harry McElroy's eldest son, Clesson R. McElroy, was a lieutenant in the army and a valiant officer, held in high esteem by both officers and soldiers, and Harry McElroy's second son, H. L. McElroy, has been superintendent of common schools in Middlesex for several years, and as such highly esteemed.

JESSE JOHNSON

was one of the first settlers, and voted for representative in 1807. He was far advanced in life in 1820. His son, Jesse Johnson, Jr., was a man in the prime of life, and lived about 50 years after 1820, and was for many years associated with Moses Holden, his son-in-law, in trade. They were esteemed by all who knew them, were good economists, and accumulated a large property, and have passed away. They have left no son to perpetuate their names.

EPHRAIM WILLEY

was one of the first settlers, and had 2 sons, Hubbard and Benjamin, who were in

29

the prime of life in 1820. They have all passed away; but have left a great number of children and grand-children to perpetuate their memory, all of whom are respectable citizens, even as their fathers and grandfathers before them were.

RUFUS CHAMBERLIN, ESQ.,

one of the first settlers, was in 1821 a man far advanced in life, and had then living 5 sons and 3 daughters. His oldest son, Clesson, died in Massachusetts. Oliver A. Chamberlin, the second son, and A. L. Chamberlin, the fourth, are still living. Rufus Chamberlin, Esq., and wife, 2 daughters and 3 sons, have passed from this life, but not without leaving children and grandchildren to perpetuate their memory, though most of the grandchildren have passed away. I will name a few: Wm. H. Holden, C. B. Holden, Martha Holden; children of Horace Holden and his wife, Mary Chamberlin, and Mary, also a daughter of Oliver A. Chamberlin. Our town clerk is a son of Harry McElroy and his wife, Mary Ann, dau. of Rufus Chamberlin, both of whom have passed away.

MERCHANTS AND STORES, 1879.

We have three stores in Middlesex village, one owned and occupied by Benjamin Barrett and James H. Holden, one by J. Q. Hobart, and one by N. King Herrick, all doing a good business without danger of failing. Our merchants are as reliable as those of Montpelier, and I choose to patronize them.

We have at this date, Jan. 1879, no physician in town. Nearly all of the people of Middlesex employ the physicians who live in Montpelier village.

MEETING-HOUSES AND CHURCHES.

We have three meeting-houses, all good; one good brick one in the village, near the passenger depot, one built of wood in the center of the town, and another of wood in the small village denominated Shady Rill. They are all kept well painted and in good repair. The one in Middlesex village is now occupied by the Methodists one-half of the time, and seldom at any other time, and it is about the same as to the house in the center of the town. The meeting-house in Shady Rill was built about 30 years ago, by the Freewill Baptists, and it is occupied by those who built it, and their posterity. There was a Congregational church in this town when the brick meeting-house was built, but there is not now. I think it passed away about 1845. The Methodist church has about 36 members at this time. The Freewill Baptist church, I think, is about the same as to numbers.

The Methodist denomination own a good and well-finished parsonage house and out-buildings, all well arranged, near the brick meeting-house in Middlesex.

MICAH HATCH

was a soldier in the Revolutionary war, and was an early settler of Middlesex. He bought two or more good lots of land, 4 miles north of Montpelier village. He had 2 sons, Micah and David; David had 2 sons, Zenas and Gardner. Zenas was drafted and lost his life in defence of his country. A daughter of Micah Hatch was the mother of the Hon. Zenas Upham, one of the side judges of Orange County Court in 1878.

SOLOMON LEWIS

was an early settler of Middlesex, and settled on the North branch of Onion river, 6 miles north of Montpelier village. William Lewis, a son of Solomon, owned and occupied the farm for many years, and said farm is now owned by Lathrop Lewis, a son of the late William Lewis. I could say much in commendation of Mr. Solomon Lewis and his son William, and of his grandson, Lathrop, all of whom have been good citizens.

EZRA CUSHMAN

was one of the early settlers, a respectable merchant, and associated as such with Theophilus Cushman, his nephew, in trade in Middlesex village in the early settlement of the town, was a man in whom the people all had the utmost confidence. He married a daughter of Hon. Seth Putnam. Their son, the Rev. Lewis Cushman, a Methodist minister much esteemed, has been engaged in the ministry more than 30 years, previous to 1879.

CAPT. ZERAH HILLS

was one of the early settlers of this town. He had 3 sons, Lorenzo, Justin and Zerah. Zerah built the house above described, and had it very nearly completed when the Rebel war commenced, and he enlisted in defence of our country, and died in its defence June 25, 1863, lamented by all who knew him.

COL. HUTCHINS

was one of the early settlers of Middlesex. He had two sons, Timothy and Solomon. Solomon married a sister of ex-Governor Paul Dillingham. Solomon Hutchins kept a public house in Middlesex village when the town was quite new. I think the house was the first public house kept in Middlesex. Solomon Hutchins and his immediate family have long since passed away, but leaving a respectable posterity of children, grandchildren and great grandchildren.

March, 1879.

MIDDLESEX CONCLUDED.

BY VOLNEY V. VAUGHN, ESQ.

The township, situated on the north side of the Winooski river, 30 miles from the mouth of the river at Burlington, lat. 44°, 20′, long. 4°, 2′, is bounded N. by Worcester, E. by East Montpelier and Montpelier, S. by Berlin and Moretown, from which it is separated by the Winooski, and W. by Waterbury.

The N. H. charter, by Wentworth, was granted " by command of His Excellency, King George III., in the third year of his reign," and provides:

The township of Middlesex, lying on the east side of French or Onion river, so called, shall be six miles square and no more, containing 23,040 acres.

The first meeting for the choice of town officers shall be held on the 26th day of July next, to be notified and presided over by Capt. Isaac Woodruff, and that the annual meeting forever hereafter for the choice of officers for said town shall be on the second Tuesday of March, annually.

The town was to be divided into 71 equal shares; each one of the 65 proprietors to whom it was granted to hold one share, and 6 shares as usual in the N. H. charters for the Governor's right, the benefit of the Gospel and schools. The Governor's land was a tract of 500 acres in the S. W. corner of the town.

The council of New York established the county of Gloucester in 1770, which included this town, and the first record of a proprietors' meeting found in our town records commences:

A meeting of the proprietors of the Township of Middlesex, on Onion River, in the *Province of New York*, holden at the dwelling-house of Samuel Canfield, Esq., in New Milford, Conn., on Tuesday, ye tenth day of May, 1770.

At this meeting Partridge Thatcher, of New Milford, was chosen moderator, and Samuel Averill, of Kent, clerk.

It was voted to "lay out said township and lot one division of 100 acres to each right," and Samuel Averill was chosen agent to agree with a surveyor and chain-bearers to do the business. It was voted to lay a tax of $3 per right, to pay the expense of surveying, and Partridge Thatcher and Samuel Averill laid out the 1st division as above voted.

The proprietors held a meeting at Kent, Apr. 13, 1773, Samuel Averill, Jr., clerk. Voted $2.50 per right instead of the $3.00 voted before to pay the expense of the surveys.

Oct. 14, 1774, Samuel Averill, Jr., collector, sold 8 lots of land at public auction, to satisfy unpaid taxes voted as above. Partridge Thatcher and Samuel Averill, Jr., bid off 4 lots each, at £1 2s., N. Y. money, per lot.

The first deed of Middlesex lands recorded is from Samuel Averill, Jr., to Samuel Averill of 5 full rights, dated Kent, Litchfield Co., Dec. 30, 1774, and acknowledged before Wm. Cogswell, justice of the peace.

The first proprietors' meeting held in Vermont was at Sunderland, Oct. 13, 1783, Isaac Hitchcock, proprietors' clerk, and the 2d and 3d division of lands were made, and surveys recorded Feb. 9, 1786.

The first proprietors' meeting held in Middlesex was at the house of Lovell Warren, Aug. 14, 1787. Choice was made of Seth Putnam, proprietors' clerk, and adjourned until Nov. 5, same year, and at this adjourned meeting it was claimed that all former surveys or pretended surveys had been made inaccurately, that some of the lots had been laid out within the limits of Montpelier, that proprietors could not find their lots, etc., and it was "Resolved to hold null and void all former surveys or pretended surveys."

It was voted to lay out the 1st, 2d and 4th divisions in 69 lots each, of 104 acres in a lot, the 4 acres being allowed for highways. Where the village now stands, 30 acres were reserved for a mill privilege, and 104 acres of the pine lands just easterly of the mill site for the first mill-builder, if he built a mill within 12 months. This reservation was the 3d, called the white-pine division, which was laid out in about 1-acre lots, and divided among the proprietors the same as the other divisions. The 1st, 2d and 3d divisions were allotted in 1787 and '88, and surveys recorded in September, 1788. Allotted by Gen. Parley Davis, surveyor; Isaac Putnam, hind-chainman; Jacob Putnam, fore-chainman. The 4th division was allotted by Gen. Davis in 1798.

This allotting, if accurately surveyed, would cover 22,162 acres, which would leave 878 acres undivided land, of which each proprietor would own an equal share. This land, which is north-easterly of the Governor's right, has been taken up or "pitched" from time to time, until it is all claimed on titles of original rights.

By an act of the legislature, approved Oct. 30, 1850, so much of the town as is contained in lots numbering 50, 55, 56, 57, 58, 63 and 64, and so much of the undivided land as lies westerly of a line commencing at the most south-easterly corner of lot number 64, and running south 36° west and parallel with the original line between Waterbury and Middlesex to the Governor's right, so called; thence on the line of the Governor's right to the original town line, was annexed to the town of Waterbury, which leaves about 22,000 acres as the present area of Middlesex.

The change in the town line was made to benefit a few families who lived in the west part of the town who could more conveniently attend meetings and go to market in Waterbury than in Middlesex, on account of living the west side of a high range of hills or mountains, that form a natural boundary, and so separate the two towns that only one carriage-road directly connects them. The change brings the town line as now established very near the summit of this range of mountains.

Near the S. E. corner of the town commences a less elevation of land, which extends in a northerly direction a little east of the centre of the town, which unites with the higher range about 4 miles from the south line, and gives the south part of the town a slope southerly towards the Winooski, and the northern and eastern part a slope easterly towards the North Branch of the Winooski, which flows through the N. E. corner of the town.

The surface of the township is somewhat uneven, but the soil is generally very fertile and productive. There are many excellent farms on the hills, and some fine intervales along the river and branch, and although the meadows are not very extensive, they are enough so to form a number of very good and valuable farms.

The land is naturally covered with maple, birch, beech, ash, elm, butternut, red-oak, iron-wood, pine, spruce, hemlock, fir and other smaller trees and bushes such as are common in this part of the State.

The N. W. corner of the town contains about 1200 acres of nearly unbroken forest, covering the mountain and lying along its base, which only needs steam-power in the immediate vicinity, backed by good mechanical enterprise and skill, to make it valuable property.

This town will compare favorably with the other towns in the County for farming and lumbering.

NATURAL CURIOSITIES.

Nature has given our territory fully an average share of the singular and odd, and of the grand and sublime.

Among the oddities is a rocking stone on the farm of William Chapin, near the Centre. This stone, weighing many tons, is so evenly balanced on a high ledge that it can be rocked forward and back with ease. On the mountain west of the late C. B. Holden farm is a high cliff of rocks, from which many heavy pieces of rock have become detached and fallen to the ravine below. These are so placed that they form some curious caverns on a small scale, which are noted hedge-hog habitations. One of these rocks, sheltered by the overhanging cliff from which it fell, which is some 6 feet long, 4 feet wide, and from 1 to 2 feet thick, lies on another rock in such a manner that it projects over nearly half its length, and is so nicely balanced that a man can teeter it up and down with one finger.

A few years ago there stood by the roadside on the farm now owned by Daniel Pembrook, an iron-wood or remon tree, which about 2 feet from the ground divided into two trunks, each about 6 inches in diameter. They grew smooth and nearly straight, and from 1 to 2 feet apart for some 10 feet, where they again united in one solid trunk, which was about 10 inches in diameter; this continued about 3 feet, where it again divided. The two trunks above were similar to the two below for about 10 feet; there it united once more, and above threw out branches and had a "top" similar to other trees of its kind. This tree was cut down by some one who had an eye keener for the useful than for the ornamental.

The only road that directly connects this town with Waterbury, about 1½ miles from the river, passes through a notch between masses of ragged ledges which for many rods rise almost perpendicular on either side to the height of 100 feet or more, with just fair room for a good carriage-road and a small stream of water between.

The channel called the Narrows, worn through the rocks by the Winooski between this town and Moretown, is quite a curiosity. Of this grand work of time Moretown may justly claim a share, but as this town is the most benefited by it, Middlesex history would be incomplete without a description. The channel is about 80 rods in length, some 30 feet in depth, and averaging about 60 feet wide. Where the bridge leading from Middlesex village across to Moretown spans the channel, the width at the top of the cut is less than the depth. Below this bridge for many rods the rocks rise very nearly perpendicular for some 30 feet, appearing like a wall. Above the bridge for many rods they rise on either side to near the same elevation, but not quite so steep, leaving the chasm only a few feet wide at the bottom, and the river runs very rapidly through the channel. At the upper end of the Narrows is a dam and the mills described elsewhere. Just below the bridge, and in direct line with the course of the river above, is a high pinnacle of rocks. When the river is low it runs the north side of this, and when the water is high it flows on both sides, or surrounds it.

By a survey made by the late Hon. Wm. Howes a few years ago, it was ascertained that the fall in the river from below the dam at Montpelier village to the top of the water in the pond at Middlesex was only 5 feet 11 inches.

There are many things that indicate that at some distant day these ledges formed a barrier that obstructed the water of the river, and raised it many feet higher than the meadows along the river above this place, forming a large pond or lake, that flowed not only these meadows but a part of Montpelier, including the greater part of the village, and a portion of the towns of Barre, Berlin and Moretown. About 2 miles above the Narrows the ledge, near where the carriage-road now is, some 50 feet above the present bed of the river, bears unmistakable evidence of the washing of the waters of the river or lake.

While gazing on this wondrous work
Of nature's law, divinely fair,
We feel how great the work of time,
How weak and frail we mortals are.

We feel the feeling grow of awe,
While looking on this rolling tide,
And think these were the works of God,
In which mankind could take no pride.

Along the mountain side in the N. W. part of the town are many rills and brooks, that come rushing down steep declivities and leaping from high precipices, forming

many beautiful cascades and miniature cataracts, which if as great as they are lofty would be supremely grand. Here, too, are found high overhanging cliffs and deep ravines, and all the sublimity common to the mountains of the Verd Mont State.

But when we stand upon the summit of the highest peak, 3,558 feet above Lake Champlain, and cast our eye at a glance over more than 10,000 sq. miles of the surrounding country, looking down over the homes of tens of thousands of our steady villagers and sturdy yeomanry, viewing the well-cultivated plains and forest-covered hills, and beholding the distant mountain scenery, the winding streams and ever-varied landscape, here we find magnificence and grandeur combined.

It might be said sublime and fair,
And lofty are our verdant hills,
And crystal streams from fountains flow
That turn with ease the swiftest mills.
Our plains, how grand, how marked with care,
While each proclaims the work of God;
And man, with thanks and willing hands,
Improves the rich and fertile sod.

For the following very good description of our mountains I am indebted to Wm. Chapin:

MOUNTAINS OF MIDDLESEX.

BY WM. CHAPIN, ESQ.

Near the South-west corner of Middlesex there rises abruptly from the south bank of the Winooski river a range of clearly-defined mountains, that extends about 20 miles, being nearly on the line between Middlesex and Waterbury, and extending between Worcester and Stowe, a little to the east of the line between those towns, and ending near Elmore pond, in the Lamoille valley. These mountains are called "The Hogbacks" in some of the earlier geographical works of Vermont, but that name now applies only to the south end of the range near the Winooski.

The most conspicuous points in Middlesex are locally known as "Burned Mountain," "White Rock," or "Castle Rock," and "Mt. Hunger." This Mt. Hunger is nearly on the line between Middlesex and Worcester, and a little east of the corners of the four towns, Middlesex, Worcester, Stowe and Waterbury. Its height is 3648 feet above the sea.

As the topmost stone of this mountain, which is the highest point in the range, is doubtless in the town of Worcester, that town may perhaps fairly claim the honor of having within its limits one of the pleasantest places of public resort to be found in New England.

The name of Mt. Hunger was given by a party of hunters who went out from Middlesex Centre on a winter's day, some 60 years ago, to hunt for deer on this mountain. Lost in the vast woods, they had to stay out all night, with nothing to eat save one partridge, and that without salt or sauce. When they got home the next day, half starved and wholly tired out, they said they had been on *Mount Hunger*. Not an inviting name, certainly, but very appropriate to the occasion.

The only comfortable way and road to the summit at the present time is in and through Middlesex. From the earliest settlement of the town this has been a favorite resort for all who have had sufficient hardihood of muscle and wind to make the first ascent. But the way was rough, tangled and steep. A better way was needed, and in due time was made. The Mt. Hunger road was commenced in October, 1877, and completed June 1, 1878. It was on its first survey 2 miles and 16 rods in length, extending from the public highway in Middlesex to the summit of the mountain. The first 500 rods was made a good, safe and comfortable carriage road. The last half mile is very steep, and only a foot-path could be made, but the path is so well provided with stairs and other conveniences that children 6 years of age have gone up safely, and men of 86 years have gone up without difficulty. [The late Hon. Daniel Baldwin, of Montpelier, twice after 86 years of age.] Many teams of one to 6 horses drawing carriages from two to 20 persons, have gone up and down this road in the summers of 1878, '79 and '80, without an accident or mishap to any one.

To build such a road, through a dense forest of spruce, birch and maple woods, was no small undertaking, requiring some courage, much capital and a vast amount of hard labor. Thousands of trees had to be dug up by the roots—giant birches that clung to the ground for dear life, well-rooted spruce, and tough beeches and maple; thousands of knolls and hills had to be graded or removed, and hardest of all, thousands of rocks and ledges to be blasted, dug out, or got around in some way.

Hundreds of feet of bridging had to be built across the many little brooks and rills that come down the mountain sides. The longest bridge is in Middlesex, near the Worcester line, and is 137 feet long. At the upper end of the carriage-road is a level plateau that has been well cleared of the undergrowth and made smooth, and here a barn has been built to accommodate travelers with teams. The grade of the road is necessarily somewhat steep, but as it is a continual rise from the foot to summit, no very sharp or steep pitches are to be found in the whole length of it.

This road was built by Theron Bailey, Esq., of Montpelier, proprietor of the " Pavilion," and is owned and occupied by him as a toll road, the various land-owners on the route having deeded him the right of way, and some 25 acres of land for building and standing ground at the top.

The construction of this road was under the superintendence of Wm. Chapin, Esq., of Middlesex Centre, and was completed, with the exception of stairs and bridges, in 60 working days, and with a gang of less than 20 men.

Whether this road will be kept up in repair or not, remains to be seen. The mountain top is one of the pleasantest places of earth, and will be visited so long as people inhabit the country; standing in an isolated position, it commands a view of the whole country; to the east, to the White Mountains, west, to the Adirondacks, north, to the Canadian Provinces, and south, to the Massachusetts line; a score of villages, many lakes and ponds, and, best of all, thousands of New England farms and homes.

Among those who visited here in the olden time was the late Daniel P. Thompson, of Montpelier, who climbed up, following the town line for a guide, about 1833, and no doubt much of the sublime mountain scenery so beautifully described in "May Martin," "The Green Mountain Boys," and other Vermont stories, was studied from nature here.

The tops of all of these mountains were covered with timber at the settlement of the town; now some 10 acres are burned down to the bare rock on the top of Mt. Hunger, about the same area on "White Rock," and on Burned Mountain the fire has cleared some 30 to 40 acres. The spaces thus opened afford the finest outlook upon the surrounding country.

> "Now on the ridges, bare and bleak,
> Cool 'round my temples sighs the gale.
> Ye winds! that wander o'er the Peak,
> Ye mountain spirits! hail!
> Angels of health! to man below
> Ye bring celestial airs;
> Bear back to Him, from whom ye blow,
> Our praises and prayers."

Middlesex Centre, 1880.   W. C.

WATER-POWER, MILLS AND FRESHETS.

The town is abundantly watered by springs, brooks and rivers. There are but very few houses in town that are not supplied with a stream of clear, pure, soft water, running from some never-failing spring.

Numerous brooks rise among the mountains and on the hills, and flow across the town. One called Big brook rises N. W. of the Centre, flows a southerly course to near the centre of the town, then flows south-westerly to the Winooski, emptying just above the village.

On this stream, about half a mile from its mouth, has been a saw-mill the greater part of the time for upwards of 60 years, and at different times there have been mills at three other places on the stream, one being near the Centre. The best of these mills, built by Solomon Hutchins about 20 years ago, was destroyed by fire soon after it was completed. The other mills have rotted down, been damaged by freshets and never repaired, or been taken down, and at present there is no mill on the stream; but there is a repair shop, owned by Myron Long, in place of the mill first described.

Along the mountains northerly of the height of land near the Centre, rise many brooks, which, flowing south-easterly and uniting, form a quite large stream, which empties into North Branch about 5 miles from Montpelier village.

The two largest of these brooks unite at Shady Rill, about one mile from the Branch, and here in the year 1824, Jeduthan Haskins and Ira McElroy built a saw-mill on the right bank of the stream, which stood about 4 years, and was washed away by a freshet. It was rebuilt soon after by Haskins on the other side of the stream. This mill stood until about 1850, when it was washed away and never rebuilt. On the east stream of the two that unite at Shady Rill, about ½ mile above that place, a saw-mill was built some years ago. In 1869, or '70, this mill was bought by Isaac W. Brown, of Montpelier, who put in a clapboard mill, which was run by John Hornbrook until 1872.

In 1872, W. H. Billings came from Waitsfield and bought the mill. He ran the old mill 2 years, and his brother, J. J. Billings, went in company with him. The fall of 1875, they built a new mill, 34 by 60 feet, and put in a small engine to run part of the machinery. In this mill they did a good business, which was increasing each year until the mill was burned, May 8, 1880. At that time they had several thousand logs in the mill-yard, and they immediately commenced clearing out the debris of the burned mill, and laying the foundation for a large new mill, 48 feet by 96. They put in a 75 horse-power engine, and commenced cutting out boards and timber July 17, and in the course of the summer they nearly finished the mill and put in all the machinery necessary for cutting, planing and matching boards, and sawing and dressing clapboards. It is now, Jan. 1881, one of the best mills in the State, and capable of turning out 10 car-loads of dressed lumber per month. There is another mill, on another stream, about half a mile west of this mill, now owned by Geo. W. Willey.

In 1815, Esquire Bradstreet Baldwin came from Londonderry, and built a mill where Putnam's mills now stand, on North Branch, about 5¼ miles from Montpelier, since which there has been a mill there.

We are favored by the following description of these mills through the kindness of C. C. Putnam, Esq:

"The north branch of the Winooski, which empties into the main stream at Montpelier, flows through the N. E. corner of Middlesex, about 3 miles, on which is situated one of the best mill privileges in the State, with a fall of 32 ft., on which was erected a mill in 1815, by Bradstreet Baldwin, son of Benjamin Baldwin, of Londonderry, Vt. The mill built by Bradstreet Baldwin, on the above-mentioned privilege, was owned and occupied by several parties until purchased by C. C. Putnam and Jacob Putnam, about 1845. At that time the capacity of the mill was about 100,000 ft. per annum. The old mill was situated on the west side of the stream at the top of the fall. In 1854, was erected a large double gang-mill on the east side of the stream below the fall to take advantage of the 32-feet fall, together with a grist-mill and machinery for dressing lumber. The latter was consumed by fire in 1862. The same year was erected by C. C. Putnam on the same site, the mill now standing, with two large circular saws. Since then have been added to the mill, planers, matchers, edging-saw, butting-machine and band-saw for cutting out chair stock, the capacity of the mill being 2,000,-000 ft. dressed lumber per year. The past year, C. C. Putnam & Son, the present owners, have shipped 150 car-loads of dressed lumber to New Hampshire, Massachusetts, Connecticut and Rhode Island, valued from $25,000 to $30,000. The most of this lumber is cut on their land in Worcester, and floated down the stream. In connection with their lumber business they have a supply store, containing all necessaries for their workmen and public generally, doing a business of from $15,000 to $20,000 per year."

Henry Perkins came to town somewhere about 1800, and built the first grist and saw-mill at the Narrows, where the village stands. He lived in the Widow Aaron Ladd house, one of the two first houses in the village. Soon after, Samuel Haskins built an oil-mill, and Thomas Stowell built a clothing-works mill.

In those early days, when news were conveyed on horseback as the swiftest means; when freighting between here and Boston was mostly done with oxen; before Arkwright had invented the spinning Jenny, or carding-machines were known; when the women did all the carding and spinning by hand; when farmers had to go a great way to mill, and carry their grist on horseback, or on their shoulders; when the meat mostly used was that of wild game, and salt to season it sometimes $3.58 per bu.; when 8 children were called an average family, and 12 or 13 not uncommon, and boys and girls were not afraid of work; when the "goode housewyfe" found ample time to spin yarn from wool, flax and tow, and weave cloth to clothe all in her goodly family, works were then in vogue and built for coloring, fulling, pressing and dressing cloth. In May, 1818, a freshet swept away the clothing-works, but they were soon built up again.

At the time of this freshet Luther Haskins was moving from the farm which he sold to Stephen Herrick in 1820, and which Mr. Herrick still owns and occupies. He got his cattle as far as the river, and could get them no farther on account of high water. Nathaniel Daniels and John Cooms undertook to go from the village in a boat to take care of the cattle. They had proceeded some 20 rods up the river, when the current upset the boat. Cooms swam ashore, and seeing Daniels struggling in the water, was about to swim in to rescue him, when some one who considered the undertaking too dangerous, held Cooms back, and Daniels was drowned.

Nov. 1821, all the mills were destroyed by fire. They were soon rebuilt, with a good woolen factory in place of the clothing-works, which was built by Amplius Blake, of Chelsea, who employed Artemas Wilder to superintend it.

In Sept. 1828, was another freshet, which swept away the factory, grist-mill, oil-mill and saw-mill. Much to the credit of the owners, they went to work with true Yankee courage immediately, and rebuilt the mills in a stronger and more secure manner, and had them all in operation within 2 years. They were not secure enough, however, to withstand the extensive freshet of July, 1830, during which the water in the Winooski probably was the highest ever known since the State was settled, being at its greatest height July 27 or 28, so high it flowed through the village, and a dam was built across the upper end of the street, to turn the current of the river back towards the Narrows. All the mills were raised by the water from their foundations, and sailed off together like a fleet, taking the bridge below with them, until they struck the high pinnacle of rocks a few rods below the bridge, when, with a deafening crash, they smashed, and apparently disappeared in the rolling flood.

The weather in the summer of 1830 was cold and wet up to July 15. From the 15th to the 24th it was mostly clear and excessively warm. During the day of the 15th, the thermometer rose in the shade to 94°, the 16th it rose to 92°, the 17th to 92½°, the 18th to 92°, the 19th to 90°, the 20th to 91°, and the 21st to 94°.

The rain commenced in the afternoon of Saturday, the 24th, and continued till the Thursday following, and is believed to be the greatest fall of water in the length of time ever known in Vermont, the fall at Burlington being more than 7 inches, 3.85 in. of which fell the 26th in 16 hours.

After this freshet, Jeduthan and Luther Haskins built here an oil-mill, which was bought by Enos Stiles in 1835, and successfully operated by him for 33 years. He sold to Y. Dutton, who now owns it. There were many oil-mills in the State at an early day, but they had all been abandoned except two, when Mr. Stiles sold his mill. Mr. Dutton kept the mill in operation for a time after he owned it, and is supposed to be the last one in the State to give up making oil from flax-seed. The Messrs. Haskins also built a grist-mill, which was afterward owned for many years by Geo. & Barnard Langdon, of Montpelier, who sold to L. D. Ainsworth. He has at great

expense fortified it against freshets, and made it a first-class, modern flouring and grist-mill, where he does a good business. He also owns a planing-mill near the grist-mill, and a saw-mill on the opposite side of the river in Moretown, which accommodates many who reside in Middlesex, and has recently bought the old oil-mill of Dutton.

In Oct. 1869, there was a freshet that did considerable damage. No buildings were carried off, but the highways were badly washed, and many bridges carried away. In the town report the following March I find, in addition to a highway tax of 50 cents on a dollar of the grand list, about $3,000 in orders drawn for extra work and expense on highways and bridges, The river was so high that Mr. Ainsworth's saw-mill teetered up and down on the water, and would have been swept away had it not been securely chained to the trees and ledges.

OF THE MINERALOGY

here but little is yet known. Rock crystal is quite common, and some very fine specimens of crystal quartz have been picked up. The largest, most transparent and most perfect specimens have been found in the north western part of the town, along the foot of the mountain. The crystal quartz found here is mostly nearly white. Some of the specimens are traversed in various directions with hair-like crystals of a reddish, yellowish or brown color, and similar to those found elsewhere along the gold formation, so called, that extends through this part of the State. Many stones are also found of which iron enters largely into the formation; and it is claimed that gold has been found in small quantities in the eastern part of the town, but no very valuable mines have yet been discovered here.

MAGNETIC VARIATION.

From an examination of the lines run when the town was alloted in 1788, it appears that the westerly variation of the magnetic needle is now very nearly 4°, so that lines in this town that were run N. 36° E. in 1787, now in 1881 run N. 40° E.

30

ANIMALS.

The first settlers found in the forest of this town, the black bear, raccoon, wolverine, weasel, mink, pine martin (improperly called sable), skunk, American otter, wolf, red fox, black or silver fox, cross fox, lynx, bay lynx or wild cat, star-nosed mole, shrew mole, Say's bat, beaver, musk rat, meadow mouse, jumping mouse, white bellied or tree mouse, woodchuck, the gray, black, red, striped, and flying squirrel, hedge-hog, rabbit, moose, and common deer.

In 1831, a very large moose left the mountain near the notch road, and wandered towards the village of Middlesex. He crossed the Winooski near the eddy just below the narrows, and went across the meadows on the farms now owned by Joseph Newhall and Joseph Knapp in Moretown, passing through a field of wheat on the latter farm. He then crossed Mad river near its mouth, and started in the direction of the large tract of woods near Camel's Hump mountain. This is supposed to be the last wild moose that ever visited Middlesex.

COUNTY MEMBERSHIP.

Middlesex has had the honor to belong to Gloucester County, established by the N. Y. Council, Mar. 16, 1770; Unity, established Mar. 17, 1778; name changed to Cumberland, Mar. 21, 1778: to Bennington, being set to this County by change of county line Feb. 1, 1779: to Addison Co., formed Oct. 18, 1785; to Jefferson County, incorporated Nov. 1, 1810; to Washington Co., the name of Jefferson being changed to Washington in 1814.

Middlesex can boast of being the first town settled in Washington County, as the county is now organized; but it was not the first town chartered, Duxbury, Moretown and Waterbury having been chartered one day first, June 7, 1763.

The altitude at Middlesex village was given by D. P. Thompson at 520 feet above the level of the ocean, probably meaning the elevation of the railroad at that place. He did not claim minute accuracy, but as his estimate was deduced from data of surveys for canals and railroads, it is probably a very near approximation.

CARRYING THEIR VISITORS HOME.

Somewhere between 1825 and 1830, a carpenter and joiner, named Downer, came with his family from Canada to build the house where Elijah Whitney now lives, for Jacob Putnam, and moved his family into a house about 2 miles easterly from Worcester Corner, and owned by Wm. Arbuckle. Downer, for some reason, went to Canada in the winter, and left his wife and four or five children in Worcester, and during his absence they were aided by the town. Danforth W. Stiles then lived where he had made the first beginning, on what is now known as the Nichols' place, above Putnam's Mills, and the Downer family came there and to Jacob Putnam's on a visit. When they were ready to return home, they procured a team, and a boy started to drive them home and take the team back, but they were met near the line by Worcester men, who turned their team around, and told them to drive back into Middlesex, and they returned to Stiles'. Stephen Herrick was overseer of the poor in Middlesex, and Stiles immediately notified him of the affair, and he started with his team to carry the family back. He took the woman and children, and accompanied by Stiles, they proceeded to within about a mile and a half of the house, which distance was through a thick woods, when they were stopped by two men who were felling trees across the road so lively that after considerable effort to cut their way through, they returned with the family to Middlesex, leaving the family at Esquire Baldwin's.

Herrick went home, arriving there about dark, and rode about that part of the town to inform the men of his defeat and procure assistance, and was soon on the road to Worcester again, accompanied by Elijah Holden, with a span of horses and double sleigh to carry the family, and by Horace Holden, Moses Holden, Xerxes Holden, Asa Chapin, Torry Hill, Josiah Holden Abram Gale, John Bryant, George Sawyer, Jeremiah Leland, Sanford White, Lewis Mc-

Elroy and others, in all 22 men, with 9 teams and plenty of axes, bars and levers, with which to clear the track, and they were joined by Stiles when they reached his place, making 23 men. When they reached the woods they were again stopped, this time by 16 Worcester men with axes, who commenced to fell trees into the road, as fully resolved to prevent any further tax to support the Downers, as the Boston "tea party" were to avoid paying the three cent tax on tea. The Middlesex men commenced clearing the road, and proceeded some distance in that way, but the 16 men kept the trees so thick in the road ahead, that Herrick ordered his men to leave the road, and cut a new road through the woods around the fallen trees. In this way they succeeded better, and when the trees became too numerous ahead, they dodged again, and brushed out a road around them, Holden following close behind with the family. As soon as it was certain that they would succeed, Herrick proceeded alone to the house, to protect that from being destroyed, and to have a fire when the woman and children should get there.

Very soon after he reached the house, William Hutchinson entered with a firebrand, and was about to set fire to the house, when Herrick seized him, threw him to the floor, and seating himself on Hutchinson, held him fast. Torry Hill soon entered, with a gruff "whose here?" Herrick answered, "I am here, and here is this little Bill Hutchinson, who bothered me yesterday by felling trees into the road." "Let me have him," said Torry. Herrick released him, when he sprang for the fire, determined to carry out his purpose, but Torry seized him by the collar, and snapping him to the door, gave him a kick that made him say, "I'll go!" "Yes, you will go, and that d—d quick, too," said Hill, giving him another kick, that sent him many feet from the house.

Soon after both parties arrived at the house, and the family was escorted in about daybreak. A war of words followed, with some threatening. One tall, muscular, Worcester man, named Rhodes, stepped out, and threatening loudly, exclaimed, "I can lick any six of you!" Torry Hill sprang in front of him, and smacking his fists together, replied, "My name is six, come on!" but no blows were struck.

Herrick was soon called before Judge Ware, of Montpelier, to answer to the charge of violating the statute against removing any person or persons from one town in this State to any other town in the State without an order of removal. It was proved conclusively that all the home they had was in Worcester, that they were visiting in Middlesex, and desired to return, and that the defendant only helped them to return to their house in Worcester. Wm. Upham and Nicholas Baylies, counsel for Worcester, and Judge Jeduthan Loomis for defendant.

Although the Worcester people were beat, they did not give up, but arranged a double sled so that the driver's seat was attached to the forward sled, and a blow or two with an axe would free the hind sled and body, and taking the family on the sled, they gave them a free ride up north, and when in a suitable place the driver detached the forward sled, and trotted off towards home, leaving the woman and children in the road, comfortably tucked up in their part of the sled, and where they would be under the necessity of soliciting the charity of Her Majesty's subjects in Canada.

POPULATION AND GRAND LIST.

1783, population 1 or 2; 1791, 60; 1793, grand list £280, 10s.; 1800, population 262; 1810, population 401, list $4770.37; 1820, 726, $7623; 1830, 1156, $5720; 1840, 1279, $8240; 1850, 1365, $2952.52; 1860, 1254, $3459.51; 1870, 1171, $3584.63; 1880, 1087, $3128; 1881, $5068.

In 1794, our votes for governor were, for Thomas Chittenden 10, Elijah Paine 4, Louis R. Morris 1, and Samuel Mattocks 1.

It was voted to raise 3d. per pound for making and repairing roads, and 2d. per pound to defray town expenses.

The 5d. on a pound was 2 1-12 per ct. of the grand list, which was a great variation from the 125 to 150 per ct. raised by the town for a few years past for necessary expenses and highways.

SCHOOLS.

The first district extended along the river, but we have not learned the exact location of the first school-house. The district was divided in 1794, the line between lots 6 and 7 on the river, and one school-house built near where the No. 1 school-house now stands, and No. 2 school-house, which was washed away by the freshet of 1818, about half way from the village to where the road leading towards the Centre passes under the railroad.

As the town became settled, new districts were organized until they numbered 13, but at present only 11 support schools, two having been divided and set to other districts. With two or three exceptions, the school-houses have been newly built or repaired within a few years, and are in good condition, and the schools will compare favorably with the common schools of surrounding towns.

The natural division of the township prevents any natural central point in town, and no high schools of any grade have been established here, but many of the larger scholars attend the high schools and seminaries at Montpelier, Barre, Waterbury and elsewhere.

The number of families having children of school age is about 170, and the number of school children only about 225, consequently our schools are all small compared with the schools of early days. About the year 1825 Stephen Herrick taught at the Centre and had 75 scholars; Hubbard Willey sending 10, Ezra Nichols 7, and others nearly as many.

TOWN OFFICERS.

REPRESENTATIVES—Samuel Harris was representative in 1791; Seth Putnam, 1792, '93, '94, '96, '97 to 1800, '3, '4, '5, '7, '8, '13 to '17, '22; Josiah Hurlburt, 1795; Henry Perkins, 1801, '2, '6; David Harrington, 1809 to 1813, '17, '19, '21; Nathaniel Carpenter, 1818, '20; Josiah Holden, 1823, '24, '28, '29; Holden Putnam, 1825, '26, '27, '34, '36, '40; John Vincent, 1830, '33, '35, '37; Wm. H. Holden,

1831; Wm. J. Holden, 1838; Leander Warren, 1841, '44, '58, '59; Horace Holden, 1842, '43; Wm. H. Holden, 1845; Joseph Hancock, 1846, '48; John Poor, 1849, '50; Oliver A. Chamberlin, 1851, '52, '55; Moses Holden, 1853, '54; Geo. Leland, 2d, 1856, '57; James H. Holden, 1860; Jacob S. Ladd, 1861, '62; Wm. E. McAllister, 1863; C. C. Putnam, 1864, '65; Rufus Warren, 1866, '67; Charles B. Holden, 1868, '69; Jarvil C. Leland, 1870; Jacob Putnam, 1872; Sylvanus Daniels, 1874; C. C. Eaton, 1876; Myron W. Miles, 1878; Wm. Chapin, 1880.

SUPERINTENDENTS OF SCHOOLS.—David Goodale was chosen in 1846; Aaron Ladd, 1847, '48, '49; Stephen Herrick, 1850, '56, '66; George Bryant, 1851; Wm. H. Holden, 1852; Wm. Chapin, 1853, '57, '69; H. Fales, 1854; Anson Felton, 1855; H. L. McElroy, 1858, '61 to '66; Marcus Gould, 1859, '60; W. L. Leland, 1867; C. C. Putnam, Jr., 1868, '70; Elijah Whitney, 1879, '80; V. V. Vaughn, 1871 to '79, '81.

FIRST SELECTMEN.—Thomas Mead, 1790, '95, '96; Samuel Harris, 1791; Seth Putnam, 1792, '98, 1803, '4, '14, '15; Levi Putnam, 1793; Josiah Hurlburt, 1794; Leonard Lamb, 1797; Henry Perkins, 1799; David Harrington, 1800, '1, '2; Ephraim Willey, 1805; Elisha Woodbury, 1806; Josiah Holden, 1807, '8; Nathaniel Carpenter, 1809, '11, '13, '18, '19, '20, '21; Joseph Hutchins, 1810; Ephraim Keyes, 1812; Daniel Houghton, 1816; Jacob Putnam, 1817; Horace Holden, 1822, '23, '27, '35, '36, '39, '46, '47; James Jordan, 1828; John Vincent, 1829, '30, '31, '34; Wm. H. Holden, 1833; Aaron Ladd, 1837; S. C. Collins, 1838; Leander Warren, 1840, '57; Geo. H. Lewis, 1841, '42, '53; O. A. Chamberlin, 1843, '44, '48, '49, '51; Samuel Daniels, 1845; George Leland, 1850, '52; C. C. Putnam, 1854, '71, '72, '73; Jacob S. Ladd, 1855; Moses Holden, 1856; Wm. D. McIntyre, 1858; David Ward, 1859, '60, '66, '67, '68; Osgood Evans, 1861; Andrew A. Tracy, 1862; Jas. H. Holden, 1863, '64; D. P. Carpenter, 1865; Jarvil C. Leland, 1869; Jacob Putnam,

1870; Gardner Sawyer, 1874, '81; Elijah Somers, 1875; Wm. B. McElroy, 1876; Hiram A. Sawyer, 1877; Norris Wright, 1878; D. R. Culver, 1879; C. J. Lewis, 1880.

CONSTABLES.—The first constable elected was Edniond Holden, in 1790; Daniel Hoadley, 1791; Jacob Putnam, 1792; Seth Putnam, 1793; Samuel Harris, 1794, '97, '98, '99; Josiah Hurlburt, 1795; Wm. Holden, 1796, 1820; Henry Perkins, 1800; Rufus Chamberlin, 1801; David Allen, 1802; Ira Hawks, 1803; Thomas Mead, 1804, '5, '6; David Harrington, 1807 to '13; Josiah Holden, 1814; Horace Holden, 1817, '19, '24; Luther Haskins, 1818; Daniel Houghton, 1821; Jeduthan Haskins, 1822; Alexander McCray, 1825; Ira McElroy, 1825; O. A. Chamberlin, 1828; Wm. A. Nichols, 1829; Luther Farrar, 1830, '31; D. P. Carpenter, 1833, '34, '36, '37; Gideon Hills, 1835; Stephen Herrick, 1838, '39, '40, '42, '45; Geo. Leland, 1841; Philander Holden, 1843, '44, '46; Geo. H. Lewis, 1847, '48, '49; Wm. H. Holden, 1850, '51; Wm. Slade, 1852; Frank A. Blodgett, 1853, '54; Curtis Haskins, 1855; Ezra Ladd, 1856, '57; Wm. Chapin, 1858, '59; C. B. Holden, 1860 to '74; Myron W. Miles, 1874 to the present, 1881.

OVERSEERS SINCE 1841.—Robert McElroy, 1842; Selectmen, 1843, '75; Jeduthan Haskins, 1844; D. P. Carpenter, 1845; Wm. S. Clark, 1846; Wm. D. McIntyre, 1847, '67, '68, '69; Enos Stiles, 1848, '49; Thomas Stowell, 1850; Benjamin Scribner, 1851, '53, '54, '64; Stephen Herrick, 1852, '58; Daniel B. Sherman, 1855, '56; Geo. R. Sawyer, 1857; W. H. Clark, 1859; C. C. Putnam, 1860 to '67; David Ward, 1870; Elijah Somers, 1871, '72, '73, '74; Seaver Howard, 1876, '77; Putnam W. Daley, 1878; H. A. Sawyer, 1879, '80, '81.

FIRST JUSTICES.—Seth Putnam, 1789, 1811, '12; Nathaniel Carpenter, 1813, '14, '15, '17, '18, '23 to '30, and '33 to '39; Rufus Chamberlin, 1816; Daniel Houghton, 1819, '20, '22; David Harrington, 1821; Wm. H. Holden, 1831, '32, '33; Horace Holden, 1839, '40, '41, '44, nearly

all the time till his death, in 1865; Wm. T. Clark, 1842; Thomas Stowell, 1843; John Poor, 1853; Jas. H. Holden, 1864, '65, '67 to '72; Marcus Gould, 1866; C. C. Putnam, 1872, '73, '74, '75; D. P. Carpenter, '76, '77, '78, '80. Seth Putnam, first justice in 1789, held the office of justice 26 years; David Harrington, 15 years; Thos. Stowell, 12 years; John Poor, 14 years; Nathaniel Carpenter, first justice, 20 years, and Horace Holden was justice at least 38 years.

TOWN AGENTS.—Stephen Herrick, 1842, '52. '57, '58, '60, '61, '66, '72; Geo. H. Lewis, 1843, '44; John Poor, 1845, '53; Holden Putnam, 1846 to '51; George W. Bailey, 1855, '56; Wm. D. McIntyre, 1859; Leander Warren, 1862, '63, '64, '65, '71, '73; D. P. Carpenter, 1867, '68, '69; David Ward, 1870; C. C. Putnam, 1874, '75; Wm. Chapin, 1876, '77, '78, '80, '81; Rufus Warren, 1879.

COUNTY JUDGES.—Hon. James H. Holden, Hon. Don P. Carpenter.

MEMBERS OF CONSTITUTIONAL CONVENTION.—Seth Putnam was member in 1793; Rufus Chamberlin in 1814, '22, '28 and '36; Wm. H. Holden in 1843; O. A. Chamberlin in 1850.

POSTMASTERS.— Theophilus Cushman was postmaster in 1824; Daniel Houghton, 1828; Aaron Ladd, 1829; Moses L. Hart, 1830; Nathaniel Bancroft, 1831; Moses L. Hart, 1832, '33; Hiram McIntyre, 1834 to '38; Ransom B. Jones, 1838, '39; Horace Snow, 1840 to '45; Wm. C. Stowell, 1845, '46; Harris Hoyt, 1847; A. A. Haskins, 1848, '49; A. H. Hayes, 1850; Jesse Johnson, Jr., 1851, '52; Anson G. Burnham, 1853, '54; Geo. H. Lewis, 1855 to '59; Simpson Hayes, 1859, '60, '61; James H. Holden, 1862 to 1881, inclusive.

PHYSICIANS.—A doctor by the name of Billings practiced and resided in Middlesex in 1821; Holdridge soon after; Joseph Lewis, 1825; Samuel Fifield, 1830; Daniel Kellogg, '33; Henry Dewey, '34; H. Dewey and Jona Webster, '35; Jona Webster, '36, '37; Rial Blanchard, '40, '41, '42; David Goodale, '44; F. B. Packard, '45; Chandler Poor, dentist, '45; David Goodale, '46,

'47; A. H. Hayes and B. L. Conant, '48; A. H. Hayes, '49; Horace Fales, '50 '51, '52, '53, '54, '55; J. W. Sawin, '58, '59; H. L. Richardson, '61, '62, '63; O. L. Watson, '65, '66; — Risdon, '79; W. G. Church, '80 and '81.

There might have been physicians in town previous to any named, but I have no such record or evidence. In addition to those named, other physicians have lived in town, among whom is Dr. Zela Richardson, a son of Frederick Richardson, who was one of the first inhabitants of Stowe. The Dr. was born in Stowe in Dec. 1799, went to Castleton when about 22 years of age, and studied for the profession under Dr. Thompson, and commenced practicing according to the Thompsonian system in Brandon and vicinity in about 1824. He moved to Stowe in 1833, and practiced some there till 1840, when he moved to where Silas Mead now resides in Moretown, where he lived until 1846, when he moved across the river to Middlesex village, where he has ever since resided, but for the last thirty years he has nearly discontinued practice.

Among others who have lived and practiced in town a short time each are a doctor by the name of Conant, and Dr. Spicer, Dr. Scott and a cancer doctor named Hill, and perhaps a few others.

THE CLERGY OF THE TOWN.

No record has been found of the first preaching in Middlesex, but it is known that about 1812 the Methodist minister of the Barre circuit preached occasionally in town, and that in 1813,

REV. STEPHEN HERRICK,

of Randolph, took the place of the Barre circuit preacher, and in his circuit visited Middlesex often, and usually held meetings in the school-house, then standing on the north side of the road, very near the present line between the farms now occupied by Stephen Herrick and Joseph Arbuckle. About the same time,

NATHAN HUNTLEY

organized a religious society, commonly called Elder Huntley's church, which in belief and manner of worship was nearest that of the Free Will Baptists. Elder Huntley continued his labors until about 1822, when through his advice the society decided to disband, and many of the members joined the other churches.

ELDER BENJAMIN CHATTERTON

was probably a resident of Middlesex longer than any other preacher that has ever resided here. He was a member of Elder Huntley's church, and was ordained Elder, and commenced preaching soon after the society to which he belonged disbanded. He was a Free Will Baptist, and continued to preach in town occasionally until near his death. He was buried on the farm where he lived, on East Hill, now owned by Charles Silloway.

A list of many of the clergymen who have labored in this town, with dates to show about what time they were preachers in Middlesex: John F. Adams, Methodist, circuit preacher in 1821; E. B. Baxter, Congregationalist, 1831; Benjamin Chatterton, Free Will Baptist, 1834; E. G. Page and Isaiah Emerson, Meth., '35; J. T. Pierce, Cong., '38; Edward Copeland, Meth., '39; Hiram Freeman, Cong., '39 and '40; W. N. Peck, Meth., '40, '41; Elbridge Knight, Cong.; and Wm. Peck and Israel Hale, Meth., '42; John H. Beckwith, Cong., and H. P. Cushman, Meth., '43, '44, '45; P. Merrill, Meth., '46; N. Webster in '47; D. Willis, Meth., '48; E. B. Fuller, Free Will Baptist, '51, '52; Joshua Tucker, Free Will Baptist, '53; L. H. Hooker, Meth., and — Cummings, Free Will Baptist, '54; E. Dickerman, Meth., and O. Shipman, Free Will Baptist, '55, '56; Abner Newton, Meth., '57; J. S. Spinney, Meth., '58, '59; N. W. Aspinwall, '60, '61; W. E. McAllister, Meth., '62, '63; T. Drew, Meth., '64; F. H. Roberts, '65, '66; A. Hitchcock, '67; Dyer Willis, '68; — Goodrich, '69; W. A. Bryant, Meth., '71, '72, '73; O. A. Farley, '74, '75; L. O. Sherburn, '76; C. S. Hurlburt, '77, '78; T. Trevillian, '79, '80; W. H. Dean, '81.

EARLY INCIDENTS AND ANECDOTES.

The following account of the hardships of the first family who made a settlement in this town, from *Deming's Vermont Officers*, 1851, written by Horace Holden:

"Thomas Mead was the first settler in the town and the first in the county. He came from Westford, Mass., having purchased a right of land in Middlesex. He came as far as Royalton with his wife and two or three children. Here he shouldered his gun, knapsack and ax, and set forward alone to find Middlesex, on Winooski river. He went from Brookfield through the woods to the head of Dog river, following that down to its junction with the Winooski, and over that river to Middlesex, having informed his wife that in a given time he should return, unless he sent her word to the contrary. On his arrival he found Mr. Jonah Harrington had made a pitch, and commenced chopping about 2 miles below Montpelier village, where he tarried till morning when he went down the river about 3 miles to the farm now owned by Thomas Stowell, where was formerly a tavern. Here he made his "*pitch*," and a very good one too for a farmer; but had he continued down to the village of Middlesex it might have been much better around the falls in that place.

"He was so pleased with swinging his ax among the trees on his own land, subsisting on such game as he took with wooden traps and his gun, that his promise to his wife was not fulfilled. She became alarmed about him, procured a horse, loaded it with provisions, and set forth to find her husband; following up White river to its source in Granville, thence down Mad river through Warren, Waitsfield and Moretown to its junction with the Winooski about half a mile below Middlesex village, crossed that river and travelled up it about one mile, where, to her joy and his surprise, she found her husband in the afternoon of the third day, doing a good business among the maples, elms and butternuts. From Royalton to Rochester she had a bridle path, then to Middlesex were only marked or spotted trees; was often under the necessity of unloading her horse to get him past fallen timber, and often had to lead him some distance. Mr. Mead's family soon moved into town. Mr. Mead's third son, Joel, was born in Lebanon, N. H., Jan. 18, 1785, she having gone there for better accommodations than Middlesex then afforded. Some time in June, 1785, Mrs. Mead was gone from home on a very cloudy afternoon. Mrs. Mead had to look for her cows, which ran in the woods at large. She started in good season, leaving three small children, one a nursing infant 5 months old, alone in the house. Not hearing the bell on the cows, she took their tracks and followed down the river about 1½ miles, found where they had fed apparently most of the day, but no bell to be heard. She then sought their tracks, and found they had gone down the river, and over "Hog back mountain" to Waterbury, one of the roughest places in all creation, almost; but cows must be found, or children go to bed supperless. She made up her mind to "go ahead," and crossing the almost impassible mountain, and following on, found the cows near the present railroad depot in Waterbury, 6 or 7 miles from home.

"By this time it had become dark, and backed up by a tremendous thundershower, rendered it so dark, that returning over that mountain in the night was out of the question. In this unpleasant situation, she found her way to Mr. James Marsh's, the only hut in that village, and stayed till the first appearance of daylight, when she started her cows for home on a double quick time, where she safely arrived before any of her children had completed their morning nap. She concluded the children had so long a crying spell before going to sleep, they did not awake as early as usual."

About 1795, Mr. Mead kept a few sheep, the only sheep kept in town at that time. He had to keep a close watch of them and yard them nights, to keep them from falling a prey to the bears that were then plenty in the woods.

One morning he found his sheep had broken out of their pen, and following them a short distance northerly from his house, he found a sheep that had been killed and partly eaten by the bears. He returned to his house, took his gun, and started in search of the intruders. He had not proceeded far into the woods before he came in sight of a bear that was on the retreat. He proceeded cautiously after bruin, keeping the bear to the windward, and followed up the hill in a northern direction, until he came near the top of the hill, when he again came in sight of his game, and was skulking along to get a better chance to shoot, when his wife, who had become alarmed by his absence and followed him, came in sight and halloed to him. This started the bear, but a quick shot rolled the sheep-thief over on the ground lifeless. The courageous woman told her husband she had seen another bear while she was searching for him, and they started back in the direction where she had seen it. They had not proceeded far when they came in sight of the second bear, which Mr. Mead also killed with one shot from his faithful gun. They then returned towards where the sheep had been killed, thinking to pick up and save the wool that had been scattered by the carniverous shearers.

As they came in sight of the spot, bruin number three was finishing his morning meal. Mr. Mead immediately settled his account with this bear in the same way he settled with the other two, and went home feeling very well after his before-breakfast exercise. He then informed the few neighbors in town of what he had done, who collected together, helped get the three bears out of the woods and dress them, and all had a "jovial time" and joyful feast.

As the number of settlements in town increased, the bears became less numerous, and when one was seen it was often the occasion of a lively and exciting chase. Sometimes nearly all the men within four or five miles would join in the chase, or surround the woods in which the bear was known to be, and lucky was the animal if he escaped unharmed. Three bears were killed one year at three such hunts. At one time, about the year 1830, a bear was discovered somewhere near the spot where the guide-board now is, near the Centre, and "all hands" started in pursuit. Geo. Holden, then living at the Centre, where Mrs. Daniels now resides, started with a pitchfork, the weapon he happened to have in his hands when he first heard the cry, "a bear! a bear!" The bear was chased down towards the Winooski, and made his way to somewhere near the river on the Governor's Rights, where, being worried by dogs and hotly pursued by men, he undertook to climb a tree that stood on a very steep side-hill. Mr. Holden, then a strong, courageous young man, was near, and ran to the foot of the tree as the bear was hitching up it, and stuck the pitchfork into the bear's posterior. Bruin, not liking to be helped up in that way, dropped upon his hind feet, and threw his fore feet around Mr. Holden's body. Holden at the same time seized the bear "at a back-hug hold," and they tumbled over on the ground, and rolled over and over to the foot of the hill, and some say into the river, where they quit their holds, and bruin ran until he was out of the way of men and pitchforks, and went up another tree. The word spread rapidly that the bear was up a tree, and the men gathered together and commenced shooting at him. Many shots had been fired when Horace Holden put in an appearance. After amusing himself and others present for a few minutes by cracking jokes and telling stories at the expense of the sharp-shooters, who were too excited to kill a bear, he expressed a desire to try it himself. No sooner did his rifle crack than the bear loosened his hold on the tree and fell to the ground.

FIRST SETTLEMENTS IN THE EAST PART OF THE TOWN.

Jacob Putnam settled where Elijah Whitney now lives in 1802; Micah Hatch on the old Hatch place, so-called, the same year; Wm. Lewis on the Lathrop Lewis farm in 1805; John Arbuckle where Putnam Daley now lives, about 1808; Lewis McElroy where Dudley Jones now lives, in 1822; Caleb Bailey and —— York lived on the George Herrick farm in 1823; Ichabod Cummings began on the Ziba Smith farm in 1824, lived there one year, and removed the next year to the farm where he with his Oramel, now live ; Daniel Colby lived on the farm where Frank Maxham and son now live, in 1826.

The most ancient writings with a pen in town, are probably in the possession of James Vaughn, among which is a book commenced by George Vaughn in Oct. 1687 ; the writing done by him being very neatly executed, and a commission of 1696, given here *et literatem :*

"William Stoughton Esqr Lieutent Governour and Comander in chief in and over his Matys Province of the Masssachusetts Bay in New England. To Joseph Vaughn Greeting, By virtue of the power and authority in and by his Matys Royal Commission to me granted, I do by these presents constitute and appoint you to be Ensign of the Foot Company of Militia in the Town of Middleboro within the County of Plimouth whereof Jacob Thompson Gent is Lieutenant. You are therefore carefully and diligently to discharge the duties of an Ensign by ordering and Exercising the sd Company in arms both Inferiour Officers and Souldiers Keeping them in good order and Discipline, Commanding them to obey you as their ensign, And yourself to observe and follow such orders and directions as you shall receive from your sd Lieutenant and other your Superiour Officers, according to the Rules and Discipline of War pursuant to the trust reposed in you. Given under my hand & seal at arms at Boston the Fifth day of August, 1696, In the Eighth year of the Reign of our sovereign, Lord William the Third, by the Grace of God, of England, Scotland, France and Ireland, King, Defender of the Faith, &c.
By Command of the Lieut. Govern'r., &c.
WM. STOUGHTON."
Jsa. Addington, Secr'y.

THE MIDDLESEX MONEY DIGGERS.

"May Martin, or The Money Diggers," by D. P. Thompson, is known to be founded upon the fact that men dug here for money, at the foot of the nearly perpendicular drop of a hundred feet or more from the southerly part of the highest peak of Camel's Hump. It was commenced by a few men in 1824 or '25, who built a shanty there, one side a large piece of detached ledge, the other three sides, log of untrimmed spruce and fir, quite young ; the

roof formed by drawing in the trees as they neared the top, until the boughs met the ledge above, which shelter being protected from the north and west winds by the high ledge, made a warm and comfortable place, under which the men professed to dig in search of the treasure supposed to have been secreted by Capt. Kidd somewhere on this continent. They were in part directed in their search by a woman living towards the North part of the State, who claimed to see into unsearchable things by looking into a transparent quartz stone or piece of glass. This company subsisted mainly by duping the nearest settlers so as to get them to furnish food. One man let them have his sheep to eat until they had devoured a large flock, he expecting good pay when the treasure should be found. Many were the conjectures as to the object of these money-diggers. Some thought they were a band of counterfeiters, others that they were a set of thieves, while a few thought they were honestly digging for money, and were hopeful for their success.

Their work was brought to a close by a party of young men from Middlesex, among whom was Enos Stiles, who gives the following account of their expedition, he being the only one of the party now alive :

Dec. 11, 1826, between 8 and 9 o'clock in the evening, Ira McElroy, Calvin Farrar, Amos L. Rice, Archy McElroy, Jerry McElroy, Alexander M. Allen and Enos Stiles started from Middlesex village for Camel's Hump, with a view to discover what they could of the work or object of the money-diggers there, and were accompanied by Nathaniel Carpenter, then a justice of the peace, who went to act as an official if any arrests should be made. As they started, it so happened Danforth Stiles, from the east part of Middlesex, one Hinkson and one Reed were on their way to the mountain, and fell in with them. There was no temperance law then to forbid, no Good Templars to interfere, and acting upon the principle that which contained the most heat and stimulus was the best beverage for a long journey in a winter's night, they took two gallons of new rum for drink with them, and what provisions

31

needed beside. Leaving their teams at Ridley's tavern, now Ridley's Station, they took their provision and drink, and proceeded on foot to the mountain, about 6 miles distant. Esq. Carpenter stopped at the last house at the foot of the mountain to await for business, if needed, and the other seven of the party kept on up the steep mountain, through some two or three miles of thick forest.

When about half way up, after crossing a spruce ridge and coming into hard wood where it was lighter, they called the roll, and found one man missing. Three men were detailed to go back and find him, which they did some one-third mile back, lying in the snow fast asleep, having apparently fallen asleep and dropped out of line unnoticed by the rest of the party. Nothing more of note occurred until they arrived in the early break of day at the headquarters of the money-diggers, where they found Rodney Clogston, of Middlesex, the leader of the band, one Shackford, Eastman, and Friezell, up, dressed, with a good fire burning before the shanty.

After looking over the premises a little, four of the party went up to the top, and were there at sunrise playing a game of cards. The south wind was blowing warm, and they suffered no inconvenience from cold. It had been warm for a number of days, and the snow was not very deep at that time. After taking breakfast, well-washed down, the Middlesex party commenced a thorough search for goods, coining implements, treasures or excavations, which continued till about 1 o'clock P. M., and resulted in finding nothing except a little digging done inside of the shanty in the ledge that formed one of its sides, about what might have been done by two men with powder, good drills and a sledge in one day.

Giving up searching, the party came together at the camp and had a social time, until some were feeling pretty well, when one man said he did not want to trouble the camp for anything, and offered to purchase one cent's worth of meat, which was dealt out to him.

Then some of the boys, being possessed

of evil spirits as well as good, commenced to break spruce twigs and put them on the fire for the fun of seeing them burn; this made a division, and two opposing parties were formed. Two of the men from the east part of the town sided with the diggers, and one remained silent and neutral, which made six against seven, when the invaders commenced piling on larger brush, and soon had the shanty in a rousing blaze. The diggers defended their property smartly by words, and declared that their things should all burn and the boys would be compelled to pay for them; but no fighting was done, and before the fire reached any of their things they made a rush and saved their trumpery, and let the shanty burn. The brush was so dry, the blaze shot into the air some fifty feet, making a splendid sight, but the diggers' lodge was reduced to ashes. In less than two hours after, the money-diggers were all on the march for home, thus ending the digging for Captain Kidd's treasures on Camel's Hump.

THE COLDEST NIGHT HERE

in the month of July since the year 1816, was probably in 1829. Enos Stiles relates that he worked at haying for Elijah Holden on the farm where Gardner Sawyer now resides, in 1829, and that he and two other men who were mowing on the 10th of July threw down their whetstones on a swath of hay, one above another, and that when he took up the upper stone on the morning of the 11th, the stones were frozen together so that he raised the three together when he lifted the top one. But he says the frost did not seriously injure the growing crops.

FIRES.

The only fire in town supposed to be incendiary was that burning the store, tavern-house and barns standing where B. Barrett's store and tavern now stand, and owned in 1835 by a man named Mann. In May, that year, the buildings, with 3 or 4 horses and one ox, were burned, and Simeon Edson, who kept tavern where J. Q. Hobart now lives, was arrested on charge of setting the fire. At a justice trial the jury found him guilty, and he was lodged in jail to await County Court trial. After being in jail for some time, he got bail, and never appeared at trial, and as there was lack of good proof, his bonds were never called for.

THE SAP-FEEDER,

so generally used by maple sugar-makers to run the sap into the pans or evaporators as fast as it evaporates, was invented by the late Moses Holden, Esq., who for many years owned and carried on the sugar-place about 2 miles from his home in the village; was a part of the Scott farm. He was a large, strong man, a great worker, and seldom had any help in sugaring, and often felt the need of having his sap boiling safely when he was away. Hearing a description of a floating contrivance for regulating the amount of water running into the flume of a certain mill, gave him an idea about regulating the sap running into his sap-pans, and he went to Montpelier and told one of the tinmen there what he wanted made. The tinman would have nothing to do with it for fear of ridicule in case of a failure; but going to another tinshop, the tinman made the feeder according to directions, and only asked for a chance to make more if it proved a success. Mr. Holden took his invention home, elevated his sap-holder, put on his feeder, and started a fire. It worked well during the day, and when he left at night, he filled his holder with sap and his arch with wood, and when he returned in the morning, found his holder nearly empty and everything right. He never applied for a patent, but used this first feeder as long as he sugared, and it is still used by Wm. Scott, who bought the sugar-place.

Moses Holden died in May, 1878, at an advanced age. He had always been a resident of the town, had represented it in the Legislature twice, and had filled many offices of trust and responsibility. Many stories are told of his physical strength, one of them being to the effect that he has been known to cut and split 8 cords of three-foot wood in one day. He could lift up a full barrel of cider, hold it, and drink from the bung-hole.

BURYING GROUNDS.

At an early date, Hon. Seth Putnam deeded his one-acre lot in the white pine division, which is in the village, on the east side of the street opposite the railroad depot, to the town for a burying ground. The yard is well fenced, and kept in as good condition as the scanty room will admit. I have not learned who was the first person buried there, and the number cannot be very accurately determined, but the cemetery is nearly all occupied.

The following names, taken mostly from the headstones there, show that there sleep some of the brave veterans who fought to establish our nation, and some of the daring pioneers who cleared the dense forest from our fertile fields:

Lyman Tolman, aged 95, Cyrus Hill, 94, Ebenezer Woodbury — Revolutionary soldiers; Hon. Seth Putnam, fourth settler in town, 93; Capt. Holden Putnam, Captain at Plattsburgh, 86; Jesse Johnson, Sen'r, 86; Luther Haskins, 84; Mary Petty Haskins, wife of Luther, 81; Sally, wife of Dr. Joseph Lewis, 83; Polly Goldthwait, 79; Elihu Atherton, 79; Moses Holden, 78; Aaron Ladd, 78: Jesse Johnson, Jr., 77.

As the ripened autumn leaves surely and successively drop from the forest trees and are borne to the silent earth, so are we, in sure succession, dropping from the stage of life, and being borne to the silent cities of the departed. And as the inhabitants of these cities will soon outnumber those living in our villages and along our valleys and hill sides, it seems just and appropriate proper mention should be made of them; and I think much credit is due the inhabitants of this town and near vicinity for the improving and adorning of their cemeteries. The ground now called

THE MIDDLESEX CENTRE CEMETERY,

is now one of the most neatly arranged country cemeteries to be found; situated in a sightly, pleasant place, on the east side of the first made and most direct road from the village to the Centre, about 2 miles from the river, on the top of the first of three elevations of rolling ground found in coming from the village on this road. Along the roadside and within the gate near the entering avenue, is a grove of handsome maples in rows, casting their shade upon the turf and over the pretty, white school house upon the left. The grounds within the cemetery are neatly arranged in 6 rows of lots, with 3 carriage avenues running the length of the ground and cross avenues. Each lot is raised above the avenues. with walk left between each 2 lots, and flowers, blooming shrubs and roses, break the mat of thick green grass and add their beauty to the sacred plots. A substantial wall and close-trimmed cedar hedge inclosing all.

But it is more the tasteful arrangement of the whole that makes the place seem beautiful for every one, than any profuse adornment. The stranger, too, pauses to admire the lovely scenery around as well, and the mourners feel a spirit of thankfulness that their dear friends are resting in so fair a place.

There are some 200 graves here now, with many monuments. Jan. 1, 1812 Nathan Benton, one of the first settlers, deeded 2 acres of land here to Joseph Chapin, Josiah Holden and 16 others: the land tc be used for a neighborhood burying ground. In the spring of 1822 there were 5 graves in this ground, but it was in an open field, and had not been exactly located. That year the neighbors met and appointed Stephen Herrick to measure and stake out the ground, and a fence was built around it.

But little was done to improve it more until about 1856, when through the influence and under the supervision of Horace Holden, the friends of the deceased buried there, and others who felt interested, began to kill the weeds and brakes that had become abundant, and improvements were continued from time to time till 1858, when everything was completed nearly as at present. In 1866, an association was formed called " The Middlesex Centre Cemetery Association," to which Aaron Ladd, Asa Chapin, and 21 others, owners of lots, deeded their right and title. Under the Association each one of those who deeded and each one who took an active part in the work of improving the ground were entitled to a family lot.

SOME OF THE OLDEST

buried here are : Elizabeth McElroy, came from Scotland to U. S. in 1740, died in 1823, aged 99; Joseph Chapin, Sen'r, 96; Susanna Chase, 89; Jeremiah Leland, 78; Elizabeth, wife of Jeremiah Leland, 88; Samuel Daniels, 87; Lucretia, wife of Samuel Daniels, 78; Polly McElroy, 84; Sanford White, 80; Maj. John Poor, 79, and Eliza M., his wife, 73—both buried in one grave; Joseph Chapin, Jr., 78; Horace Holden, 74; Marian Leland, 92; Abram Gale, 78, and Mary, his wife, 92; Margaret Mead, 79; Benjamin Willey, 72; Mary Wilson, 73; Hosea Minott, 74; Knight Nichols, 81, and Mercy, his wife, 92; Geo. H. Lewis, 71.

THE NORTH BRANCH CEMETERY.

On North Branch, about 1 mile below Putnam's Mills, is another cemetery, of which Mr. Putnam furnishes the following description :

"About 1810, Jno. Davis was buried on land then occupied by him, known as the Scudder lot, nearly in front of his house, on the opposite side of the road. After that time the place was used for a burying ground, and ¼ of an acre was enclosed with a log-fence. At that time a man by the name of Flanders lived where Chester Taylor now lives; Levi Lewis and wife, Polly, lived where G. M. Whitney now does. Jno. Davis and wife, Nancy, were the first who lived on the Stiles place. James Pittsly and wife, Esther, commenced on the place known as the Bohonnon place, on the east side of the stream, now occupied by Jacob Putnam. After this, Wm. Lewis purchased the Scudder lot and the inhabitants erected a board fence around the burying lot. Oct. 8, 1863, an association was formed called the North Branch Cemetery Association. The trustees purchased 1½ acres, together with the old ground of Lathrop Lewis, son of Wm. Lewis, for $150, and built a good, substantial fence around it, erected a hearse-house and purchased a hearse. The location being on the main road, and the soil dry and sandy, makes it the most desirable cemetery in the town."

Some of the oldest buried in North Branch Cemetery were: Clarissa Gould, aged 66; Ruth Minott, 66; Daniel Russell, 68; his wife, Temperance, 81; Reuben Russell, 78; his wife, Susannah, 69; John Gallison, 83; his wife, Phebe, 85; Allen Gallison, 68; Enoch Kelton, 64; his wife, Huldah, 72; Josiah Wright, 76; his wife, Betsy, 84; Nathaniel Wentworth, 71; Elizabeth, relict of Moses Wentworth, 87; William Lewis, 88; his wife, Hannah, 67; Jacob Putnam, 73; his wife, Polly W., 57; Betsy Thayer, 67; Isaac Batchelder, 61; his wife, Mary, 68; David Herrick, 86; his wife, Mary, 85; Stephen C. Jacobs, 76: Andrew Tracy, 75; his wife, Levina, 84; Ebenezer Cummings, 94; Abel H. Coleman, 75; David Gray, 82; David Hatch, 63; his wife, Sarah, 57; John McDermid, nearly 77; his wife, Adelia, nearly 72; Louiza Lane, 72; Margaret Smith, 81; Thomas Culver, 71; his wife, Anna, 73; Zeley Keyes, 76; Micah Hatch, 83; his wife, Mary, 69; Ephraim Hall, 68; Timothy Worth, 84; Solomon Lewis, 89; his wife, Susannah, 70; his second wife, Lucinda, 68; Elizabeth Church, 60; Sabra Burrell, 85; Wm. R. Kinson, 56; Hannah Kinson, 73; Eunice Edgerly, 64.

MRS. LYDIA KING, widow of Elder Nathaniel King, died at the house of her son-in-law, Stephen Herrick, at the age of 91 years, and was buried in Northfield.

REMARKABLE CASE OF PETRIFACTION.

In March, 1846, James Vaughn (the writer's father,) and family, which included his father, Daniel Vaughn, moved from Pomfret, this state, on to a farm in the N. W. part of Middlesex.

"Uncle Daniel," as he was universally called in Windsor County, was a man about 5 feet, 10 inches in height, broad shouldered, stout built, and weighing some more than 200 lbs. He was noted for his remarkable strength, his strong, heavy voice, his sociality, his song-singing and story-telling, and was a notedly robust man, the solidity of muscle increasing as age advanced to such an extent as to make it necessary for him to use a cane or crutches for the last 15 years of his life.

He died of dropsy June 3, 1846, aged 78 years, and by his request was buried in a place selected by himself in a sightly spot near the house where he died. The following March the eldest daughter of James Vaughn, aged 16, died of consumption, and was buried in a grave near her grandfather. In Feb. 1855 their remains were taken up to be removed to the family burying-lot in Woodstock cemetery. The remains of the young lady were found in the usual condition of those buried that length of time.

The uncommon heft of Mr. Vaughn's coffin led to an examination of the remains, when it was found that the body had become petrified. Every part, excepting the nose, was in perfect form, nearly its natural color, but a little more of a yellowish tinge, hard like stone, and it weighed 550 lbs. The petrified body was viewed by Mr. Vaughn's family and many of the neighbors in Middlesex, and was also seen by many at Woodstock. A somewhat minute examination by physicians and scientific men revealed the fact that the fingers, toes and the outer part of the body were very hard and brittle, but that the length of time had not been sufficient to so fully change the inner portions of the most fleshly parts of the body and limbs. But it was generally believed by those who made examination that a few years more of time would have made the work of petrifaction complete, and changed the entire body to a mineral formation, that would perhaps endure for ages.

A biographical sketch of him we have not given, as it properly belongs in Pomfret history, of which town he was an early settler.

SUDDEN AND ACCIDENTAL DEATHS.

Luther Haskins, aged about 80, died in a chair in Barrett & Holden's store. He sat leaning slightly back, and was first noticed to be dead by Will Herrick, who happened to go into the store.

Nancy Hornbrook, aged 16, daughter of Wm. Hornbrook, dropped dead at a party at Alfred Warren's, about the year 1856.

When the railroad was being built, Lovina Cameron, aged about 13, dau. of Ira Cameron, of this town, was visiting in Berlin. She and a cousin and another girl were walking over the railroad bridge near Montpelier Junction, stepping from one stringer to another, all having hold of hands, when one made a misstep, and Miss Cameron and her cousin fell through into the river and were drowned.

U. W. Goodell, nephew of L. D. Ainsworth, was struck on the forehead by a stick thrown by a circular saw while working in Mr. Ainsworth's saw-mill, and lived but a few hours.

Chester Newton, while working in the same mill, helping to saw logs, was twitched upon the large circular saw, by the saw catching a board he was moving, and so horribly mangled that he lived but a short time.

Alvaro, son of Frederick Richardson, brakeman on the cars, aged 26 years, was killed by his head striking the timbers overhead in the dry-bridge at Waterbury, in 1879. Hinkley Chapin, aged 22, was killed at the same place, and in the same way, in 1851.

In 1872, Louis Amel's house, on east hill, caught fire from smoking meat in the wood-shed, and Mr. Amel was overcome by the flames while removing property, and burned with the house. Age, 51 yrs.

Nathaniel Daniels was drowned in 1818; see account of freshets. George, a son of Hiram Williams, was drowned in the river below the Narrows, while bathing, aged about 16. Frank, son of Osgood Evans, was in a boat above the Narrows, one paddle broke, and he went over the falls and was drowned. His body was found in the eddy below the Narrows. The only son of Asa Chapin, was drowned in a spring while drawing water for use in the house, and a little son of Samuel Mann was drowned in a spring on the Stephen Herrick farm.

James Daniels, aged about 78, living at Lawrence Fitzgerald's, was found dead in bed in the morning.

There have been 10 cases of suicide in the last 60 years by Middlesex people, 7 of which were committed in town.

STEPHEN HERRICK.

BY THE EDITOR.

We do not usually give sketches of the living, but the senior writer of this town history being so aged a man, and it being somewhat remarkable in his case that of 210 men living in the town when he settled here, who had families, that he has been the last survivor of them all for eight and a half years past, it seems a moderate autobiographic record in such circumstances is admissible.

Mr. Herrick is of English and Scotch descent, son of Stephen, senior; born in Randolph, Vt., Feb. 19, 1795. In the fall of 1820, he came to Middlesex, and selected his location, bought in October, but returned to Randolph, taught school that winter after in Brookfield, and returned to Middlesex in April, 1821. He bought his farm of Reuben Mann, son of Samuel, who was one of the first settlers, and where Mr. H. has continued to reside for the past 61 years. He married Lydia, dau. of Rev. Nathaniel King; their children: Eliza—mar. 1st, Chester Pierce of N. H., 2d, Samuel Warren of Middlesex, 3d, Adin Miles of Worcester, has three children living: Nathaniel King, the only son, who m. Jane Foster, 3 children, 2 living—King Herrick, as he is always called, is a merchant at Middlesex village; Emily R., who died at 22; Harriet, who m. Abram S. Adams, had 5 children, and is deceased; Laura Jane, who m. John McDermid, had 2 daughters, buried one; Nancy Jane, who m. Arthur McDermid, bro. to John, 3 children, her husband dying, m. 2d, Frederick A. Richardson; Lydia Ann, who mar. Heman Taplin, no children; and youngest, Alma R., born In 1842, married V. V. Vaughn, Mar. 8, 1865,—children, Mabel, died at 10 years, Wilmar Herrick, Ida Alma, and Frank Waldo.

Mr. Herrick has been a man of great physical strength and vigorous mind. The following will evince what his mental ability has been:

When the Vt. Central R. R. was being built, Abram B. Barker and Thomas

Haight contracted to build 2 miles of it below Middlesex village. They carried on work for about a year and failed. Stephen Herrick took a contract to finish the work; carried it on about 13 months, and in consequence of short estimates also failed—but for which he immediately commenced a suit against the R. R. Co., and afterwards was retained for and commenced a suit in favor of Barker and Haight as agent for their creditors. After carrying on these suits for 8 years he got a decree against the R. R. Co. in his own case for about $9000; the Barker & Haight suit he prosecuted for 20 years before getting a final decree.

In these suits he took all his testimony himself, examined his witnesses himself in court, and wrote out his own pleas. In a word he was his own lawyer. It is said he once appeared in Supreme court with his case written out, filling 300 pages, that Gov. Paine, the president of the road, said that that book would be the death of him. Mr. Herrick tells the story now well, and adds *that it was*. When Gov. Paine was summoned, he told the officer he had rather meet the devil than that Stephen Herrick in the court.

He has also successfully, as town agent, managed many suits for the town, including the noted Wythe pauper suit with Moretown, the Beckwith suit in regard to settling the 3 ministerial lots, and the East Hill road suit, and has managed many grand jury suits, in all of which he acted as his own counsel and made his own pleas.

The Saturday before the death of the late Hon. Daniel Baldwin, these two old men met upon the street at Montpelier village. Said Mr. Baldwin. "We two old men, the two oldest inhabitants of our respective neighboring towns, should have a visit together." Mr. Herrick assented, and asked where it should be. "It must be at my house," replied Mr. Baldwin, "and next Saturday, one week from to-day." The following Wednesday Mr. Baldwin died. Mr. Herrick seems remarkably hale and hearty yet.

REVOLUTIONARY PENSIONERS.

No official list of Revolutionary soldiers who have resided in Middlesex can be obtained, but the following-named men are said to have been Revolutionary pensioners who have lived in town: Estes Hatch, — Sloan, Jas. Hobart, Cyrus Hill, Micah Hatch, David Phelps, Col. Joseph Hutchins, Joseph Chapin, Sr., Lyman Tolman.

Seth Putnam was one of the first three settlers in Washington County, having moved into Middlesex in 1785. He was a cousin to the noted Israel Putnam, and as a subaltern in Col. Warner's celebrated regiment of Green Mountain Boys, participated in their battles and marches in the old Revolution. He related many of his adventures of the first settlement, and among them one of a remarkable march which he made through the wilderness in a snow-storm, from Rutland, where he had been in attendance as a member of the legislature during the month of November. The only traveled road to his home was then around by Burlington.

SOLDIERS BURIED IN TOWN IN THE WAR OF 1861.

S. F. Jones, Jacob Jones and Zenas Hatch,—in North Branch Cemetery.

Chester Newton,—in the Cemetery at the Center.

Nathaniel Jones,—in the village Cemetery.

Mrs. Esther Shontell, of this town, sent seven sons into the army in this war: William, who measured 6 feet 8 inches in height; Benjamin, 6 feet 4 inches; Frederick, 6 feet 3 inches; Leander, 5 feet 9 inches; Lewis, 6 feet 1 inch; Joseph, 6 feet 7 inches; Augustus, 6 feet. Two of the brothers were killed; and the mother draws a pension for one of them. Another left a widow, and two are pensioned on account of wounds.

O, the strong Middlesex boys
Were mad for the war!
And the name of each hero
To the ages afar
Shall leave a track like a comet—
Each shine as a star.

LIST OF MEN CREDITED TO THE TOWN OF MIDDLESEX, 1861–1865.

BY STEPHEN HERRICK.

VOLUNTEERS FOR THREE YEARS.

Names.	Age.	Reg. Co.	Enlistment.	Remarks.
Brown, Harvey W.	19	2 F	May 7 61	Died Feb. 4, 63, at Point Lookout, Md.
Smith, William S.	22	do	do	Died Sept. 5, 61, at Washington, D. C.
Ripley, William C.	21	3 H	June 1 61	Discharged Nov. 8, 62. [23, 65.
Scribner, Walter	21	4 G	Aug 22 61	Corp : pris. June 23, 64 : must. out May
Herrick, George S.	23	do	Aug 29 61	Discharged Jan. 21, 63.
Leonard, Alonzo R.	21	do	Sept 3 61	Discharged Dec. 18, 62.
Leonard, Charles P.	19	do	do	Re-en. Feb. 8, 64 : must. out May 23, 65.
Cushman, George H.	34	do	Aug 22 61	Corp : killed at Weldon R.R. June 23, 64.
Evans, Goin B.	21	6 G	Feb 18 62	Discharged April 24, 63. [June 26, 65.
Gould, Page	21	6 H	Aug 14 61	First Serg : wd. April 16, 62 : must. out
Gould, Worthen T.	18	do	do	Died Jan. 4, 63, at Belle Plains, Va.
Jones, Stephen F.	44	do	do	Died Feb. 63, at Brattleboro.
Jones, Jacob G.	18	do	do	Died Jan. 24, 62, at Camp Griffin.
Divine, John	30	6 G	Oct 15 61	Re-en. Dec. 15, 63 : must. out June 26, 65.
Lee, John Jr.	32	do	Sept 20 61	Re-en. Dec. 15, 63 : must. out July 15, 65.
Sweeny, James	35	do	Sept 23 61	Discharged Jan. 8, 62.
Leonard, John R.	26	6 F	Oct 3 61	Mustered out Oct. 28, 64.
Whitney, Elijah	31	do	Oct 8 61	First Lieut : resigned June 19, 62.
Hogan, John	22	6 H	Aug 14 61	Wd. April 16, 62 : deserted Jan. 19, 63.
Shontell, William	25	8 E	Oct 21 61	Corp : discharged Feb. 12, 63.
Shontell, Benjamin	24	do	Dec 16 61	Discharged Oct. 16, 62.
Shontell, Frederick	22	do	Jan 10 62	Died May 16, 62.
Shontell, Leander	19	do	Dec 16 61	Wd. Sept. 4, 62 : must. out Aug. 3, 64.
Amel, Louis	38	do	Oct 7 61	Re-en. Jan. 5, 64 : must. out June 28, 65.
Warren, Lorenzo S.	22	do	Dec 7 61	Wd. Sept. 4, 62 : dis. April 6, 63.
Warren, Alonzo S.	20	do	do	Died March 19, 63.
Kinson, Benjamin H.	26	do	Oct 3 61	Died June 18, 62.
Wilson, Francis	28	do	do	Corp : died Dec. 5, 62.
Nichols, Roswell S.	41	do	Nov 30 61	Musician : discharged June 30, 62.
Lewis, Frederick A.	18	Cav C	Sept 13 61	Paroled pris : must. out May 23, 65.
Lewis, DeForest L.	20	do	Nov 12 61	Mustered out Nov. 18, 64.
Scott, Elisha	50	do	Sept 20 61	do [Nov. 18, 64.
George, Albert	21	do	Sept 13 61	Pro. Corp : wd. Apr. 1, 63 : mustered out
Smith, John W.	41	do	Sept 12 61	Corp : discharged Oct. 9, 62.
Chase, Austin A.	21	do	Oct 3 61	Discharged Nov. 27, 61.
Spencer, George W.	28	do	Sept 20 61	Discharged Oct. 3, 62.
Hastings, Sidney B.	42	do	do	Discharged Nov. 18, 64.
Dudley, William N.	32	do	Sept 12 61	Discharged Jan. 13, 63.
Preston, Philander R.	27	do	Sept 21 61	Wd. July 6, 63 : Re-en. Dec. 31, 63 ; taken pris. June 29, 64 ; died at Florence, S. C., Jan., 65.
Wells, Warren O.	38	1st Bat	Dec 3 61	Corp : mustered out Aug. 10, 64. [La.
Hills, Zerah	34	do	do	Corp : died June 25, 63, at Port Hudson,
Oakland, George	24	2d Bat	Oct 23 61	Corp: re-en. Feb. 20, 64 : mus. out July 31, 65
Hogan, Henry	20	9 I	June 18 62	Pro. Corp : do. Serg : mus. out June 13, 65.
Smith, William P.	19	do	June 30 62	Died Oct. 12, 62.
Cushman, Holmes	27	10 B	July 25 62	Mustered out June 22, 65.
Williams, Hiram	29	do	Aug 1 62	Died Feb. 17, 65, at Washington, D. C.
Morrisett, John	28	do	July 30 62	Mustered out June 22, 65.
Patterson, Robert	35	do	Aug 6 62	Wd. Oct. 19, 64 : dis. May 27, 65.
Scaribo, Fabius	28	do	Aug 4 62	Mustered out June 22, 65. [15, 65.
Lewis, Charles J.	25	11 D	Aug 12 62	Sec. Lt : pro. 1st Lt : do. Capt : dis. May
Fifield, William C.	41	6 F	Aug 15 62	Must. out June 19, 65. [out June 19, 65.
Tobin, John W.	18	do	do	Wd. Sep. 19, 64; pro. Corp: do Serg: mus.
Cameron, Sylvester	25	do	do	Mustered out June 19, 65.
Ward, Tertullus C.	26	do	do	Killed in ac. at Gettysburgh, July 3, 63.
Bean, Albert	23	2 D	do	Died Oct. 3, 64, at Sandy Hook, of wds.
Bruce, George W.	23	10 K	Aug 11 62	Deserted July 5, 63.
Jones, Jabez	19	11 I	Dec 5 63	Died at Middlesex, July 10, 65.
Chase, Amos J.	40	Cav C	Nov 24 63	Mustered out Aug. 9, 65.
Buck, William H. H.	22	Cav G	Dec 11 63	Discharged Sept. 15, 65.
Templeton, James A.	45	Cav C	Dec 8 63	Mustered out Aug. 9, 65.
Cameron, John	26	do	Dec 18 63	Wd. May 6, 64 : discharged Feb. 22, 65.
Rublee, Otis N.	18	3d Bat	Sept 5 63	Musician : mustered out June 15, 65.
Herrick, Geo. S.	25	do	Nov 2 63	do do
Amel, Louis	19	do	Sept 15 63	do do

www.ingramcontent.com/pod-product-compliance
Lightning Source LLC
Chambersburg PA
CBHW030619270326
41927CB00007B/1242